M000289666

"There's no one better able than Matthew Taylor to s[...]
gence framework can be applied to school leaders. *T[...]
ratizes leadership excellence."

— Daniel Goleman, author of *Primal Leadership:*
Unleashing the Power of Emotional Intelligence

"Matt has created a new approach that takes the concepts of emotional intelligence and makes them specific to the lived realities of school leaders. You will see yourself reflected in this book, and you will walk away with deepened insight and actionable strategies for shifting the deep mindsets that can hold us back."

— Sara Keenan, founder and CEO of AF Accelerate

"When Matt was a principal, he led his school to be the #1 middle school in the entire state for student growth – and then he went on to coach hundreds of other school leaders to achieve remarkable success for their students. Matt has always deeply believed in the potential of all students. What he figured out is how to help leaders develop the emotional intelligence they need to unlock the potential of the adults on their team – an essential and too-often overlooked pre-requisite to student success. As we navigate the unprecedented challenges facing education right now, Matt's practical wisdom will help all of us see and break through our self-limiting 'brick walls' so that we can be the leaders our students and teachers deserve."

— Dacia Toll, founder and former CEO of Achievement First

"Matt's ingenious five-square approach provides a practical way for everyday people like you and me to bring emotional intelligence up off the page as a concept and into our daily lives as parents, spouses, colleagues, leaders, coaches, and educators. Often what stands between us and actualizing our own capacity is a sound approach, a method by which we can again and again activate our own wherewithal and potential irrespective of the situations we find ourselves in. His years as a teacher, school administrator, leadership coach, and emotional intelligence practitioner have resulted in the practical wisdom and insight he has brilliantly weaved together and is sharing in this book. Matt's five-square methodology will forever transform how you think of yourself, your students, and your own capacity to become an emotionally intelligent person and noble school leader!"

— Michele Nevarez, founder and creator of the
Goleman EI suite of Coaching and Training

The Noble School Leader

The Noble School Leader

The Five-Square Approach to Leading Schools with Emotional Intelligence

Matthew Taylor

JB JOSSEY-BASS™
A Wiley Brand

Copyright © 2022 John Wiley & Sons. All rights reserved.

Jossey-Bass
A Wiley Imprint
111 River St, Hoboken, NJ 07030
www.josseybass.com

Except as expressly noted below, no part of this publication may be reproduced, stored in a retrieval system, or transmitted in any form or by any means, electronic, mechanical, photocopying, recording, scanning, or otherwise, except as permitted under Section 107 or 108 of the 1976 United States Copyright Act, without either the prior written permission of the Publisher, or authorization through payment of the appropriate per-copy fee to the Copyright Clearance Center, Inc., 222 Rosewood Drive, Danvers, MA 01923, phone +1 978 750 8400, fax +1 978 750 4470, or on the web at www.copyright.com. Requests to the Publisher for permission should be addressed to the Permissions Department, John Wiley & Sons, Inc., 111 River Street, Hoboken, NJ 07030, phone + 1 201 748 6011, fax +1 201 748 6008, or online at www.wiley.com/go/permissions.

Certain pages from this book (except those for which reprint permission must be obtained from the primary sources) are designed for educational/training purposes and may be reproduced. These pages are designated by the appearance of copyright notices at the foot of the page. This free permission is restricted to limited customization of the DVD-ROM materials for your organization and the paper reproduction of the materials for educational/training events. It does not allow for systematic or large-scale reproduction, distribution (more than 100 copies per page, per year), transmission, electronic reproduction or inclusion in any publications offered for sale or used for commercial purposes—none of which may be done without prior written permission of the Publisher.

Limit of Liability/Disclaimer of Warranty: Although the publisher and author have used their best efforts in preparing this book, they make no representations or warranties with respect to the accuracy or completeness of the contents of this book and specifically disclaim any implied warranties of merchantability or fitness for a particular purpose. No warranty may be created or extended by sales representatives or written sales materials. The advice and strategies contained herein may not be suitable for your situation. You should consult with a professional where appropriate. Neither the publisher nor authors shall be liable for any loss of profit or any other commercial damages, including but not limited to special, incidental, consequential, or other damages.

Jossey-Bass books and products are available through most bookstores. To contact Jossey-Bass directly, call our Customer Care Department within the U.S. at 800–956–7739, outside the U.S. at +1 317 572 3986, or fax +1 317 572 4002.

Wiley also publishes its books in a variety of electronic formats and by print-on-demand. Some material included with standard print versions of this book may not be included in e-books or in print-on-demand. If this book refers to media such as a CD or DVD that is not included in the version you purchased, you may download this material at http://booksupport.wiley.com. For more information about Wiley products, visit www.wiley.com.

Library of Congress Cataloging-in-Publication Data is Available:

9781119762874 (Paperback)
9781119762867 (ePDF)
9781119762928 (ePub)

Cover Design: Paul Mccarthy
Cover Art: Courtesy of the Author

SKY10033203_030422

Contents

Introduction

This book is about a kind of leadership development that we haven't paid much attention to in the education sector. Every school leader experiences the need for this approach when they have been working hard to grow a technical leadership skill and inexplicably hit a brick wall. We double down on skill and knowledge building over time, and still there's no movement. As managers we begin to assume that our leaders may not have what it takes, or that there's some fixed trait that will keep them from getting there (they just have a low bar . . . their awareness is too low). As leaders we just can't figure out why we don't do something (delegate to our teammates, show vulnerability) that we deeply want to do. Or we assume that some competencies are just not our strengths and that we are fixed in certain ways (I will never be good at conflict. That's just the way I am.).

We've gotten increasingly good in our sector at technical leadership skill and knowledge building in the areas of instructional leadership, data practices, and building school-based systems. But this brick-wall phenomenon falls into a different category of leadership competency building that calls for a very different approach. We can't see the obstacles to growth because they are hidden inside of us—or below the surface—and they're very personal. So even when we are teaching and learning discrete skills, we're not getting to that level of figuring out the real obstacles. Practicing skills without figuring out a leader's inner obstacles is like riding a merry-go-round that never stops.

I have been obsessing about these brick-wall leadership competencies for close to a decade now. Through hundreds of coaching and training sessions with school leaders across the leadership pipeline, I have built a development model based on Daniel Goleman's Emotional Intelligence (EI) theory. EI brings an essential lens to leadership development with its focus on self-awareness, self-management, and social awareness—what we need to know about ourselves and others before we ever engage them. In the book, I share how we have operationalized EI to create a common language and road map for building personal leadership competencies. My framework—The 5-Square—is applicable across competencies and across all levels of the leadership pipeline. This book introduces the 5-Square, takes readers on a guided tour for applying it to their personal leadership challenges, and provides practice opportunities to build those brick-wall leadership competencies over time.

The leaders who have used my 5-Square have experienced significant growth in competencies that they often believed were fixed, and the impact of that growth has been evident in their 360 feedback, org health data, staff retention, and other organizational outcomes. Just as importantly, this work has reduced suffering, sparked hope, and helped leaders and the people they lead thrive in their work and their lives.

This book is essentially an EI-based, replicable approach to social–emotional learning for leaders. Social–emotional leadership is a prerequisite to student growth because leaders are the creators and the keepers of the conditions for learning in our schools. Students depend on us to create the conditions for learning that everyone in our schools—from students to teachers to principals—needs to meet their full potential. I have learned that these conditions primarily result from the way that people feel. Because these conditions are difficult to name and measure, they tend to be overlooked and undervalued

Since the days when I first started teaching 27 years ago, our profession has been moving toward an increasingly technical approach to teaching and learning. We have reacted to the pressures to improve student achievement—increased exponentially with the arrival of Common Core—by building more efficient systems to grow academic skills as fast as possible, for as many students as possible. I have watched as these technical practices that serve us in improving student achievement have also led to disconnection, inequitable conditions, and a limited growth trajectory.

As a sector we have arrived at a moment of reckoning. Schools that have taken an increasingly technical approach have become increasingly unhappy places for both the adults and students. The conditions we have created hold everyone back— adults and students—from reaching their potential. This is because emotions are contagious, and they are most contagious when they come from leaders. When adults are working under leadership and conditions that are antithetical to social–emotional health and growth, they create those same conditions in their classrooms for students. Very few students will develop the social–emotional competencies to be strong learners in spaces that are unhealthy for adults. The learning and life outcomes of our children depend on healthy adults, and leaders create adult conditions to thrive. This has become even more painfully clear as we have all experienced the trauma of the Covid pandemic. Academic growth has stagnated for sure, but our collective emotional capacity to teach and learn as educators and students is at rock bottom. Without addressing the affective—the social–emotional—obstacles of the moment, most of us and our students will remain academically incapacitated.

It is time to rebalance the conditions for learning in our schools. That rebalancing must start with the adults; not the kids. And it must come from the leaders.

When I was immersed in schools as a teacher and then a leader, I felt but did not understand all of this. My eyes were opened when my work training school leaders collided with my introduction to Goleman's work on Emotional Intelligence (EI).

I became a principal after 11 years of teaching in urban neighborhood, magnet, charter, international, and private schools. Amistad Academy Middle School was the flagship school of the three-school Achievement First (AF) charter network. When I left the principal seat six years later, we had expanded to 31 schools. During my tenure, I experienced a shift from an entrepreneurial spirit of "build it yourself while flying the plane" to a determined focus on aligning to a set of organizational systems. From student discipline and culture to curriculum and instruction, we were leveraging our collective wisdom and energy to create best-in-class resources for teachers and school leaders so that kids were consistently receiving the very best teaching in the very best schools we could build—and fast! Our sense of urgency came from the belief that kids who were behind simply did not have time for adults to slowly get better at teaching. We had to develop the very best teachers and leaders as fast as possible.

During my last two years as principal, we launched three major systemic initiatives. Our school was one of the first in the network to turn our merit/demerit-based student culture approach into a tight, aligned system. We used Doug Lemov's *Teach Like a Champion* book and teaching model to double down on the technical training of core teaching strategies. This enabled us to take a giant leap forward in our ability to systematically and quickly teach teachers common instructional moves. Finally, during that same year, we launched a robust instructional coaching system in which every teacher was observed and received feedback and planning support weekly.

These three initiatives, supported by a data-driven culture that regularly reflected on whether we were doing what we said we would do, and that we were doing it well, were some of the foundations on which we built breakthrough levels of student achievement across our network. We were proving that Amistad was not an anomaly, and that we could replicate its breakthrough results for kids. Meanwhile, we were also seeing early signs that our systemic approach might have an unintended effect on morale. These early signs didn't get much attention because of our focus on instructional expertise and student outcomes.

Then Common Core dropped like a bomb on public schools. We were horrified when we saw our students' test scores plummet; the new assessment showed that not half as many reached proficiency compared to the previous year's state test scores. We had thought that our kids were closing in on their counterparts in the wealthiest public school systems in the country. We were wrong. But we were not alone. Almost every public charter and district had the same wake-up call. AF's response to this crisis was one of humility, accompanied by an all-out instructional leadership campaign to build our capacity to meet the rigorous expectations of Common Core. I was proud of our organizational response. It was not long, however, before I started to understand the unintended consequences of our reaction.

During that first year's push to align to Common Core, I left Amistad to start a leadership development partnership with our district counterparts in New Haven, Hartford, and Bridgeport, CT. In this new program, built on the medical residency model, district leaders spent a half year in AF schools and then a half year in a strong district school, working with a principal mentor to apply what they had learned. Our pitch to Residents: "You are smart, passionate professionals. We are going to expose you to the best of what charter and district schools have to offer, and we expect you to make your own decisions about what works and doesn't work."

Over time, clear themes emerged about what district leaders experienced at AF: "These instructional approaches and the teacher coaching practices are INCREDIBLE! But the student and adult culture systems and approaches? We can't figure out why you would do those things."

With time, it became difficult to give my Residents a compelling rationale for some of our core practices around student and adult culture. From my new perspective gained from observing schools, I was seeing large numbers of unhappy, disinvested students on a spectrum from apathetic compliance to outright resistance. I was seeing many teachers, deeply invested in our teacher taxonomy skills, hanging their authentic selves up at the door of their classrooms and adopting a teaching persona—a kind of performance—that often disconnected them from their students. I was seeing teacher coaches who excelled at teaching instructional skills but were often stuck in a leadership persona that disconnected them from teachers and students. And I was seeing principals who, having been promoted because they were really good at teaching instructional moves to teachers, struggling mightily and sometimes failing miserably with the real, messy human aspects of their jobs.

Meanwhile, I was getting to know district schools that were happy, inclusive places for kids and adults. The challenge many of them faced, however, was that large percentages of their students were significantly underperforming academically. Between district and charter schools, I was experiencing a wide range of learning communities that fell on a continuum between two poles: on one end happy yet underperforming and enabling, and on the other negative, controlling, yet (relatively) academically high performing. I saw very few schools that were hitting the sweet spot where inclusive, nurturing cultures and high academic performance were embodied simultaneously.

A year into this work, I found myself questioning my beliefs and my training. I loved AF, our people, and our mission. I deeply believed in the direction that our curriculum and pedagogy was heading. And yet some of our schools were unhappy places for adults and kids.

I was in the midst of this internal struggle when I discovered Daniel Goleman's Emotional Intelligence (EI) theory. To support my principals-in-residence as a coach, I enrolled in an executive coaching training course at the Teleos Leadership Institute that was grounded in EI. The training opened my eyes to both the emotional conditions necessary for learning and the personal leadership competencies it takes to create those conditions. I came to understand the extent to which learning is inherently emotional and deeply personal. The competencies of EI gave me a language to make sense of what I was experiencing.

My epiphany also sent me straight into therapy. The Teleos coaching experience awoke parts of myself that I had been neglecting for years. I realized that as a school leader and trainer of school leaders, the intensity of my work, my total immersion in it, and the technical way I had learned to approach it had led me to disconnect from myself and many of the people I loved. Focusing on my own self-awareness and self-management led me to experience transformative personal growth. It changed the way I show up as a leader and also as a person, and I know that I am still evolving because of it.

Learning is much more dependent on the emotional conditions we create than our sector's collective approach to teaching and learning suggests that we believe. For people to experience deeply transformative learning, we need the right combination of two elements: personal connection and challenge. The more challenging the learning, the more the personal connection matters. Each person requires a different balance of these elements, and to get the right balance, we have to know a person well enough to understand where they are and what they need. To create these conditions is human work, and it takes emotional intelligence.

I returned from Teleos seeing opportunities to apply this new EI language and understanding everywhere I looked. I came to see the conditions we are currently creating by default in our schools as an emergency. Our overreliance on data-driven systems and protocols leaves adults and children in our schools feeling less connected and experiencing less care from one another. Classrooms and adult teams are less inclusive of the identities people bring to them. The structures and pace of the work take away the space and time that the adults need to be able to ground themselves in their personal WHY for doing the work, and to be able to be fully present as themselves in the moment. I find myself working with a generation of highly technical school leaders in highly structured schools who are deeply unhappy and feeling unsuccessful in their work. Many feel stuck and cannot figure out why. Others know why they are stuck but feel powerless to change within their existing system. Most of them wonder how long they will be able to last as school leaders.

With the perspective gained through the EI coaching, I felt called to advocate for change. Doug McCurry and Dacia Toll, AF's co-CEOs, embraced this work and created the opportunity to share it with our AF principals through cohort training and one-on-one leader coaching. I had the privilege of making my passion for EI leadership my day job for seven years. During that time, I trained and coached many of the leaders in our organization. It was through that work that my colleagues and I created the tools for the practical application of EI theory. We discovered that the training and coaching is relevant for leaders at every level of seniority. Actually, there is usually a greater need for this social–emotional approach to development the higher one travels up the leadership pipeline. We also found that, unless the leaders at the top of an organization are doing their own social–emotional work, it is not likely that others down the chain will be able to do so effectively.

Since starting the Noble Story Group, I have worked with hundreds of leaders in over 60 school and nonprofit organizations across the country. This work has confirmed in very powerful ways that what I experienced as a teacher and school leader is playing out all across the education sector and beyond. A lopsided focus on building and measuring technical skills has created organizational conditions that are not conducive to people—children and adults—reaching their full potential. All of my clients share the same top three organizational challenges: people experiencing inequitable and exclusive conditions across lines of difference; teachers and leaders feeling that their work is not sustainable over time; and leaders not knowing how to challenge people while staying personally connected. Everyone I work with feels a deep desire to change. Harnessing EI has proven to be an effective way to support them.

Science can broadly be separated into the theoretical and applied. EI theory is not new. What we have done is develop a practical, applied approach to using EI in leadership development. This means helping leaders build the awareness of self and others and generate effective self-management and relational strategies to become stronger adaptive leaders. Over time, clear patterns have emerged about the internal obstacles—the self-limiting mindsets—that get in the way of this growth. I have found that there are archetypical self-limiting mindsets that leaders at all levels of leadership must contend with inside of themselves to reach their potential. This book describes these seven self-limiting mindsets in detail and offers an approach to enable leaders to transcend them.

I wrote this book for school leaders and for their managers who are looking for ways to overcome their brick walls. I introduce readers to the seven most common school leader self-limiting mindsets that have emerged as patterns of behavior as I have applied it over the last decade. Leaders will determine which of the seven self-limiting mindsets hold them back and develop their own self-management strategies to overcome them. For leaders, this is a self-guided tour "below the surface" to build self-awareness about both self-limiting mindsets that get in their way and the source of their personal power that will support them to build new mindsets and behaviors. For managers it is a field guide for supporting leaders "below the surface" and creating the learning conditions that make that work possible. Adopting its language and approaches with fidelity can jump-start transformative learning at every level of a learning community.

I know school leaders. We choose this work because of our personal commitments to children and to making this world a better place. I hope that you chose this book to become a better leader. I hope your personal mission and commitment to students helps you stick with the deep personal learning you will be asked to take on in these pages. The learning below the surface will make you a better human being for your students, your team, your family, and the rest of the world.

Acknowledgments

I would like to thank Delea Deane-Allen, Brian Behrman, and my editor Adaobi Obi Tulton for their wise feedback through the writing process; my family and my Noble Story Group partners for their unflagging support; and most of all my dad for editing every inch of this book with his writer's eagle eye.

About the Author

Matt Taylor is the founder and CEO of The Noble Story Group, a consulting group that leverages emotional intelligence to unleash leadership potential through the power of social–emotional leadership to promote sustainable, thriving, and equitable communities. He is a co-author of Daniel Goleman's *Building Blocks of Emotional Intelligence* primer series and a contributor to *School Administrator* magazine, the Fordham Institute's *Education Gadfly*, and other coaching blogs.

Preparing to Do Mindset Work

1 Seven Invisible Obstacles to Strong School Leadership

Every school and educational organization is led by leaders who are seeking to develop and get better. All are learning skills and knowledge that will make them stronger, but few of them are able to focus on what is truly holding them back from succeeding, or from reaching their next level of personal growth.

The most significant obstacles to growth are "below the surface" of skills and knowledge. This book will refer to what lies below the surface as mindsets. Mindsets are made up of the elements that dictate our habits of human interaction: values, beliefs, motives, traits, and other personal attributes.

Every leader arrives in their role with mindsets that serve them and mindsets that get in their way, or self-limiting mindsets. Leaders will work through some of these self-limiting mindsets on their own, but with others they will hit a brick wall. These more elusive, deep-seated habits of mind and behavior have been with leaders most of their lives. They tend to be so deeply engrained that leaders—and people in general—think of them as "just the way I am." When we step into the role of leadership for the first time or are promoted to a new level, these self-limiting mindsets often become more pronounced or take on new significance.

Over the last decade I have been immersed in the coaching and training of adaptive leadership—the human, emotions-driven side of leadership where there are no right or wrong answers and decisions come down to choosing between competing values. Developing leaders through this adaptive lens, my colleagues and I have noticed several archetypes emerging in the kinds of self-limiting mindsets that are common to school leaders at all levels. While these archetypes aren't new (most are leadership types that have been widely studied in the fields of social psychology and business), we are bringing them together in a new way and applying a new lens to addressing them. We have identified a group of seven self-limiting mindsets that we see in various combinations across leaders, roles, and schools.

They are:

- The Transactional Manager
- The Unintended Enabler
- The Negative Controller
- The Pacesetter
- The Doer
- The Imposter
- The Implementer

The Transactional Manager

There is much written about the transactional manager management approach (McClesky 2014; Spahr 2014; and Hargis et al. 2011).[1] My use of this term emphasizes its technical, compliance-driven aspects that can demotivate stakeholders when the approach is overused.

Transactional managers assume that the world is a mostly rational place, that adult human beings are rational creatures that receive clear (to me) information, process it (like I do), and then behave according to the expectations I have communicated: a simple transaction. They under-prioritize understanding other people's needs, and inevitably tell too much and listen too little. When these leaders do not know where their people are and what they need, they are likely to misdiagnose the problem and choose the wrong leadership action to accomplish their objectives. These errors can lead the transactional manager to make the *fundamental attribution error*—the assumption that *people themselves* are the reason for their lack of growth and not the conditions in which they are working, which the leader is largely responsible for creating (Heath and Heath 2010).[2]

The Unintended Enabler

The concepts of unintended enabler and negative controller (the next self-limiting mindset) have been applied effectively to the education sector in the last decade by the CT3 professional development group (CT3 2018).[3]

Unintended enablers are uncomfortable with conflict and are afraid of damaging relationships. These leaders often hold a negative view of positional power. When acting from an unintended enabler mindset, leaders default to attempting to build or preserve positive relationship and inspire stakeholders, even when those approaches will not achieve the outcomes they desire. Enablers "let things go this time" and retreat to silence when observing behavior that doesn't meet their standards.

When leaders enable, what they allow becomes the unwritten rule. When their teams and students know that they are not going to be held accountable, leaders lose credibility, and inadvertently communicate that they don't believe in their people. Schools led by unintended enablers may be positive on the surface but lack real investment in learning, and they are marked by underperformance in all substantive areas.

The Negative Controller

Negative controllers assume that, when people struggle, there is something wrong with *them* (CT3 2018).[4] When driven by the negative controller mindset, a leader who sees a teacher struggling thinks, "This teacher is struggling because he/she is not committed, or not willing to work hard enough, or blames kids, or is an excuse maker, or a racist." Like the transactional manager, the negative controller misdiagnoses leadership challenges by making the *fundamental attribution error*—the assumption that *people themselves* are the reason for their lack of growth, rather than the conditions in which they are working. This assumption lets the negative controller off the hook. It also leads to negative relationships, insecure learners, and an emotionally toxic organizational culture.

The Pacesetter

The pacesetter is one of Daniel Goleman's six leadership styles (Goleman, Boyatzis, and McKee 2002).[5] Pacesetters are driven by an admirable desire to reach and exemplify excellence. In schools, excellence is often equated with the social justice–related drive to close the opportunity gap for students, as measured by outcomes on achievement tests. This is mission-driven work that attracts mission-driven people. Leaders create organizational cultures around this goal that both deeply resonate with educators and create intense urgency. School leaders often assume that embodying this ideal means sacrificing themselves for the mission. This is an emotionally contagious phenomenon. When school leaders lead this way, their teams respond in kind.

While this approach may work for short periods of time, such as during start-up or turnaround, it is not sustainable. Staff perceive their pacesetter leader as not caring about them as people. Schools and leaders who attempt to maintain the pacesetter approach to teaching and learning experience chronic stress. Teachers pass on their stress to students, who respond in kind. Performance of both adults and students decreases. Over time, there is significant teacher and leader attrition. The constant turnover of staff leads to even more urgency to develop new people quickly, which intensifies the pacesetter response over time.

The Doer

Doers believe that their job is to the be the #1 performer (Charan 2011).[6] Leaders who demonstrate this mindset are usually promoted to their new roles in part *because* they were great doers in their previous roles, so the mindset and behaviors are deeply engrained. Often the doer hasn't been taught that, in their new role, they are supposed do less and instead direct other doers. Even when they have been taught, they struggle to let go of what served them and made them feel competent in the past. (In this way a mindset can shift from being a strength to an obstacle as one climbs to new levels of leadership.)

Doers do not delegate well, if at all. They tend to take on the work of others at the expense of doing their own work (which they are likely the only person in the organization qualified or tasked to do). They send the inadvertent message to their teams that they do not trust them to do their own work. Their teams become increasingly dependent on the doer to solve their problems for them. Doer leaders take on more and more while their teams do less. They become overwhelmed, drop balls more and more frequently, and communicate reactively. Doers lose credibility and sink into chronic stress, while their teams become less empowered and less effective over time.

The Imposter

While all seven of these self-limiting mindsets are very personal in nature, this one—commonly called imposter syndrome or imposter phenomenon—is anchored most deeply in self (Mount and Tardanico 2014; Mount 2015).[7] Leaders struggling with imposter syndrome believe that they aren't really qualified for their job, that others believe this too, and that sooner or later they will be confronted about this ugly truth by the people they lead. In challenging moments, imposter syndrome sends leaders into their head, causing disconnection, indecisiveness, and avoidance of difficult decisions or actions in the moment. It leads to the very loss of credibility that the leader fears.

The imposter syndrome may be the deeper mindset at work when one or more of the other mindsets on this list shows up in practice. When combined with any of the others, the impact on leader behavior is multiplied.

The Implementer

Implementers believe that the leader's primary job is to execute on the best practices they are given by others. The implementer should not be confused with the doer, who is driven by the desire to be the performer. Implementer believes that the results will be better, and the process will be more efficient if they fully follow the school leadership playbook that they are given by their manager or their organization.

Our sector has done a lot of great work on building efficient systems in schools. We have gotten smarter about how to pool our resources to build better and better curriculum, and then to share it efficiently and widely, resulting in a significant, positive impact on student achievement. We have increasingly valued the implementer competency in our selection of leaders. And implementers are not wrong about the importance of being able to replicate great practices! Where they go wrong is in the degree to which they try to replicate.

When implementers lead from someone else's playbook without connecting to their values, they may inadvertently lose touch with their own visions. Implementers tend to lead from a persona that is not authentic to who they are and to what they believe. They are less likely to truly connect with others, particularly when confronted by adaptive leadership challenges that require authentic influence and inspiration to be able to solve.

Why These Mindsets Matter

These self-limiting mindsets have a deep impact on the leaders whose behaviors are governed by them. These obstacles lead to constant overwork and significant emotional turmoil that has become known as chronic stress or power stress.

In their book *Becoming a Resonant Leader,* Boyatzis and McKee refer to the cycle of constant stress as the sacrifice syndrome, which ultimately leads to burnout and diminished effectiveness (Boyatzis and McKee 2005).[8] Leaders who can't find their way through these obstacles suffer. They do not live the lives that they imagined for themselves. Further, they will not realize their potential for growth as leaders and human beings, and they know it. While all of this is terrible for the leaders themselves, the negative impact of their self-limiting mindsets on the people they lead, and their educational outcomes, is much greater. This is because teaching and learning are emotional work, and emotions are contagious.

School Leadership Is Primarily Emotional Work . . .

In our focus on educational outcomes, we often lose sight of the fact that learning and teaching are fundamentally emotional work. People need to feel emotionally safe to learn. There have been multiple studies showing that emotional connection is a condition for learning:

- A concept from graduate school that has stayed with me is Vygotsky's Zone of Proximal Development theory. The idea here is that, for people to learn new skills, a trusted "knowledgeable other" must guide and encourage them as a first step (Penguin Dictionary of Psychology 2009).[9]
- Research on memory has made it very clear that what makes its way into long-term memory is almost always associated with a strong emotion (Bloom 1956).[10]
- Bloom's Taxonomy identifies the affective domain—marked by feeling tone, emotional acceptance, or rejection—as one of three domains for learning. The affective domain is the gateway to learning. If the emotional gates aren't open, learning can't get in. Research on memory makes sense when considering the affective domain. What makes its way into long-term memory is almost always associated with a strong emotion (Conway, Anderson, and Larsen 1994).[11]
- Goleman writes that how the brain's reaction to emotional stimuli shows that negative emotions shut down cognitive function while positive ones both reinforce existing synapse connections *and* create new neural pathways (Karen 1998).[12]
- Attachment research shows that connection and trust is a prerequisite to learning for people who have experienced trauma, and that this connection does not come easily (Boyatzis in Coursera).[13]

Meeting a human being's needs for connection is a prerequisite to their being able to learn from their teacher. Once a teacher has met their student's need for connection, the work of learning can begin. The second core ingredient then comes into play: challenge. The education sector is much more fluent in the challenge component of learning. Academic rigor is the focus du jour, and as a sector we are making headway on the "what" of academic skills. However, effective challenge in teaching and learning is both a "what" and a "how" endeavor. Effective challenge stimulates intrinsic motivation and energizes a learner to strive to meet their full potential. This is a largely human, emotional endeavor that is inextricably linked to the connection between teacher and student.

This book is grounded in the belief that a school leader's job is to create the conditions for the people in their schools to reach their full potential. The two conditions leaders must create for each individual are connection and challenge. These conditions are emotional conditions. They are necessary for both students and teachers alike because emotions are contagious. If the connection and challenge needs of teachers are not being met, then the teachers will not be able to create the right conditions for students.

. . . And Emotions Are Contagious

The biggest challenge and opportunity of creating the right conditions for people to learn is that emotions are contagious. Significant and astonishing brain research has proven this to be true. We have what scientists call mirror neurons that react to the emotions of those around us. These neurons dance with each other in our separate heads and hearts. The same research shows that the emotions of the person with the most power in a room are significantly more contagious than those of others (Goleman and Boyatzis 2008).[14]

These findings have proven what many already knew: that a school reacts to the emotions of its leader. If a leader struggles to manage chronic stress, then so will everyone else in the school. The leader's emotions and the behaviors connected to them tend to be internalized by other leaders and teachers. That's where the most frightening emotional contagion begins. A classroom of students reacts to the emotional contagion of their teacher. If a teacher is experiencing chronic stress, then so will everyone in their classroom. Consider the impact of this emotional contagion on the conditions for learning.

The science of emotional contagion teaches us that emotional conditions for learning are delicate, tenuous, and very dependent on leaders. This is true from the superintendent all the way down the chain to the teacher. There is a far more powerful and complex emotional interdependence between us than we think that impacts our ability to create emotional conditions. Everyone in a school's emotional chain is responsible for the conditions that actually come to pass. The higher up the leader, the more impact they have on the system and the more responsibility they bear for ensuring that a healthy climate of connection and challenge is present.

We Cannot Teach Mindsets . . .

To understand why we can't teach new, productive mindsets, we must begin with Daniel Goleman's definition of a competency. According to Goleman, competencies consist of a combination of characteristics that are best described using the analogy of an iceberg. Below the water's surface we know that there is not only more iceberg, but significantly more than what we see above the surface. Leadership competencies are like icebergs in that there are the aspects that we can see in a leader's knowledge, skills, and behaviors, but there is much more to the competency below the surface—inside of the leaders or between them and others—that is not visible. In this book we roughly equate the concept of mindset with what is below the surface of Goleman's competency iceberg (Figure 1.1).

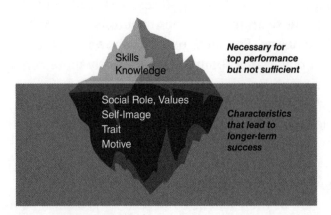

Figure 1.1: Goleman's competency iceberg.

Source: Goleman's competency iceberg. Goleman Daniel. 1995. *Emotional Intelligence: Why It Can Matter More Than IQ* (Bantam); but may be property of Korn Ferry consulting.

Unfortunately, we cannot just read books, integrate some sentence starters, or practice some leadership skills to change self-limiting mindsets and behaviors. The root causes are not knowledge- or skill-based, and the behaviors we see are just the tip of the iceberg of the obstacle. The problems that self-limiting mindsets cause are invisible to the human eye because they are personal and internal, or as I will refer to them, "below the surface." What's below the surface may be something inside of me, or it may be something between you and me.

Internal Below-the-Surface Obstacles

The leader brings a complex stew of emotions, experiences, identities, beliefs, values, motives, and character traits that have a much larger impact on the leader's competency level than what we are aware of above the surface. If the leader's below-the-surface characteristics do not align with their above-the-surface knowledge, skills, and intended behaviors, then it is not likely they will be able to "perform."

We can teach to the above-the-surface competency gaps by practicing skills and building knowledge. Sometimes skill building is all a leader needs to become competent. This is often the case with leaders who are new to a competency. These leaders find that new knowledge and skills fit nicely with their existing beliefs, motives, values, etc. Through practice, they grow quickly.

Unfortunately, we cannot teach to the below-the-surface competency gaps. If there is misalignment between skills, knowledge, and behaviors and a person's values, beliefs, identities, motives, and character traits, there is no amount of teaching that will change that. No one can teach us to shift these deeply personal aspects of ourselves. Others can support us to make those shifts, but the new awareness and strategies come from within ourselves.

Interpersonal Below-the-Surface Obstacles

What is invisible below the surface between leaders and the people they lead also contributes to self-limiting mindsets. In her Six Circle Model, leadership consultant Margaret Wheatly created the simple but powerful concept of the Green Line to illustrate this social version of the below-the-surface concept (Perrius 2014).[15] The three circles above the Green Line (the horizontal line in Figure 1.2) embody the conversation we tend to focus on with our stakeholders, in essence, what's on the agenda.

THE GREEN LINE

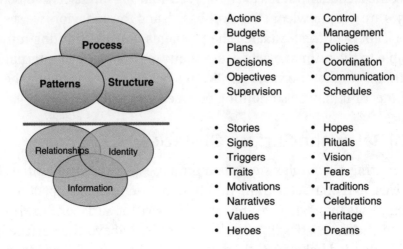

• Actions	• Control
• Budgets	• Management
• Plans	• Policies
• Decisions	• Coordination
• Objectives	• Communication
• Supervision	• Schedules
• Stories	• Hopes
• Signs	• Rituals
• Triggers	• Vision
• Traits	• Fears
• Motivations	• Traditions
• Narratives	• Celebrations
• Values	• Heritage
• Heroes	• Dreams

Figure 1.2: Wheatley's graphic illustration of the Green Line concept.
Source: Margaret Wheatly, 1992.

The three circles below the Green Line represent another entirely different, potentially high-stakes level of interaction that may go unnoticed and unaddressed. This interaction is emotional and personal. It is the interaction of identities, values, assumptions, emotions, histories, and more. What is happening below the Green Line is always in the room, whether we are aware of it and engage with it or not.

Strong leaders value what is happening below the Green Line and they are adept at surfacing this material, and then engaging with it. Part of this strength is skill, and part of it is mindset. We can't teach this essential leadership mindset just by telling leaders what others are experiencing and having them read books, though these can be part of the solution. Leaders must shift their value systems and learn to exercise new muscles like empathy and compassion to do this well.

. . . But Productive Mindsets *Can* Be Learned

We cannot teach below-the-surface competencies, but they can be learned. More aptly put, people can change deeply engrained habits of mind and behavior that often seem like permanent aspects of who they are.

Neuroscientists have discovered that our habits of mind and behavior become encoded in our brains as neural pathways. The deeper the habit, the stronger the neural pathway. Our oldest and deepest habits are neural superhighways that are very easy for us to travel. We follow them almost automatically when they are triggered by our environment, our emotions, and our thoughts. The exciting news about neural pathways is that we can deconstruct and replace them with new neural pathways through intentional focus and practice. We can intentionally rewire our brains! (Goleman, Boyatzis, and McKee 2001).[16]

Not surprisingly, rewiring our brains takes significant effort and time. New pathways start out as footpaths that we carve with a machete in the wilderness, even as we long for the comfortable old neural superhighway of habits in the distance. We have to carve the new path over and over again for it to evolve—and stick. We must face the triggers of old habits and force ourselves to choose a new behavior over and over again. Over time, the paths become wider and easier to travel, and our old pathways begin to shrink. When we are successful, the new habit becomes the superhighway and the old one becomes the small dirt path in the forest.

. . . And EI Is the Key

Emotional Intelligence leadership theory, when applied effectively, provides a method to support leaders to rewire our brains, and overcome our deepest self-limiting mindsets. We cannot teach ourselves out of the seven self-limiting mindsets discussed earlier in the chapter, but we can build new mindsets and internal habits with a deliberate focus on self-awareness and self-management. Once we are aware of our "stuff," we can build self-management strategies that will help us to construct new neural pathways. As we begin to shift our internal patterns of thinking and behaving, we draw in social awareness to help us make changes in how we see the world. The self-work inevitably leads to acquiring a new perspective about others. Productive new leadership behaviors are the inevitable culmination of this type of deep, internal work.

The next chapter will ground you in EI theory and our 5-Square method for supporting leaders to shift their mindsets and behaviors. The foundational concepts are Goleman's, but we have made them operational in our 5-Square. Once you understand how the 5-Square supports personal leadership transformation, you will be ready to begin the personal leadership work of this book.

Endnotes

1. McCleskey, J.A. (2014). Situational, transformational, and transactional leadership and leadership development. *Journal of Business Studies Quarterly* 5(4), 6–9.; Spahr, P. (November 25, 2014). What is Transactional Leadership? How Structure Leads to Results. Retrieved November 8, 2016, from http://online.stu.edu/transactional-leadership/ (accessed 18 November 2016); Hargis, M.B., Wyatt, J.D., and Piotrowski, C. (2011). Developing leaders: Examining the role of transactional and transformational leadership across contexts business. *Organization Development Journal* 29 (3): 51–66.
2. Heath, C. and Heath, D. (2010). *Switch: How to Change Things When Change Is Hard.* New York: Random House.
3. CT3 Web Admin (2018). A powerful paradigm shift for educators. https://www.ct3education.com/2018/05/08/a-powerful-paradigm-shift-for-educators/.
4. Ibid.
5. Goleman, D., Boyatzis, R., and McKee, A. (2002). *Primal leadership: Learning to Lead with Emotional Intelligence.* Cambridge, MA: Harvard Business School Press.
6. Charan, R., Drotter, S., and Noel, J. (2011). *The Leadership Pipeline: How to Build the Leadership Powered Company*, Second Edition. San Francisco: Wiley; Batista, E. (2013). Doing less, leading more. *Harvard Business Review* https://hbr.org/2013/12/doing-less-leading-more.
7. Mount, P. and Tardanico, S. (2014). Beating the impostor phenomenon. Greensboro, NC: Center for Creative Leadership; Mount, P. (2015). Impostor phenomenon. *Training Journal*, 5(8).
8. Boyatzis, R. and McKee, A. (2005). *Resonant Leadership: Renewing Yourself and Connecting with Others Through Mindfulness, Hope, and Compassion.* Cambridge, MA: Harvard Business School Press.
9. Zone of proximal development. (2009). *Penguin Dictionary of Psychology.* Retrieved from Credo Reference database Affective Domain.
10. Bloom, B.S. (Ed.), Engelhart, M.D., Furst, E.J., Hill, W.H. et al. (1956). *Taxonomy of Educational Objectives, Handbook I: The Cognitive Domain.* New York: David McKay Co Inc.
11. Conway, M.A., Anderson, S.J., Larsen, S.F. et al. (1994). The formation of flash bulb memories. *Memory and Cognition.* 22 (3): 326–343. doi:10.3758/BF03200860. PMID 8007835.

12. Karen, R. (1998). *Becoming Attached: First Relationships and How They Shape Our Capacity to Love.* New York: Oxford University Press.
13. Boyatzis, R. The Positive (PEA) and Negative (NEA) Emotional Attractors. Coursera. Case Western Reserve University. https://www.coursera.org/lecture/emotional-intelligence-leadership/watch-the-positive-pea-and-negative-nea-emotional-attractors-4GRcY.
14. Goleman, D. and Boyatzis, R. (2008). Social intelligence and the biology of leadership. *Harvard Business Review* magazine.
15. Perrius, C. (2014). An integrated approach to improving school systems. National Equity Project. https://blog.nationalequityproject.org/2011/05/23/an-integrated-approach-to-improving-school-systems/.
16. Goleman, D., Boyatzis, R., and McKee, A. (2001). Primal leadership: the hidden driver of great performance. *Harvard Business Review* magazine (December).

2 Building New Mindsets and Behaviors with Emotional Intelligence
(How You Will Drive Your Learning Using This Book)

There are four domains of Emotional Intelligence in Daniel Goleman's theory. The 5-Square—my method for applying Goleman's theory—adds a fifth. In this chapter you will build a deep enough understanding of these domains to apply them to your own below-the-surface learning in the following chapters. You will also see how the domains work together to support leadership growth in ways that a skill-building approach never could.

I tell my own story of developing school leaders in two parts: what I did before I discovered EI and what I have done since then. First as a principal and then as a trainer of school leaders, I was fortunate to receive strong leadership training: from graduate school, KIPP's Leader in Training Institute, and later KIPP's Leader Development Fellowship. Achievement First's (AF's) internal leadership development was excellent, too, particularly when it came to instructional skill development.

My training and coaching approaches were grounded in knowledge acquisition and the gradual release model of skill building. My trainees built their knowledge from the readings and models that I provided; they practiced with my support; and then they practiced independently while I observed them and provided feedback. For example, when I facilitated my "difficult conversations" sessions, they would read some chapters from *Crucial Conversations* as prework (Patterson et al. 2011).[1] I would provide them with sentence starters, a high-level agenda, a set of criteria for success, and I would model in a role play and case study. Trainees would engage with additional case studies and role-play conversations using the resources I provided.

I was proud of these development sessions. They were well planned, rigorous, and practice based. Then I discovered EI and realized I was largely missing the mark.

What I learned from Emotional Intelligence theory is that I was only focusing on about 25% of the competencies my trainees needed to excel as leaders.

Goleman's EI model has four domains: two are focused on self and two are focused on others. The four domains are self-awareness, self-management, social awareness, and relationship management.

> **Self-awareness** encompasses our connection to our values and intuition, our awareness of our internal obstacles below the surface, and our awareness of how others perceive us.

> **Self-management** is our ability to leverage our values and intuition and manage our internal obstacles to show up as our most effective selves.

> **Social awareness** turns our focus from self to others. It is our ability to understand—to really see—other people and groups.

> **Relationship management** is the culmination of the dimensions that precede it. Once we are managing ourselves and can see others clearly, we are able to choose the most effective leadership approach in the moment to meet others' needs and to achieve our goals.

The four domains can be applied in another important way: to distinguish awareness from action (Figure 2.1). The awareness domains are about the understanding of what makes us and others tick. The management domains focus on the actions we choose to take, either internally, or in relationship with others.

An epiphany when I discovered EI was that almost all of my leadership development experience (skill building to engage others) was within the relationship management domain. Absolutely none of my training addressed either of the two "self" domains. I failed to understand that practicing moves in fictional case studies never challenged my trainees to think about their inner obstacles—their triggers, emotions, limiting stories about themselves or others—that might get in their way. Without this self-focus, they were likely to continue enacting self-limiting leadership behaviors no matter how many trainings on courageous conversations they attended.

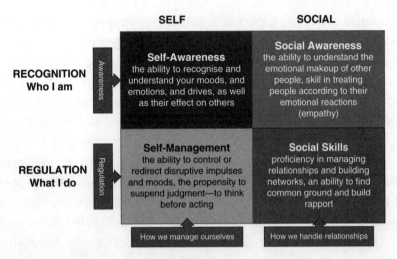

SELF   SOCIAL

RECOGNITION
Who I am

Awareness

Self-Awareness
the ability to recognise and
understand your moods, and
emotions, and drives, as well
as their effect on others

Social Awareness
the ability to understand the
emotional makeup of other
people, skill in treating
people according to their
emotional reactions
(empathy)

REGULATION
What I do

Regulation

Self-Management
the ability to control or
redirect disruptive impulses
and moods, the propensity to
suspend judgment—to think
before acting

Social Skills
proficiency in managing
relationships and building
networks, an ability to find
common ground and build
rapport

How we manage ourselves   How we handle relationships

Figure 2.1: Goleman's model. From GS-4 Paper. (2015). A Self Study History (5 April). `https://selfstudyhistory.com/2015/04/05/concepts-of-emotional-intelligence/`.

Furthermore, my training paid very little attention to the social awareness domain. This is about leveraging empathy to understand where people are and what they need. Where people are is partly about what can be observed on the outside (what people say and do), but much more about what is usually hidden from the external observer, which is their emotional reality below Wheatley's Green Line (see Figure 1.2 in Chapter 1). Social awareness means *listening with empathy and compassion*. My training was mostly about *talking, presenting, and teaching*—communicating information in order to get people to complete a task well.

EI leadership theory begins with the premise that leadership is as much about us as it is about the people we lead. To effectively engage with others, we need to work the other three EI domains *first*. We need to understand and get ourselves right before we can understand where others are and what they need. If we can do all that inner work effectively, then we are prepared to choose the most effective engagement approach to achieve our goals in unique contexts with unique human beings.

Goleman's framework turned my leadership development approach on its head. While technical skill building is important, especially for new leaders, I began to build in training for the other domains of Emotional Intelligence as well. Doing so led me to a second epiphany: by focusing on the self and getting below the surface, my trainees started to overcome skill deficits that they had been struggling with over time, regardless of how much skill building support they received. The focus on EI forced them to confront what was actually the biggest obstacle to their growth that had previously been hidden—a self-limiting mindset—and then supported them over time to rewire their brains and build new habits.

We cannot teach—either ourselves or others—when we are stuck in self-limiting mindsets, because these obstacles are usually so personal and below the surface that we don't know what they are. And what we are not aware of we cannot address. What we *can* do, with a deliberate focus on self-awareness and self-management, is bring unknown obstacles to the surface and build internal strategies to shift patterns of thought and behavior. As we shift our internal patterns of thought and behavior, we begin to draw on social awareness to help us shift how we see others. That is inevitable; self-work leads to a new perspective on others. Enlightened leadership behavior is the culmination of this internal work.

Applying EI with the 5-Square

At the Noble Story Group, we have over time turned Goleman's four EI domains into a leadership development and strategic planning tool. The foundational concepts are Goleman's, but we (and others like us) have made them operational. We think of this as the difference between theoretical and applied science. Our one theoretical contribution is our fifth domain. We took values, intuition, and self-care out of self-awareness and created a fifth domain to highlight these aspects of self that we have found to be the key to accessing personal leadership power. We call this coaching tool, simply, the 5-Square.

The 5-Square is our approach to putting EI to work in our lives and leadership.

Over time and training, we have distilled the EI development journey through the five squares down **to seven core questions** (Figure 2.2).

When leaders apply these questions to their work and their lives, they begin to shift their own deep-seated, self-limiting patterns of thinking and behavior. *No one is teaching them anything*—they already have what they need within themselves to build new competencies. The learning journey is building awareness of their own power and inner obstacles, then learning to leverage this power and manage obstacles. A coach or coaching-manager can help guide this work, but the content and strategies come from the leaders themselves.

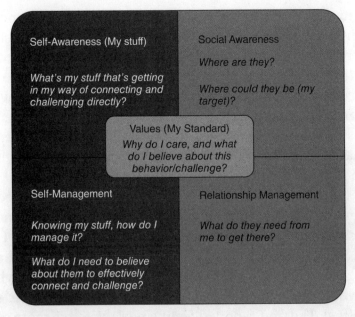

Figure 2.2: The Noble Story Group's basic 5-Square.

How the 5-Square Works: A Personal Case Study

I wish I had known how to apply the 5-Square to my own leadership as a principal. It took me years to become aware of what was getting in my way below the surface. Had I been aware of my internal challenges earlier, my path to effectiveness would likely have been much faster and less painful.

My leadership trajectory was pretty typical. I did well as a middle manager. In my first school administrator role I was half teacher, half extended-day director. In a school where every student participated in a 90-minute enrichment block from 3:30 P.M. to 5:00 P.M. four days a week, I was for all practical purposes the afternoon principal. From soup to nuts, I built and managed the administrative systems of the program. I hired and managed the team of artists and coaches who came in to teach in the afternoons. I was present across the building during those 90 minutes, managing every student or adult challenge that came up. And it was good! Feedback was positive, my manager was happy, and I loved the adrenaline rush of swooping in to solve problems. After a year in this position, the founder chose me to be her successor.

Fast-forward 18 months to the winter of my first year as principal, and the scene had shifted. I still had the credibility I had earned and strengths that served me in my previous role, but the days felt darker. I could not believe how much of my time I spent dealing with the emotionally charged challenges of adults! In most of these cases, there was no rational or right answer that could solve a problem. I found myself dragging other people's problems around with me, and I was unable to let them go. Another unpleasant surprise for me was the reactive nature of my work. I was good at swooping in and solving classroom challenges, but suddenly they filled my entire day. While I had a leadership team now to help, there seemed to be more to fix than all three of us could handle. I found myself working 11- to 13-hour days and weekends on a regular basis. This did not go over well at home, where my wife and I were raising two toddlers. I did two things in my life: I worked and I took care of infants. Everything else had disappeared. I sometimes felt near panic when thinking about how I would make it to the end of the year. Meanwhile, the energy in the school had shifted. The staff reported feeling more stressed, more overwhelmed, and increasingly negative.

Fast-forward again another 18 months and I was a third-year principal. I was carrying around significantly less of my team's emotional burdens. I seemed to be developing a thicker skin, and I was showing up more grounded in challenging, emotional conversations. I also noticed that the energy in the school felt more positive. I was not sure why because nothing substantial had changed, but I was thankful. I had become more efficient at the administrative tasks of the job, so I was spending slightly less time working. But still too much time. I still worked many 12-hour days and at least one day out of every weekend. I still could not consistently hold sacred work time during a school day because I was responding to crises in the building. I was increasingly aware that I was doing work that others should be doing, and that I needed to delegate that work. I had attended some really good delegation training and had (on paper) strong protocols and systems for delegating tasks and managing others to outcomes. I was highly motivated to delegate more, but something was holding me back. I knew that I did not like to ask other people to work harder, but I was unable to figure out why that was getting in my way given my desire to change and the delegation skills I had in my toolbox.

The Left Side of the 5-Square: Doing Our Self-Work

When leaders have acquired a technical skill like delegating, but struggle to perform it in practice, they probably have a self-limiting mindset getting in the way. There were several mindsets I had as a leader that got in my way, but the doer mindset was at the top of the list in terms of impact on effectiveness. If I had been my manager or coach, knowing what I know now, I would have stopped training my principal-self to delegate and started focusing on how I was getting in my own way at the mindset level. The personal below-the-surface reflection is what I call self-work.

Grounding in My Power (What's My Standard?)

Self-work begins by connecting to the source of *my* power as a human being. While there are four aspects of this power—or drivers, as my colleague Michele Nevarez calls them (Nevarez 2020)[2]—I would have begun with my core values. I would have started by asking, "Why do I *care* about delegating and prioritizing my time effectively?" The answers to that question, if I had been able to reflect deeply, would have been:

- Health and family—I want to live a sustainable, healthy, and full life. I want to be a good father to my children and partner to my spouse.
- Growth and development—I want my team to grow in their leadership. If I do their work for them, I am holding them back.
- Empowerment and social justice—I am doing this work to create the opportunity for people to reach their full potential, and to fight back against the systematic injustice of our country. I am not empowering my people to lead. I am enabling. I am disempowering. This is the opposite of my values.

As a new principal, I was like a boat without a rudder in a storm. I was making leadership decisions in the moment that seemed right, but that were not focused. I may have been keeping everything afloat, but we were going in circles. Rarely did I think about my core values, and never did I deliberately use them as my rudder to make day-to-day decisions. I am sure they guided me on some big things at a subconscious level. The challenge is that leaders make hundreds or thousands of decisions every day. If many of them are technically right decisions but are not grounded in that leader's values, the overall direction—the vision—may be unclear.

As a new principal, I was not tapped into my values. If I had been, I would have felt even more dissonance, and I would have felt compelled to do something more about my delegation and life balance problems. As a third-year principal I was tapped into the values of health and family, and my energy and determination were gathering behind it to make a change in the way I was leading. It took another year for my motivation to reach a level that led to deliberate action. If I had been as tapped into my values of growth, empowerment, and social justice, I know my power would have grown more quickly and I would have acted sooner.

To really understand and access our power, we must be aware of its connection to our identities. This is because our values are closely tied to our identities. According to the idea of intersectionality, we all have many identities, or facets of self, that make up who we are. Some of these include gender, race, sexuality, class, ability, place of origin, and religion, but the list is really only limited by the number of social constructs we use to make sense of ourselves and each other in the world. These identities are not neutral. We know that multiple forms of discrimination accumulate across identity markers, marginalizing or privileging groups and individuals. Yet we also know that our identities are a source of our power. They weave together to shape our cultures, from family culture to our many different group cultures. From all of these interwoven identity groups, we learn what matters to us in the world.

Social justice is a core value of mine that fuels my power. I value social justice in part because I am aware of my outsized power and privilege as a white man, and I feel a responsibility to use my power to create a more equitable distribution of power in the world. I have colleagues of color who also hold the value of social justice at their core. However, we hold this power in different ways because of our identities and life experiences. We all need to be aware of how our identities connect to our values to maximize them as our power source, and to make sure they do not become an obstacle to reaching our goals. More about that last point later.

Building New Mindsets and Behaviors with Emotional Intelligence

Other Core Power Drivers

Our power comes from the things that fuel us as human beings. Michele Nevarez at Goleman EI calls this fuel our core drivers and has bucketed them into four motivational spheres (Figure 2.3).

The values I explored earlier are part of the life path sphere. While our values are our anchor in challenging leadership decisions, we must stay grounded in all of our drivers to sustain ourselves over time as leaders and show up consistently as our most effective selves.

Until I became a principal, I had always had some kind of athletic activity that I practiced on a regular basis. I had always been part of a vocal music group of some kind, and I read a lot of fiction. All contributed to my well-being from an early age. During my early years as a principal, I decided that I didn't have time for these things because I had too much work to do. The years when these core aspects of my well-being were absent were a dark period of my life. I was doing the hardest work I had ever done while taking away the physically and emotionally fulfilling activities that renewed and sustained me.

In retrospect, I was probably functioning at about 60% of my leadership capacity. It was not until sometime in my third year as a principal that I started paying attention to my drivers. But more on that when we come to self-management.

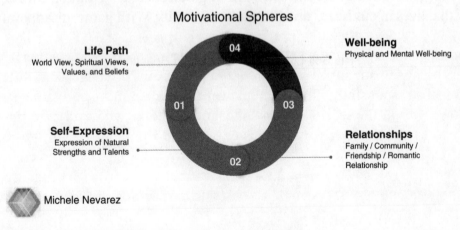

Figure 2.3: The motivational spheres from Goleman EI (2019).

Building Self-Awareness (What's My Stuff?)

 My next move, if I had been coaching my principal self, would have been to dig into what was getting in my way. We have chosen to distill a complex set of psychological factors into a simple label we can remember and that does not sound overwhelming: our *stuff*. Exploring my stuff as a principal would have gotten me further under the surface to understand the emotional reactions that led to the behaviors that were getting in my way. That kind of exploration is most fruitful when done in the context of our work—the micromoments when we live out the behaviors we want to change. In my coach training I learned to call these "behavioral moments." Analyzing the actual moment when I chose to do someone else's work rather than delegate it to them, I can identify the chain reaction of emotions and thoughts that lead to my bad habit (Figure 2.4). For me a common **trigger** was suddenly realizing, as I was planning my week, that something urgent needed to be done and should have been started days or weeks ago.

This realization would trigger a complex soup of **sensations** and **emotions**. A sinking, tight feeling in my chest would be followed immediately by a hot flash up my neck and to my forehead. My first emotion was usually panic, followed by disappointment and anger with myself. Guilt and indecision came next, and all were eventually wiped away by determination and some kind of grim pride connected to self-sacrifice.

Our emotions don't live by themselves. They come with stories, or beliefs. The ones that get in our way we call **self-limiting beliefs**. Each emotion connects to a story that lives in our heads and becomes our reality. With panic, disappointment,

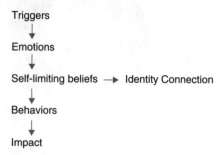

Figure 2.4: The self-limiting mindset chain reaction.

and anger comes, "Oh my God, what did I do?!? I am f#*!ed! How could I have dropped this ball. I really screwed up this time. This is going to cost me." With guilt and indecision comes, "I know my assistant principal should be doing this, but how can I ask her at this point? She is already working so hard and is so stressed, trying to find balance with two young kids at home. How could I ask her to do this, so reactively? If I do give her this work, then I will cause real stress and unhappiness here and she might quit. I will also reveal myself to the world as an ineffective leader." Then with grim determination and pride comes, "Well, I know I can fix it myself if I just bite the bullet, take one for the team, and grind for three extra hours. The product will be good, I can afford to take another hit, and no one will ever know I dropped the ball." Our awareness of how these stories play out in the moment is key to shifting the behaviors we hope to change. Changing our stories empowers us to change our behaviors.

To reach a deeper awareness of our self-limiting beliefs we must again explore their connection to our intersectional identities and the factors of power, privilege, and oppression that come with them. As a white, cis-gendered, heterosexual, upper-middle-class male, I held several identity-based stories that got in my way as a principal. I grew up in a family that went silent and stoic rather than engage in direct conflict. According to Tema Okun's 2019 article "White Supremacy Culture,"[3] fear of open conflict is a white norm that my BIPOC leaders may not share. My conflict-averse behavior surely got in their way, as they sensed my dissatisfaction and holding back but having to create their own story about why. Further, I now realize that my desire not to overburden at least one assistant principal was connected to my white privilege guilt. Knowing his life challenges connected to structural racism (both in his past and present) and how privileged my own path has been in comparison made me question my judgment about what was right and fair to ask of him. So I stayed silent, lowering the bar for him and possibly contributing to his own questions about our relationship and his performance. Awareness about how my identity played into my mindset issues would have helped me see how I was not leading from my standard and would have helped me understand how I was holding my assistant principal back. Even now with all the work I have done on my mindsets, I sometimes have to actively manage these stories in challenging leadership moments across lines of difference.

We all have self-limiting stories that connect to our identities. While I spoke from my privileged identities, there are self-limiting stories connected to the experiences of marginalized identities as well. In conversation with Black colleagues who lead this work with me, several have shared about grappling with imposter stories connected to their experiences of exclusion. From being the only Black person in a room to feeling that their voices were not valued, my colleagues internalized stories of self-doubt that led to behaviors ranging from overcompensating to passive and compliant management rather than leadership. Even now as highly successful senior leaders they must actively manage these stories as they continue to experience the inequitable conditions that caused them.

All our stories, identity-based or otherwise, work with our sensations and emotions to make up our *self-limiting mindsets*. These mindsets are patterns of emotion and thought that have become deeply engrained in us over time, and they dictate our habitual behavior. Unless we deliberately attempt to uncover them, we are usually not very aware of them because we don't *want* to have to face them. However, when we do become aware of them, we are able to see what is causing us to do the things we want to stop doing.

After unpacking our self-limiting mindsets, we continue building new awareness by focusing more deeply on our behavior and its impact. I knew that I was doing other people's work and that I was burning myself out. It would have taken deeper analysis with support, however, for me to realize that I was also *not* doing my principal work of proactive planning and communication, which no one else in the organization could do. That choice to not do that was also a behavior. So was isolating myself to hurriedly do complicated visioning and planning work that touched many people, behind closed doors. That was a behavior, too. Uncovering the many behaviors that accompanied the core problem would have helped me to see the myriad ways that I was impacting not only myself and my assistant principals but everyone else in my world. I was modeling dysfunctional leadership behavior to my leadership team and creating a pacesetter culture by working all the time. By not allowing them to own their own work I was disempowering and enabling my team, sending the message that I did not trust them to lead. Adults in my building did not feel comfortable making decisions without checking in with me first. More fundamentally, adults did not feel comfortable taking intellectual risks. They inevitably spread this emotional contagion to our students, making it feel unsafe for them to take intellectual risks.

I wish I had had the language of EI to help me become aware of my "standard" and my "stuff" and its impact on me and my school as a principal. Awareness is power. Knowing my deeper impact and how out of sync that was with my values would have sparked the intrinsic motivation to change that I did not have at the time. Seeing the patterns of emotion and story would have empowered me to act. We cannot control our emotional reactions, but we *can* manage them. We can also manage our stories—the mental narratives that become our internal reality.

Building Self-Management: Leveraging Our Standard, Managing Our Stuff, and Plugging into Our Drivers

Our triggers, sensations, emotions, and stories dictate our behavior, for better or for worse. When we are triggered by something that happens around us, we experience a physical and emotional reaction that our thinking brain attempts to make sense of with a story. These stories can be grounded in our standard (our values, intuition, and self-care), our stuff (our self-limiting beliefs and behaviors), or a mixture of both. The better our self-awareness in the moment, the stronger our ability to answer a fundamental question of emotionally intelligent leadership:

Is this my standard or my stuff?

It takes self-management for us to be perceptive enough in triggered moments to answer that question accurately. If we succeed at the awareness level, it takes even more self-management to choose new stories and new behaviors (rather than our self-limiting habits of mind and behavior) to show up in new ways as leaders.

Based on our training, research, and experience supporting leaders at Noble Story Group, we have prioritized three general strategies for managing triggers, emotions, and self-limiting beliefs in moments of challenge:

1. Creating space
2. Positive self-talk
3. Choosing noble stories

Creating Space Between a Trigger and My Response

We are hardwired to respond to threat with fight or flight. These are physiological reactions that are inherited patterns of emotion and behavior. When we are really triggered, our response amounts to an emotional hijack in which we lose our ability to use our thinking brain. The good news of EI is that, while we cannot control our physiological reaction to threat, we can manage our response.

Creating space between stimulus and response, or perceived threat and what we actually do, is the prerequisite to accessing any other self-management strategy. Creating space begins in our bodies, managing our sensations to create a window of time for us to slow down and return to our thinking brains. The most common of these strategies is intentional deep breathing. Two or three deep breaths can be the difference between disastrous and successful outcomes in a challenging conversation or a high-stakes decision-making moment. For me as a third-year principal trying to stop doing other people's work, the trigger moment was often the discovery that something needed to be done in the near future that was my assistant principal's responsibility. I needed to create space between that realization and my automatic self-limiting narrative to access new productive narratives about delegating. A deep breath and five seconds probably would have been enough to interrupt my self-limiting reaction and access those stories.

Breathing is one example of many physical actions we can perform in a moment of trigger to create space. More formal mindfulness meditation practices can be extremely effective as proactive techniques. There are less formal micropractices that we can access in the moment. I know leaders who, in a triggering moment during a conversation, will take a long sip of water before responding. For some it's as simple as leaning back, or leaning forward, in their chairs. I know one leader who discovered that taking off his sports coat allowed him to shift from leading in an inauthentic controlling persona to leading from his authentic values and emotions. Many school leaders I know manage their internal (rather than interactive) triggers by stepping into a classroom for five minutes and watching great teaching and learning happen. The keys to all these simple actions are 1) they are a physical response to their trigger sensations and 2) they deliberately create space between the trigger and our behavioral choice. We can all find a micropractice that works for us to create the space that is essential for responding to our triggers with an intentional response.

Self-Talk Grounded in Core Values

Creating space makes it possible to access other self-management strategies. One of the most important of these is to intentionally connect to our standard—the beliefs, values, and intuition that drive us as human beings. I like to think of this as accessing our gut. An effective way to do this is to develop meaningful self-talk.

As a coach and trainer, I love supporting people to build their self-talk. I help them explore what is at their core in the context of their challenge, and to articulate this to themselves in a way that lights their fire. Essentially, I am helping people find their power. When they find it, I can see them transform in front of me. Their energy shifts and they seem to get bigger somehow.

Remember the classic cartoons where Bugs Bunny or Elmer Fudd ponders a decision, and a devil and angel appear on their shoulders? That is what is happening with self-talk. With our big self-limiting mindsets, we have an oversized devil yelling in one ear and a very tiny, weak angel whispering in the other. By deliberately articulating alternative personal narratives grounded in our values—in our power—we are building our angel and shrinking the devil. With practice over time, the power balance shifts. We create new neural pathways of thought. These allow us to create new neural pathways of behavior.

Self-talk is most effective when it is simple and the language deeply resonates with us. An effective piece of self-talk should read like a bumper sticker or a message on a T-shirt. For me as a principal struggling to delegate to my APs, this self-talk would have been impactful:

> *If I'm not delegating, I'm enabling and disempowering.*
> *I either blow this [work/delegation pattern] up, or I quit.*

These statements connect directly with the values I discovered when exploring my standard. As a principal, it actually was a version of this second message that moved me to finally change my behavior. I came to a decision that my job was untenable the way I was doing it and gave myself permission to take what felt at the time to be dramatic steps.

Choosing a Noble Story

This third approach to self-management is so fundamental to strong leadership—even to being an effective human being—that we decided it deserved to be one of the seven questions in the 5-Square. Managing our stories is one of the most powerful things we can do to manage our self-limiting mindsets because our stories essentially *are* our self-limiting mindsets.

Our stories about ourselves and other people determine our reality. We compose these stories to make meaning and explain what we experience. In the absence of actual data, we fill in the blanks with our assumptions. If we are feeling positively about a situation and the people involved, and our experience with them has built trust between us, our stories tend to be positive. In challenging situations with people we may not know or who do not belong to our group, we tend to create stories that magnify our fears. The same can be said about our stories about ourselves. When we are feeling safe and in our element our stories about ourselves are positive. When we feel out of our element and unsafe, our stories about the context and ourselves tend to reflect our fears.

The good news is that we have the ability to change our stories about other people and even about ourselves. We can flip our stories by training ourselves to build and hold onto noble stories rather than negative stories. Developing this muscle of rewriting our stories gives us power over even our deepest fears. I coined the phrase "noble story" to describe this self-management work.

The concept has its roots in what EI theorist and author Annie McKee calls noble purpose (McKee 2017).[4] McKee's noble purpose refers to a person's or group's values that drive their actions. My concept of the noble story, while still grounded largely in values, takes the noble concept in different directions. The basic idea is that everybody has their own noble story about themselves. Everyone believes that what they do comes from a noble intention—one that connects to values that we hold dear to us. Even the lowest bad guys have their noble story. Think about every superhero movie that you've ever seen. At some point the villain's narrative comes out, usually tied to a value of justice in some way. If you have ever watched *Scooby Doo*, then you know how this works. At the end of every episode the villain who scares Scooby and his pals half to death in a monster costume shares why they have been scaring people away from the old hotel, ranch, or theme park. Money is sometimes a theme, but there is always something deeper there, too, about a wrong being righted. Even these villains have noble stories.

Building and holding a noble story is an act of leveraging empathy and compassion. If we listen for it, we will hear seemingly "bad" people connect their actions to intentions based on values and beliefs that we hold too. A Christian colleague of mine likens the noble story to what her pastor calls "finding Jesus in everyone." Building a noble story starts by being honest with ourselves about our negative stories. It takes emotional muscles and discipline to do it, but if we are aware of our negative stories, we can manage ourselves to keep them at bay. Then we can deliberately build a noble story by thinking about what we already know about the other person's values, strengths, and positive contributions to our lives and the world.

The fundamental question we ask to develop a noble story:

> *What do I need to believe about the person (or myself) to be able to accomplish my goal?*

As a principal struggling with delegation and doing other people's work, I needed to work on my noble story for myself and for my leadership team. I needed to hold the noble story that my leaders *wanted* to do the work I was hesitating to give them. I needed to believe that my leaders wanted to own their portfolios because they wanted to lead and to grow. I also needed to believe that my leaders would not write me off as their leader if I asked them to do work on a short deadline. They may be angry with me and they may push me to delegate better, but they wouldn't write me off. For myself, I needed to believe that this growth area did not define me as a leader. This was one growth area among many strengths. As a matter of fact, I could leverage some of my strengths to improve in this area.

Shifting our stories shifts our mindsets and our emotional energy. Given that emotions are contagious, this last piece is essential to leading in new and effective ways. We can radically shift the emotional energy and the outcome of challenging conversations when we start with a person's noble story and focus on building that story by listening with curiosity for values and beliefs. We can also radically shift our ability to engage resonantly when we start with our own noble story rather than a story grounded in our fears and perceived inadequacies.

Holistic and Proactive Self-Management: Plugging into Our Core Drivers

While most self-management strategies considered in this section are for use in moments of challenge, there is an entire world of self-management strategies that are holistic and not connected directly to managing challenges. We deploy these strategies proactively day to day. They are deliberate choices about how we live our lives to maximize our purpose, our power, our joy, and, by extension, our leadership. When we use these strategies consistently over time, we feel that our lives are sustainable, and that we are consistently showing up as our best selves. When we go through stressful periods that call for unsustainable sacrifice of our energy and well-being, these are the strategies that help us renew, or recharge, and get back to equilibrium.

Goleman's drivers, again, are life path, self-expression, well-being, and relationships. When we are being intentional about how we live into these motivational drivers, we are practicing self-management. Sometime in the third year of my principalship I made a very deliberate decision to change my life (see "blow it up" earlier) and started focusing on my drivers. I joined a gym and bought a jogging stroller. I can still feel the joy of walking into the gym at 4:30 on a Wednesday afternoon and stepping onto the elliptical. This was the only place in my life where I wasn't someone's principal or someone's father or spouse. I was just a random guy at the gym, and I was moving my body. During that same period, I rejoined my former church choir for the Christmas holiday concert. Sacrifices were made to do it, but I attended six weeks of rehearsal and sang in the Christmas Eve service. I get emotional now remembering the joy and gratitude I felt during those rehearsals and on that Christmas Eve, when I found myself too overcome to sing a good quarter of the service.

Slowly over the later years of my principalship I added back into my life the emotional drivers I had sacrificed for the work. As I did, I realized that those personal practices were an essential source of power for me to show up as my best self and leader in my school. I was calmer, and the self-doubting voices in my head had lost some of their power. Somehow a space was created inside of me to think more clearly and proactively about my work and my life.

Sleeping, exercising, practicing hobbies, connecting with family and friends, cooking, spiritual practices, meditating, being in nature, journaling, reading for pleasure—these are self-management strategies. We need them in our lives to be at our best. When we are not doing these things that make us whole as human beings, our ability to shift our self-limiting mindsets and behaviors are significantly compromised.

The Right Side of the 5-Square: A Focus on Others

Doing our "self" work—managing our stuff and our standard—is a prerequisite to effectively understanding and engaging others. Our focus on others begins with social awareness: leveraging empathy and compassion to truly see people—as individuals and as groups—to understand where they are, and then to set our leadership objectives (our targets) accordingly. Once we have built this awareness about where they are and where they need to be, we are ready to make decisions about how to best engage them to meet their needs and achieve our common goals.

Social Awareness: Where Are They and Where Do They Need to Be?

In the opening paragraph of *Primal Leadership*, Goleman writes, "Great leadership works through the emotions." He goes on to say that leaders who work through emotions build *attunement*—a direct connection with people's emotional centers.[5] It takes strong social awareness to become attuned to others.

Leaders with strong social awareness intuitively keep one eye below Wheatly's Green Line, which we discussed in Chapter 1 (see Figure 1.2). They understand that there are always two conversations happening: the one above the line that is about the work and the one below the line that is about emotions and relationships. The attuned leader knows when to lean into which conversation at any given moment. It is as if they have radar that tracks the invisible emotional path of the conversation.

In fact, the attuned leader *is* the radar—a finely tuned instrument that is sensitive to what others are feeling. The leader becomes the instrument by working the muscles of empathy and compassion. Empathy is our ability to take perspective on another's emotional experience by connecting to a similar emotional experience in ourselves. Compassion is our desire to help. When we put empathy and compassion together, we get empathic concern: we not only understand a person's predicament and feel with them but are spontaneously moved to help. In a talk I heard Goleman give at his Coaching Certification Program in July 2019, he explained that empathic concern is also a component of our parental care circuitry. It is hardwired in a parent's brain and it leads to the parenting behavior that every child needs to become a secure human being.

Attuned leaders exercise empathic concern with groups as well as individuals. When attuned to groups, they are like spiders, aware of even the most subtle vibrations across their organizational webs. Attuned leaders are able to predict how emotional energy will travel across their web of stakeholders when they make a leadership decision. They value and monitor their team's emotional energy, reading people and actively seeking information about people's beliefs before they act.

Strong social awareness is also about understanding social systems beyond the school community that impact it. The web extends to the full community of stakeholders, including parents, boards, governing and credentialing bodies, and even sector- and society-wide forces that impact schools. One of these forces is structural racism and other forms of systemic marginalization. An understanding of how identity, privilege, and power work both systemically and interpersonally in our country is essential social awareness for a leader to understand what is happening in their school.

Leaders with strong social awareness determine where their teams are before they decide how they will engage them. In other words, their social awareness determines their objectives, or targets, for engaging people. These targets determine *how* to engage. Socially aware leaders act *after* they have diagnosed the emotional needs of their people.

I walked into my principalship with a dangerous underappreciation for social awareness. I was fortunate to be part of an organization with robust leadership development, but almost all of it was above the Green Line. I assumed as a new principal that I would spend most of my time above the Green Line but was shocked and overwhelmed to find that I spent most of my time below it, struggling to manage other people's (mostly adults') emotional reactions. And, like many new leaders with strong technical training and little adaptive training, I made several big mistakes leading from the wrong side of the Green Line. I tried to treat some pretty significant below-the-Line challenges as above-the-Line challenges. When I independently changed my school's schedule to add an intervention reading block and sent it to the staff, I was shocked by my team's reaction. It took a near mutiny for me to see that there were rituals and traditions that many staff held dear that would be affected by the new schedule. This was one of several unforced errors that led me to start thinking about what was happening with my team below the Green Line.

Some version of my social awareness story is playing out in many schools. We under-prioritize the human side of learning and teaching while over-prioritizing the technical instructional work of school. There are legitimate reasons for this. We have a horrifying, unjust opportunity gap in our country that mirrors the structural oppression built into our social, political, and economic systems. The Common Core curriculum and testing were created to set high standards for all children and hold schools accountable for reaching them. Schools feel tremendous pressure to meet these standards, while working on tight budgets and competing for talent that could choose much easier, more lucrative work. Most of the education sector has responded by doubling down on teaching academic skills and training teachers to teach them by the most efficient means possible, at the expense of training on the more adaptive skills of leading and teaching. The unintended consequence is that our social awareness muscles as a sector have been neglected and allowed to atrophy. I have found that building these muscles is at the center of many school leaders'—and teachers'—growth needs.

Relationship Management: What Others Need from Me to Reach My Targets

Strong relationship management is the outcome of effective self-awareness, self-management, and social awareness. Strong relationship management is not likely to happen when a leader is not aware of and managing their standard and their stuff and attuned to where their people are and where the school needs them to be. Hence the iceberg metaphor: most of strong leadership happens below the surface—or inside of us—before we ever engage with other people.

Goleman has broken down relationship management into five subcompetencies that are leadership disciplines:

- Conflict management
- Coaching
- Influencing
- Inspiring
- Teamwork

In applying Goleman's theory to the education sector, I have found it more effective to divide relationship management into three more basic, emotional components that align with the core conditions that people need to learn: **connection, care,** and **challenge**. Goleman's subcompetencies and mine are not mutually exclusive. Leaders will choose one of his subcompetencies as the right approach to meet the needs of the others that they are engaging. I consider connection, care, and challenge to be the core emotional ingredients for any approach a leader chooses. Each person or group and context will require its own unique blend of these ingredients. When we get connection, care, and challenge right, we create the conditions for people to reach their full potential.

Connection: Authenticity, Presence, and Attunement

Think about a conversation you had recently where you felt unusually present, like *all* of you was there. Your defenses were down, you were not posturing or hiding a part of yourself or acting out a persona. At the same time, you felt that the walls between you and the other person were down. There was no ego between you in the moment; no fluff, no subtext, nothing being hidden. The world around you fades into the background. The curtains are somehow drawn back and you feel that you can see the other person clearly. You feel safe yet vulnerable, and somehow locked in. This is real connection.

Connection happens when we are able to self-manage to both be fully present in the moment with another person and show up as our authentic selves. If we can do that, we can leverage our empathy and compassion to invite others to also be fully present and authentic. The degree that we can connect like this determines the degree to which we get to attunement—that direct connection with another's emotional center.

Looking back, I can see that I made most of my biggest mistakes as a principal when I was not listening below the Green Line and connecting. Leading change usually worked when I listened to and connected with my people before making a decision, and then planned to meet their emotional needs accordingly. I managed conflicts and crises much better when I made the effort on the front end to connect. As long as the connection was there, the other person and I could wade through the mess together.

A common misconception about connection is that it should feel good. While that is often true, connection can also feel challenging. The goal of connection is neither positive nor negative emotions. The goal is to get to what is real. What is real can be any emotion. We know this from experience with connecting in our personal lives. When I engage to establish real connection with another human being, I need to be prepared for them to share whatever is real for them. As leaders who are often engaging to remediate adaptive challenges, we have to be prepared for all the emotions that people bring when they are struggling. We also must be prepared to share our own real emotions and beliefs—connection has to go both ways for it to be real. To be clear, our goal is not to be in our emotions, but to be able to share what they are as a kind of data with others. It takes considerable self-management to be able to share our emotions without being in them, while holding the space between us when we are connecting. Leaders should be mindful of that when they consider what contributes to their stress and what they need to renew themselves when engaging in adaptive leadership.

Care: Investment and Belief

Connection and care are often confused with each other because they seem so similar. In the 5-Square model, connection and care meet different emotional needs of the people we lead. Connection is about creating a space together where we can be real and see each other. This is usually a first step to effectively engaging with others as their leader. We need to know where people are and create a space together before moving toward a target.

Care is the embodiment of compassion. We care when we authentically feel invested in someone else's growth and success, and when we believe that they are capable of growing and succeeding. We can express this in words, but care is most powerfully expressed through our energy and our actions.

Think back to a challenging learning experience that turned into a transformative one because of an extraordinary teacher or a coach. You were probably afraid that you would fail and to some extent doubting your abilities. That teacher, their actions, energy, and maybe their words, made you believe that you could do it, and somehow made it safe enough for you to try. I have heard so many people say that these teachers "saw something in me that I didn't see in myself." This expression of belief and investment is the essence of care.

As leaders manage challenges with staff, students, or parents, holding real care for them gives us influence and creates safety for them. If we truly care, then our self-limiting mindsets lose their hold on us in the moment. If we truly care, others will feel that, and we will build the trust they need to take the risks required for them to grow and succeed. Great teachers know this. When I ask them to "think of a student that you just couldn't get yourself invested in or believe in," they cannot do it. They are unable to imagine what it would be like to work with a student and not care for them. Yet these same teachers, when they become leaders, often struggle to hold the same care for adults. This is the work of adaptive leadership: bringing the same level of care to adults that we do to children.

As a school leader I learned that the worst parts of the job could become opportunities if I could hold care for others. Even engaging with nonrenewing staff—always a challenge—could end well if I held onto my investment and belief in the person. Conversely, if I stopped caring, I set people up to fail. Because emotions are contagious, people know when we do not believe in them even if we think we are doing a great job of faking it. When we engage without care we create negative conditions for others that lead to self-doubt, isolation, decreasing effectiveness, and usually a voluntary or involuntary exit from the job. To engage with care often takes deliberate and intensive self-management, but we can do it by building and holding onto our noble stories for those we lead and teach.

Challenge

Recall your transformative learning experience with that transformative teacher or coach. Care was an essential ingredient in their work with you, but it was not the only essential ingredient. Care without challenge is enabling and disempowering. I am sure that this teacher also challenged you.

In her 2017 book *Radical Candor*, Kim Scott speaks compellingly about the role of both care and challenge in leadership. She makes the important point that when leaders challenge, we are providing our people with the information that they need to grow and succeed—the ultimate goal of the leader. When we don't challenge appropriately, we are denying our people the opportunity to grow and succeed, which is unfair. Scott flips a common self-limiting belief about challenge on its head by claiming that challenging is the best way to show that you care.

Challenging means holding people to high standards and naming it when they don't meet them. Challenging means speaking our truth and not trying to soften our words to spare feelings. As Scott puts it, when we challenge, we have to accept that "we are sometimes going to piss people off," and we cannot pretend it does not hurt. Scott also points out that challenge is a two-way street. When we challenge, we have to be ready to welcome challenge right back. To challenge effectively while maintaining connection, one needs to be good at accepting challenge as well.

As a new principal my discomfort with challenge was at the root of what held me back. I was an unintended enabler. When I hesitated to delegate or point out when someone was not meeting an expectation, I was undermining my credibility and others' opportunities to grow. A failure to challenge sent the implicit message that I didn't believe they could do it, thus potentially impacting their belief in themselves. Later, when I was at the top of my game, it felt normal to my team that I would challenge them regularly. My comfort with challenge—bolstered by connection and care—communicated trust and an expectation of growth.

Challenges should be attached to well-defined goals, which we call **targets**. We pressure test these targets when we engage others based on new information that we receive from them. Our target is our True North if we get lost in the mess of an adaptive engagement. If our target is our True North, then our standard is our steering wheel. If we find ourselves going in circles when trying to challenge, regrounding in our values and why we care about the conversation allows us to grab the wheel and steer.

We can and should plan ahead for how we might connect, care, and challenge when we engage in adaptive leaderships situations. However, we have to accept that we cannot follow a script. We won't really know where people are below that Green Line until we engage them, and we have to be ready to meet them where they are and go from there. Focusing on people's need for connection, care, and challenge helps us in the moment to make emotionally intelligent decisions about how to engage. It gives us some structure to maneuver in a messy, human leadership endeavor.

Applying the Five Domains to Grow

When we become more aware of our stuff and our standard, we can leverage our power to manage our internal obstacles. Once we are aware of and managing ourselves effectively, we are able to see others more clearly. We can leverage our empathy and compassion to figure out where they are and make informed decisions about our leadership targets (where they need to be), both above and below the Green Line. If we can manage our selves and stay attuned to others in the moment, we can stay connected even while we both challenge and hold our care for them.

That, in a nutshell, is how we apply the domains of the 5-Square to help leaders develop otherwise unteachable leadership competencies. The rest of this book will lead you on a personal growth journey through these five domains. You will apply them to the self-limiting leadership mindsets that are your deepest obstacles.

Repetition alert! If you were to read this book straight through you would notice many of the same big ideas and questions coming up in every chapter. That is because the same 5-Square domains and their core ideas and questions will support you to work through any of the mindset obstacles. My intention with this book is for leaders to identity the mindset chapters that connect to their personal growth areas and go deep. You might read the first few pages of the mindset chapters that are not challenges for you, but I would expect you to skip ahead to what is personally relevant after that. Those chapters that you do connect with should yield a plan that captures new awareness about yourself and others, and strategies you can use to build new mindsets and behaviors. This plan should help you grow over months and years, and can evolve over time if you stay focused on it.

Before moving to the mindset chapters, however, we will start with important personal work that everyone should attend to. We begin by exploring the sources of our power as leaders and as human beings.

Endnotes

1. Patterson, K., Grenny, J. McMillan, R.et al. (2011). *Crucial Conversations: Tools for Talking When Stakes Are High*. New York: McGraw Hill.
2. Michele Nevarez. (2020). Values and Drivers. Goleman Emotional Intelligence Coaching Certification Program.
3. Tema, O. (2019). White Supremacy Culture. DRWorksBook, www.dismantlingracism.org/.
4. McKee, Annie (2017). *How to Be Happy at Work: The Power of Purpose, Hope and Friendships*. Cambridge, MA: Harvard Business Press.
5. Goleman, D., Boyatzis, R., and McKee, A. (2002). *Primal Leadership: Learning to Lead with Emotional Intelligence*. Cambridge, MA: Harvard Business School Press.

3

Preparing for the Learning Journey by Connecting to Your Power

Chapter 1 described seven common self-limiting mindsets of school leaders and explained the need for the EI approach to shift them. Chapter 2 presented the 5-Square approach to applying EI theory, which is the tool you will use throughout this book to drive your learning. Each chapter after this one will tackle one of the seven self-limiting mindsets using the 5-Square. These chapters are the meat and potatoes of your below-the-surface learning journey. However, you are not quite ready for that work yet.

You know from Chapters 1 and 2 that what lies ahead is personal and emotional learning. You are going to dig deep below your surface to explore emotions, self-limiting stories, and bad habits that might be hard to face. Then you will practice new internal and interpersonal behaviors that may feel uncomfortable. The good news is that you already have what you need to do this learning inside of you. When you intentionally access this power that you have, it grounds you, renews you when you are depleted, and provides you with the fuel you need to succeed in the transformative learning journey ahead.

The term power may sound a bit dramatic, but it is as good a term as any for the internal resources and beliefs at our core. When we talk about power in this book, we are referring to the center square of the 5-Square. This chapter is about harnessing that power. You will come back to this center square in every chapter as you generate strategies to manage yourself and others.

It is likely that you are not fully aware of your power, even though it consists of the values, behaviors, and people you hold most dear. It takes a certain level of emotional and physical balance and mindful focus to become aware of and access our power. Unfortunately, this kind of balance and focus is something that few of us create for ourselves. School leadership makes doing so difficult, since our work tends to create power stress—an unending series of heavy, emotional challenges that cause chronic stress and burnout. The structure and nature of our work keeps us on a hamster wheel of self-sacrifice that, over time, causes us to lose touch with our power. We often tell ourselves we don't have time for it and, in our exhausted never-ending sprint, we forget what it is. See Chapter 7 on pacesetter leadership for more on this phenomenon.

Accessing your power will be necessary for the work ahead. We can internalize new ideas and practice technical skills when we are running on fumes, but we can't reflect deeply at an emotional level or change deeply engrained habits. To do this kind of learning, we need to be physically, emotionally, and spiritually grounded and able to focus. If we were to translate Maslow's Hierarchy to social–emotional learning, the learning you are about to do would be at the top of the pyramid (McLeod 2020).[1] By recharging you power sources in advance, you are preparing the base of your pyramid for what is coming in the chapters ahead.

In this chapter, you will shift from using the intellectual part of your brain to using the emotional part. You will assess different aspects of your power, set new intentions, and experiment with new behaviors to connect with it. Prepare to engage people you trust in your life to help you reflect. You will need a journal for this and all of the following chapters. You may want to spend two to three weeks on this chapter both before and during your work in subsequent chapters. Finally, if you find reflecting on and doing the work of this chapter particularly difficult, you will want to immerse yourself completely in Chapter 7 on pacesetter leadership.

Our Power Map

Michele Nevarez at Goleman EI has created a very effective framework for mapping out our power. Her Four Motivational Spheres framework, introduced in Chapter 2 and shown here in Figure 3.1, will be our guide.

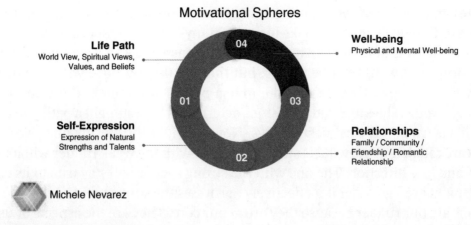

Figure 3.1: Motivational spheres.

Core Driver 1: Life Path

The first emotional driver, Life Path, is about core values, beliefs, and spiritual center. This driver is what guides us through life, like the rudder on a boat.

All boats, regardless of type or price tag, share some basic components, shown in Figure 3.2. Of these, the least visible and recognizable to people unfamiliar with boating is probably the rudder. This simple slab of wood, fiberglass, or metal hangs straight down from the hull of the boat. There is nothing exciting about the rudder, but without it, the boat goes anywhere. No matter how high tech or well made the rest of the boat, without the rudder it would go in circles.

Our core values and spiritual beliefs are our rudder. No matter how smart and skilled we are, and no matter how up to date our technology, without our core

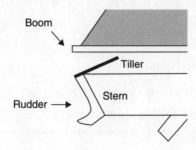

Figure 3.2: The rudder.

values and beliefs we would not get anywhere. Consider how many hundreds or thousands of decisions you make in a day. Many of them—especially the adaptive ones—have multiple right answers or no right answers. As a leader you can make decisions that would not be wrong, but that would not move you or your team forward if together they do not add up to a *path*. The strength of the connection between your values and your decisions determines how straight a path you are on.

This is true on the calmest of days. Now consider the stormy ones, when the seas are rough and the wind is strong. The boat with the weak rudder will toss and turn and lose direction. The one with the strong rudder will stay true to its course and might even go faster if it effectively harnesses the strong wind. Our values and beliefs are our rudder because they are at our core. They are the aspects of us that are the pillars of our identity. No matter the challenge, if we are able to connect to our core values and beliefs—what most defines who we are—we can find the power we need to move forward.

Unfortunately, we tend to think less about our core values in the midst of adaptive challenges and chronic stress when we need them the most. Over the next few pages, you will connect—or reconnect—with your values and beliefs. Over three different activities, you will both build awareness about your rudder and intentionally exercise the muscle of connecting your values and beliefs to real challenges you face right now in your life and work.

Activity 1: Lifeline

Many of you have probably done a lifeline exercise in the past. This activity is great for team building, but it is just as impactful as an exercise to explore our life path driver. The exercise of creating our story, the felt experience of sharing it, and the mirror that others hold up when they react all help us understand who we are and what drives us in the world.

Step 1: Create Your Lifeline

It is time to get your creative juices flowing! Your first task is to create a visual depiction of your life story. Consider the events and decisions that have made you who you are and that have brought you to where you find yourself today, both personally and professionally. You should consider challenges and successes, setbacks, and opportunities. You are aiming for somewhere between 10 to 20 events across your life from birth to now. This is for you, so get as creative as you want with how you depict your story (pictures, words, pencils, crayons, markers, watercolors, paper, canvas, computer programs . . . whatever works for you). Take your time and do not ignore key elements, even if they are uncomfortable.

Step 2: Share Your Story

Once you have finished drawing your lifeline, choose someone to share it with. This should be someone who you feel safe being vulnerable with, but who doesn't know your story intimately (your coach, a trusted colleague or manager, a friend). Feel free to share with more than one person. The more people you share it with, the more insight you will receive. Set aside 20 to 30 minutes when you can sit down with this person in a quiet space where you aren't likely to be interrupted. When you share, you should plan on narrating your story while you share the visual representation of it. This should take 10 to 15 minutes. Know that the in-the-moment narration is key to building your new awareness.

Before you start, frame the following question.

> *I created this story in the hopes of raising my awareness about the values and beliefs that drive me. When I am done, I am hoping you can answer this question: What does my story tell you about what values and beliefs drive me in my life and work?*

Step 3: Reflect with Your Partner

After you finish sharing your story, stop talking and listen. Let your partner be the first one to speak. When they do, just sit back and listen to what comes up for them until they are done talking. Then consider the following questions.

1. For you to answer about your own experience: What came up in my story that surprised me? What did I share that I wasn't planning to share? In what places did I experience emotions that I wasn't expecting to feel?
2. For your partner to answer: What does my story tell you about what values and beliefs drive me in my life and work?

Journal Reflection

What are you taking away from this activity about who you are and what drives you? Record your thoughts in your journal.

Activity 2: Values Sort

I find that this exercise always sheds new light on our core values because we are in a different place, or considering values through a different lens, each time we complete it. After having completed the lifeline activity, and in the context of the personal change work you are preparing to do in this book, this exercise should yield new insights.

Following you will find a list of values from the Goleman EI Coaching Certification Program.[2] It is not exhaustive, and you should add your own if the ones you care about most are not on the list. You are going to go through a three-step process of whittling these values down to the ones that mean the most of you. As you move through this exercise, consider what drives you as a person, an educator, and a leader.

Accountability	Cheerfulness	Drive	Honesty
Accuracy	Collaboration	Effectiveness	Honor
Achievement	Comfort	Efficiency	Hope
Adaptability	Commitment	Empathy	Humility
Adventure	Community	Enthusiasm	Independence
Agility	Compassion	Excellence	Influence
Altruism	Consistency	Excitement	Initiative
Ambition	Continuous	Expertise	Innovation
Appreciation	improvement	Fairness	Inspiration
Art	Control	Faith	Integrity
Assertiveness	Cooperation	Family	Intelligence
Autonomy	Courage	Flexibility	Joy
Balance	Creativity	Focus	Justice
Beauty	Curiosity	Freedom	Kindness
Belonging	Daring	Friendship	Knowledge
Benevolence	Decisiveness	Fun	Learning
Boldness	Dependability	Generosity	Loyalty
Bravery	Desire	Gratitude	Mastery
Calmness	Determination	Happiness	Meaning
Candor	Dignity	Hard work	Mentoring
Challenge	Diplomacy	Health	Mindfulness
Change	Discipline	Helpfulness	Openness

Organizational awareness	Purpose	Speed	Tolerance
	Reliability	Spirituality	Trust
Passion	Reputation	Spontaneity	Truth
Peace	Resourcefulness	Stability	Understanding
Perfection	Responsibility	Strength	Variety
Perseverance	Sacrifice	Structure	Warmth
Playfulness	Self-awareness	Success	Wealth
Positivity	Self-control	Sympathy	Whimsy
Pragmatism	Selflessness	Teaching	Will
Precision	Service	Teamwork	Wisdom
Preparedness	Simplicity	Thoughtfulness	
Professionalism	Sincerity	Timeliness	

Step 1: Top 10

Choose the 10 values from the preceding list that most drive you as a human being, a leader, and an educator. Give yourself no more than 5 minutes to choose (part of the exercise is the pressure to make a gut decision).

Step 2: Top 7

Now give yourself 3 minutes to narrow your list to a top 7 by crossing out 3 values from your list of 10. To help you prioritize, think about what situations and actions of others cause a dissonant emotional reaction for you when they cross your values. For example, seeing someone cut in line might make me feel an anger connected to my value of fairness or justice. What seven values on your list would elicit the strongest emotional response if someone were to violate them?

Step 3: Top 3

I am asking you to make a false choice, but I'm going to do it anyway in the spirit of forcing you to dig deep. To help you prioritize, imagine that you are 95 years old and contemplating your legacy. What three values do you want to be remembered for embodying in your life and work? Narrow your list of seven to three.

Journal Reflection

Write about what came up for you in this activity about what drives you. Consider:

- What resonated with your lifeline takeaways? What new came up?
- How do these values connect to your desire to work on your self-limiting mindsets?

Activity 3: Connecting to Values in Context

For values to serve us as a rudder, we have to become aware of and access them in our day-to-day life and work. This in-the-moment self-awareness is like a muscle: the more we intentionally use it, the stronger the muscle gets. An intentional core values workout starts with noticing emotional reactions, which alerts us to the fact that something is happening that we care about. When this emotional early warning system goes off, we have to create the space to think about what values are being activated and why.

Over the next three days, schedule 10 minutes at the right time for you to journal about how your values are being activated. You can write as you always do, or you can create a thought catcher like Table 3.1. Either way, make sure you respond to the following prompts.

Journal Reflection

After your three days of journaling about your values in context, what patterns are you noticing? What does your lived experience of what values keep coming up tell you about your true core values? How does this confirm your takeaways from the last two values exercises? What is new?

Table 3.1: Sample thought catcher.

What happened	Why I care	My value(s) at play
Someone cut in line at airport security check	Everyone else had been waiting for a long time, following the rules, respecting each other. This guy disrespected us all. Such arrogance! Such white male privilege!	Equity Integrity

You will return to this practice of finding your values in context in every chapter of this book.

Core Driver 2: Well-Being

We will now move from the life path driver to the wellness driver.

Wellness has become a familiar word in our culture, particularly through the Covid pandemic. While that collective experience has made us all more aware of our unique wellness needs, it certainly does not mean we are good at prioritizing them. The metaphor of the airplane oxygen mask helps to think about wellness, but it is particularly useful for those of us whose mission in life is to educate our children. Mission-driven educators do not put their own oxygen masks on first. We choose this work because we see an emergency—structural inequality, the opportunity gap, insufficient schools for children—and we sign up *expecting* to make significant personal sacrifice. Once we are in it, the structures and cultures of mission-driven, "better faster" schools conspire with our own mindsets to create chronic stress. This is true all the time in schools. Oxygen masks are popping out of the ceiling of our planes every day, yet we consistently fail to put them on ourselves first. For many of us, not putting on our oxygen masks is a badge of honor and reaching for them seems selfish. For many others, we are so stuck in the work hamster wheel that we cannot figure out how to reach for it.

If the center "power" square of the 5-Square were a pyramid, wellness would be its base. Wellness refers to how we care for our physical and mental selves. This includes sleep, nutrition, exercise, medical care, emotional grounding practices like meditation, and more. The following two activities will reconnect you with what you need to be at your physical and mental best, and help you prioritize what might be missing at the moment. The second activity will also help you build new awareness about your needs.

Activity 1: Wellness Audit

The following checklist includes five pillars of wellness and related criteria to consider for each pillar. Consider this a place to start your reflection, as it is not an exhaustive list and you may think of more aspects of wellness that are important to you. In your journal, create your own thought catcher similar to Table 3.2. Celebrate your good habits and zoom in on the places that feel like opportunities for improvement.

Table 3.2: Sample thought catcher for journaling.

Wellness Category	To consider	Score (scale 1 to 5, poor to excellent)	Start doing/ stop doing
Sleep	Timing (Circadian rhythms)		
	Bedtime rituals		
	Technology at bedtime		
	Impact of dinner time and what you eat, drink (especially alcohol and caffeine)		
Nutrition	Meal timing and size		
	Balance of food groups		
	Research on gluten and carbohydrates		
	Potential food allergies		
	Caffeine and alcohol intake		
Exercise	Your optimal timing		
	Strength vs. cardio vs. stretching		
	Group vs. solo		
	Consulting a trainer to get started		
	Consulting a physical therapist about physical obstacles (chronic aches and pains)		
Medical care	Overdue wellness checkups		
	Nagging issues that haven't reached the urgent threshold		
	Preventative health habits (flossing, vitamins, etc.)		
Emotional grounding	Intermittent breaks to ground self, including:		
	Mindfulness practices		
	Yoga		
	Walks and other activities outdoors/ in nature		
	Walks		
	Music, art		
	Presence of social media		
	Pets		

Wellness Category	To consider	Score (scale 1 to 5, poor to excellent)	Start doing/ stop doing
Physical space	Cleanliness, clutter Silence vs. sound Light vs. dark Presence of plants Color		

Reality Check

Once you have a draft plan, share it with someone in your life who knows your patterns well and will be honest with you about where you are and what you need. Listen and try not to defend and explain (it might be hard to hear this feedback). When you have taken a deep breath and allowed your immediate reaction to pass, make revisions accordingly.

Activity 2: My Ideal Wellness Schedule

In the context of your *real life,* what would you ideally be doing to prioritize your wellness? Create a thought catcher like Table 3.3. I have shared some personal examples to get your thoughts flowing.

Journal Reflection

What did you learn (or relearn) about what you need to do to recharge your physical and emotional batteries? What is one wellness practice that you are motivated to commit to after this exercise? How will this practice support you in your efforts to shift your self-limiting leadership mindsets?

Table 3.3: Sample wellness schedule.

	Mon	Tues	Wed	Thurs	Fri	Sat	Sun	Monthly/ Quarterly
Morning	Run		Yoga		Run	Sleep in Big breakfast and the paper	Run Big breakfast and the paper	Church
Midday	Short walk Read fiction for 10 minutes	Short walk Read fiction for 10 minutes	Short walk Read fiction for 10 minutes	Short walk Read fiction for 10 minutes	Lunch with teammate		House cleaning	Hiking with the family
Evening	Walk the dog with wife	Walk the dog with wife	Swim	Walk the dog with wife				
Night	Read in bed 10:30 lights out	Read in bed 10:30 lights out	Read in bed 10:30 lights out	Yoga 10:30 lights out	Pizza and movie night		Yoga	Date night Dinner with friends

Core Driver 3: Relationships

Human beings are wired to connect (Goleman 2007).[3] Our drive to connect has allowed us to live in larger and larger groups, collaborate, build language, exchange knowledge, and evolve as a species into what we are. Given our wiring, relationships are necessary for our emotional health. We need connection to recharge our batteries. According to my mentors at Teleos, mindfulness, hope, and compassion are the three emotional building blocks of renewal after a period of intense sacrifice (McKee, Johnson, and Boyatzis 2008).[4] We practice compassion through our relationships.

It is very easy for school leaders to deprioritize relationships given the intensity and hours of our work. As a principal with two babies at home, I was fortunate to have a close group of local friends (thanks to my wife) but many of my closest long-distance relationships fell by the wayside. I lost touch with my best friend from college, and that relationship has never been the same. My extended family was easiest to deprioritize for me, as they seemed the easiest group to take for granted. For years my brothers and I only connected around the holidays. I did not really appreciate the impact that had on me until years later. I now realize that the absence of these relationships contributed to my feelings of isolation and general emotional numbness. By not exercising love and compassion with the people I cared about the most I was depriving myself of a primary power source for recharging my batteries.

Activity: Relationship Mapping

This relationship mapping activity will help you reflect on the state of the relationships that are most important to you. As you create your map, notice where you feel the most emotion and the most desire for more connection.

Your map begins with a big circle in the middle of your paper to represent you. From there you will add up to five or six more circles that represent the groups of relationships that are most important to you. It is completely up to you who you put in these circles and how you define important (there are no wrong answers or approaches here). What will be important is the size and proximity of each circle. The size of each circle signifies its importance to you. The proximity of each circle

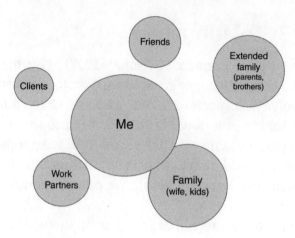

Figure 3.3: Sample relationship map.

to your circle in the middle signifies the current presence of this group in your life. Figure 3.3 captures my own relationship map. I was surprised to notice how far my extended family circle is from me at this moment in time.

Journal Reflection

At what points did you experience the most emotion during this exercise? What does that tell you about the state of those relationships in your life?

What relationships will support you most through the below-the-surface learning you have chosen to do with this book?

What commitments do you want to make to strengthening relationships in your life right now?

Core Driver Four: Self-Expression

When we think of the sources of our power we are less likely to think about self-expression than well-being. Expressing ourselves seems like more of a nice-to-have than getting enough sleep or eating right. There may be a more immediate negative impact from suboptimal sleeping and nutrition, but we will not thrive if we are not experiencing the unique energy we receive from self-expression.

With self-expression we use energy in a way that creates more energy. Exercising self-expression produces fulfillment and validation at the core of our identity. We nurture self-expression in two basic ways. One is identifying and then developing talents. The other is bringing our unique voice into the world. While interconnected, the first of these is more about personal fulfillment and the second is more about interpersonal fulfillment.

Self-Expression and Flow

Mihaly Czikszentmihalyi's concept of flow helps us understand the personal aspect of self-expression (Oppland 2021).[5] Flow is the state we reach when are practicing a skill at the just-right level of challenge. The higher our skill level, the higher the rate of challenge must be to get to flow. This is our optimal state between boredom and anxiety. In this state we are so immersed in something we are good at that everything else—worries, stress, self-consciousness—fades away and we are completely in the moment. We are in the zone.

Czikszentmihalyi refers to the "flow channel" as the way we grow in our talents over time. We move up the flow channel as we get better while increasing the level of challenge. When we effectively match our skill level with the optimum challenge level, we will not only stay in flow but experience deeper levels of flow over time (Figure 3.4).

Flow happens in our work lives and in our private lives. At work I am in flow when I am coaching a leader. Everything else fades away and I feel electrified. When my coachee says, "That's a great question. I never thought about that before," I feel deep fulfillment. I also can achieve flow when I am writing. I don't hear voices or noises outside my window, and I have to set a timer to remember when to stop. The energy I feel when I have expressed an idea in a new way makes it hard to stay in my seat. In my personal life, I am in flow when I am playing my favorite card game (Hearts) and when I am doing a puzzle. My grandmother was apparently a world-class crossword puzzler. As a kid my brother could kick a soccer ball against a wall for hours at a time. There are as many sources of flow as there are hobbies, sports, art forms, and pastimes.

Flow should not be confused with the feeling we get when we are scrolling through our social media feeds. These apps may provide in-the-moment distraction, but the experience is not flow because it is passive. Czikszentmihalyi actually calls this state apathy, which lives between boredom and worry in Figure 3.4. Flow requires challenge and the exercise of a skill.

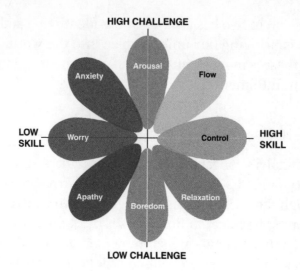

Figure 3.4: Flow model diagram.

Activity 1: Finding More Flow

Are you experiencing enough flow in your life to keep your power source charged? Complete the flow audit in Table 3.4 to evaluate and set some goals to move toward your flow potential.

Make a list of the activities in your life in which you reach a state of flow. Reflect not only on your current reality but also about other times in your life when you may have been engaged in flow activities that you have put to the side. Make sure you are listing both work and personal activities.

Evaluate your current level of engagement with this source of flow. Are you practicing it as much as you would like to? What would the ideal be, given the reality of your life and work? What are the obstacles to accessing this source of flow? What opportunities might you pursue to increase frequency? What opportunities are there to increase challenge and get better?

Reality Check

Once you have a created a draft flow plan, share it with someone who knows you well now and someone who has known you most of your life. Listen to what they say about what they think are the sources of your flow without explaining and justifying. Add their wisdom to your plan.

Table 3.4: Flow audit.

	Presence in my life (scale 1 to 3)	Obstacles to practice	Opportunities to increase practice or increase challenge
Personal Flow			
Work Flow			

Journal Reflection

What are you taking away about the state of flow in your life?

What commitments do you want to make to increasing your flow?

Which sources of flow will most support the below-the-surface learning you have chosen to do?

Self-Expression and Personal Voice

What we do in flow may or may not be interactive, and the fulfillment we get from flow is mostly about the internal gratification. The interpersonal side of self-expression is about sharing our authentic selves with the world in a way that validates us and makes us feel like we are contributing to something collective and greater than ourselves. Harvard psychologist Judith Glaser writes that this kind of self-expression is one of the most important ways people connect, navigate, and grow as human beings (Glaser 2015).[6] Spiritual teacher and author Christian de la Huerta similarly writes that self-expression is about a journey of self-discovery that leads to our life fulfillment and reaching our full potential.[7]

What they say resonates with my experience as a learner. My most powerful professional growth experiences have been team projects that involved creating new teaching or learning approaches. In these groups my ideas are validated and honored, and they become part of a collection of ideas that are greater than what I could have accomplished alone. A similar experience I have in my personal life is singing in choirs. Some of my moments of greatest joy in life have been on a stage with hundreds of other singers and instrumentalists. There are infinite ways, both big and small, that we can express our authentic selves. These range from the microdecisions that we make about how we walk through the world every day (think hair, clothing, movement, body language, who we engage, what we say and how we say it) to weighty decisions we make at pivotal moments in our lives. In all these decisions, we contribute who we are to the collective.

Activity 2: Where and How Am I Bringing My Voice?

Consider all the ways, both big and small, that you express your authentic self. It may help to view the last few weeks of your life as a movie or montage in your mind, envisioning yourself moving through your day-to-day life. For the bigger things, do an emotional memory scan for the most socially fulfilling moments of your life in the last six months or beyond. Add what comes up to a Personal and Work Life Venn Diagram (in your journal, on butcher paper, on your computer . . . whatever works best for you). List actions from your personal life in the left circle, work life in the right circle, and the things that show up in both personal and professional in the middle. Give yourself at least 15 minutes to reflect. See my example in Figure 3.5.

Reality Check

Share your list with two people who know you well—one personally and one professionally, ideally with some overlap. Listen to their reaction and ask them

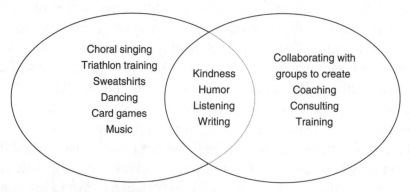

Figure 3.5: Sample self-expression Venn diagram.

what they think is missing based on their experience of you. Add what resonates to your lists.

Journal Reflection

What aspects of your self-expression were less present than you would like? What appeared in one circle or the other that you wish appeared in both the personal and professional parts of your life?

What aspects that came up here will support you in your below-the-surface learning journey ahead?

What intentions do you want to create about bringing your authentic self into the world?

From Plan to Practice

With the exercises in this chapter you have identified, assessed, and set goals to engage the sources of your personal power. It has been important self-awareness building work. Now the work of turning your plan into practice begins. In the weeks ahead, I hope you are able to maintain your focus on connecting to your power. Mindful follow-through on the goals you set will change your quality of life for the better. It will also provide you with the fuel you will need do the personal, emotional learning in this book as well as the adaptive work of school leadership. The key word here is *habit*. Once your intentions become habits, practicing them will take much less effort.

Now we begin your below-the-surface learning journey. Each of the chapters that follows will be a stand-alone learning project of overcoming a single self-limiting mindset. You will work the 5-Square by increasing your awareness about yourself and others, and building new internal and interpersonal strategies that, when they become habit, will be the measure of your learning. Not every chapter will be relevant to you. Given your own awareness about your growth areas as well as the feedback you have received about your leadership, you will choose the chapters that represent your biggest obstacles and work through them over time. You likely already know which ones you want to focus on, but you should read the first few pages of each chapter to test your assumptions before skipping ahead.

Endnotes

1. Mcleod, S. (December 2020). "Maslow's Hierarchy of Needs." Simple Psychology. https://www.simplypsychology.org/maslow.html.
2. Values list from Goleman EI Emotional Intelligence Coaching Certification Program.
3. Goleman, D. (2007). Why aren't we more compassionate? TED2007. https://www.ted.com/talks/daniel_goleman_why_aren_t_we_more_compassionate.
4. McKee, A., Johnston, F., and Boyatzis, R. (2008). *Becoming a Resonant Leader: Develop Your Emotional Intelligence, Renew Your Relationships, Sustain Your Effectiveness*. Cambridge, MA: Harvard Business Review Press.
5. Oppland, M. (2021). Eight ways to create flow by Mihaly Csikszentmihalyi. Positive Psychology.com. https://positivepsychology.com/mihaly-csikszentmihalyi-father-of-flow/.
6. Glaser, J. (2015). With this exercise, talk your way to your best self. *Entrepreneur* (29 January). https://www.entrepreneur.com/article/242304.
7. De La Huerta, C. The power of self-expression. Soulful Power. https://soulfulpower.com/the-power-of-self-expression/.

II Working the 5-Square

4

The Transactional Leader

In this chapter you will deeply explore the first of this book's seven self-limiting mindsets. Each of the ensuing chapters will be a self-guided journey of one mindset. You will decide within the first two pages whether that chapter's mindset is a challenge for you, and then choose to keep reading or move on to the next chapter. Transactional leadership is the mindset you will consider in this chapter.

Transactional leadership assumes a simple agreement: the leader tells you what to do, and you do it because you want to be successful. This assumption rests on the belief that the world is a mostly rational place, that adult human beings are rational creatures that receive clear (to me) information, process it (like I do), and then behave according to the expectations I have communicated: a simple transaction. Consider Isabel's story:

> *Isabel traveled up the ranks of leadership from teacher to assistant principal to principal because of her ability to build and manage schoolwide systems and her strength as an instructional coach. The administrative tasks that she owns all turn to gold. Her teacher portfolio consistently makes the most growth as measured by teacher taxonomy (skill) data. However, now that Isabel is a principal, new leadership challenges arise. It doesn't occur to her to question how people will feel about changes to the school schedule to make space for an intervention block. She doesn't ask anyone for feedback or share any details about her plan until unveiling it in a Friday staff meeting. On Monday she is surprised to hear gossip about how she treats people and how arrogant she is to just "take over" the schedule. Hurt and disoriented, Isabel did not see this coming. She feels like she has been ambushed. Isabel has a new appreciation for those who say that leadership is a lonely path.*

Meanwhile, people are pushing back on expectations that Isabel feels are no-brainers. She is shocked, frustrated, and disappointed by people when this happens. When she steps up to the challenge of holding the line on her expectations, Isabel gets feedback that she comes off as cold and uncaring, she never listens, and people feel disconnected from her. Isabel is now hurt, angry, and perplexed. What is there to listen about when people are not complying with basic-level expectations?

Does Isabel's story resonate with you? Read this chapter if you:

- Focus most of your time and energy on managing structures and systems.
- See learning as mostly a process of acquiring skills and knowledge.
- Believe that sharing one's personal self is not appropriate at work.
- Believe that emotions have no place in leadership.
- Do not spend much time considering the feelings of others when you make decisions.
- Are often surprised to discover that your decisions or people's interactions with you personally have evoked negative reactions.
- Feel frustrated and impatient with others when they have these negative reactions.
- Highly value control when it comes to managing your team.

Transactional Leadership and Its Costs in Learning Organizations

There are forces in our sector that encourage transactional leadership, and for noble reasons. When transactional leadership works, goals are accomplished quickly. We see it in our sector's "better faster" mindset that assuages our urgency to close the opportunity gap. Better faster leads to expedited skill and knowledge breakthroughs for the majority of our students. It has also led us to prioritize transactional adult learning and transactional leadership approaches. Many of us reading this book learned everything we know about teaching and leading in these transactional school systems. We were likely selected to lead because our skills and mindsets matched institutional approaches and culture. However, as we rise through the ranks of leadership, the work becomes increasingly adaptive and we discover the downsides of an overly transactional approach.

Smart, passionate, ambitious young adults do not respond well to transactional leadership, which is largely about control and compliance. Transactional leaders take away space for creativity and true ownership over one's work. The approach seeks to create an external locus of control that replaces internal motivation with fear of consequences. People with transactional bosses tend to become dependent on them and do not feel comfortable making decisions without consulting them first. Smart, passionate, and ambitious young adults do not tend to stay in these kinds of environments. If they do, they internalize the approach and excel at it, becoming transactional teachers and transactional middle managers themselves, thus perpetuating the cycle. It probably goes without saying, but the conditions I describe here are not those that support most people—kids or adults—to reach their full potential. The effects of these conditions are amplified for marginalized groups, as overly transactional leaders reinforce the exclusion and disempowerment already endemic in society's systems of structural racism, sexism, and other forms of oppression. Keep reading for more on equity implications later in this chapter.

The Work Ahead

If you know that transactional leadership is getting in your way, keep reading. If you do not see yourself in the preceding checklist or case study, then maybe this chapter is not for you. Ask for feedback from your manager and a few trusted staff before making that decision. If others confirm your opinion, then skip ahead to the next chapter.

This chapter is a self-contained learning journey. If you take it on, you could spend several months focusing on changing deeply engrained habits and building new adaptive muscles. Use the 5-Square shown in Figure 4.1 and download a 5-Square learning plan template from www.noblestorygroup.com to build your plan. You will also need a journal to explore new ideas.

Let's get started.

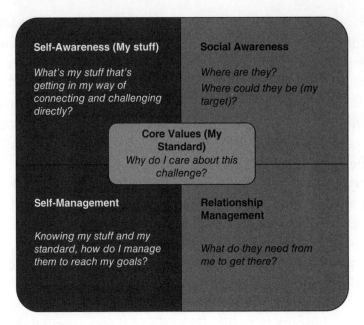

Figure 4.1: The EI 5-Square.

Step 1: Start with the End in Mind

This journey starts by thinking about what success will look like when you are leading as an effective adaptive leader. Use your imagination to envision what you will be doing differently and how it will feel ideally to lead with connection, care, and challenge. Pay particular attention to the situations you find most challenging (the preceding checklist might help you with that) but remember that your goal is to envision your *ideal* self in these situations. To help you drill down, consider what it will look like and feel like to:

- Spend more of your time focusing on people challenges.
- Be present and attuned to others' emotional needs.
- Shift from a technical conversation to an adaptive one in the moment.
- Engage in challenges at the level of emotions and values.
- Have your finger on the emotional pulse of your learning community.

You should record this reflection on the first page of your 5-Square worksheet. Journal first and then transfer to the 5-Square if journaling helps you think creatively. Give yourself uninterrupted time (at least 30 minutes) and emotional space to do this reflection. You might find it helpful to see an example vision from another 5-Square, and there is one in Appendix A. You will use this vision of success during this journey to generate awareness and strategies, and to measure your progress over time.

Step 2: Building Self-Awareness

When you have thought deeply about the leader you want to be, you are ready to hold up the mirror and explore what is getting in your way. As you think about this, push yourself to remember specific times when your transactional approach was an obstacle to reaching your desired outcomes. It may help to revisit the checklist at the beginning of this chapter as you think of examples. Once you have two or three in mind, choose one example to use as a case study over the rest of this chapter. In coaching we call these case studies behavioral moments. When we zoom in on these moments of emotional cause and effect, decision, and behavior, we are able to identify the chain reaction of a self-limiting mindset.

What Are Your Triggers?

First, identify the trigger moment in your case study. What happened that started you down the transactional path? Something in your environment—another person's behavior, receiving a text or email, looking at your to-do list—triggered a feeling. For transactional leaders, the trigger can be a moment that we are faced with a messy human challenge. It may be that we are surprised when what we assumed was a simple technical process gets complicated by human emotion or struggle. Be as clear as you can about the specific moment in your case study, then think more broadly about how this kind of trigger shows up regularly in challenging leadership moments. Write down what comes up in the self-awareness box of your 5-Square.

What Sensations and Emotions Do You Experience?

Our triggers cause a self-limiting chain reaction that starts in our body. Neurological research shows that we process stress physiologically before we process it emotionally or intellectually. Our body is our early warning system—a fundamental aspect of self-awareness that most of us do not pay enough attention to. Think back again to your trigger moment. Where did you feel your reaction in your body? Was it a sinking in the chest, burning ears, or urge to tap your foot? Note your physical reaction in your 5-Square.

Soon after the physiological reaction comes an emotional one. Our emotions in our moment of trigger are more complicated than we might think. We experience emotions about ourselves and also emotions directed at others. We often experience a contradictory blend of positive and dissonant emotions at the same time. Transactional leaders often feel surprised by, frustrated, and impatient with stakeholders who veer from the transactional path. At the same time, they may also feel stuck, confused, and afraid of mishandling non-transactional leadership moments. Write down all the emotions you tend to experience in these moments. Push yourself to name as many as you can.

What Stories Get in Your Way?

Our stories—the inner narratives and assumptions about ourselves, others, and context that help us make sense of the world—come next. Here we specifically focus on the stories that feed your self-limiting behaviors. In your case study, what were you telling yourself about others, yourself, and the situation that got in your way? It might help to connect each emotion with the thoughts that accompanied it. For example, if I am feeling frustrated and impatient with someone who seems to be pushing back on my transactional request, I might be thinking, "These people should be able to do their jobs without this emotional drama!" When feeling stuck I might be thinking, "I don't understand or have any idea what to do with this reaction, and I'm going to really mess this up."

Our Stories and Our Identities

The deeper our stories, the more connected they are to our identities. Growing up in America, with our 400-year history of white male supremacy, it is inevitable that racism, sexism, and other forms of privilege and oppression impact our perceptions of self. Transactional leadership is a style that has many connections to white supremacist cultural norms. In her 2019 article "White Supremacy Culture,"[1] Tema Okun lists at least four white cultural norms that are hallmarks of a transactional leadership style:

- Objectivity—*I believe in a rational "neutral" and invalidate people who show emotions, which are inherently destructive, irrational, and should not play a role in decision-making.*
- Urgency—*fast, highly visible results are more important than building collaboration, allies, and the interests of communities.*
- Quantity over quality—*valuing and directing resources to what can be measured, while devaluing things that are hard to measure like process and relationships.*
- Progress is bigger and more—*measuring success by how we are expanding and the number of people we serve, while paying little attention to the costs to people, learning, and organization.*

Regardless of our identities we all may be performing these white cultural norms. While they are not harmful in and of themselves, they can be when they are the unconscious default and are overplayed to the detriment of other non-white groups, as in the case of overly transactional leadership. The stronger the dominant white culture is in your organization, the more pressure we feel to perform these norms. Consider how these white cultural norms may be at play for you.

Write down all the self-limiting stories that come up in your case study moment and consider how they feed your transactional behaviors.

Then What Do You *Do*?

When you are triggered, experiencing all of those sensations and emotions, and telling self-limiting stories to yourself, what do you do that gets in your way? What did you do in the behavioral moment you chose as your case study? Consider the sequence of actions in that moment and in follow-up interactions. As a transactional leader you are likely identifying behaviors related to staying technical—above the Green Line—when others need you to engage at an adaptive below-the-Green-Line level. Consider not only your words but your tone, body language, and maybe even what you did *not* say or do that got in your way. Write it all down.

What Is the Impact of Your Behaviors?

Now reflect on impact. We rarely explore the full ripple effect of our impact across social webs. This effect goes much further than we might think. Unpacking the deeper impact of our actions is usually both a sobering and galvanizing experience.

Wheatly's Green Line (see Chapter 1 and shown in Figure 4.2) helps us reflect adaptively on our impact. Start by considering the impact of your actions on yourself. Considering the three circles above the line, compare your intended outcomes for the interaction with the actual outcomes. Consider the ripple effect of these actual outcomes on your staff and students. What is the connection?

Now go below the Green Line and consider the social and emotional implications of your behavior. Again, start with self and follow the ripples out. How did your actions impact your self-perception? How did your behavior affect your relationship with that person or group? How might it have affected their ability to be successful and reach their full potential in their work? Remember that emotions are contagious. How do you think their emotional contagion leaving your interaction influenced the conditions they created for others to learn and thrive in their work?

Finally, consider your reputation as a leader. How has this episode affected your credibility with this person or these people? What will they tell their colleagues?

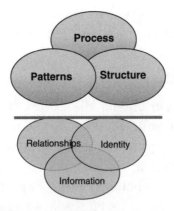

Figure 4.2: Wheatly's Six-Circle Model.

Their friends and family who live and work in your community? What will others see and feel when you and this person (or these people) are interacting in the hallway or in staff meetings? How does the state of your reputation affect your ability to achieve your leadership goals and your ultimate student outcomes?

Take a few minutes to journal on the ripple effect across your world. When you think you have a pretty exhaustive list, consider sharing with a trusted colleague or manager to see if they can think of anything you might have missed or that might not be likely (we all have blind spots about our impact, especially when it comes to our reputation). Then return to your 5-Square and record the levels of impact that matter the most to you.

Pause and Reflect

At this point, I encourage you to take both a literal and metaphorical deep breath. Step back and offer yourself grace and gratitude for the work you have done so far. You have gone well below the surface and explored the emotional chain reaction behind your transactional leader mindset. It is painful to confront self-limiting stories and behaviors and it is natural to feel down on yourself at this moment. However, when you confront personal obstacles, you open the door to change and growth. With self-awareness comes an opportunity you may not have known you had: to choose a more empowering and effective way of being.

This choosing begins with building self-management strategies that can shift your stories and behaviors.

Connect with Your Power to Choose New Ways of Being

Building self-awareness is partly about recognizing the dissonance you feel when facing your self-limiting stories and behaviors. Thinking about why you feel the dissonance is one way you can access your standard: the power of your true values in context.

To mine for the standard that can empower you most to disrupt your transactional leader behaviors, go back in your case study to the self-limiting stories, behaviors, and their impact you recorded earlier in your self-awareness square.

Why do you care about rejecting those stories and leaving overly transactional behaviors behind? Your answers likely connect to who you want to be, what you want to accomplish, and why you do this work. In your journal, start listing all of the reasons you care that come up. When you think you have a relatively complete list, review and prioritize your top five. This should be an emotional exercise that you feel in your gut.

Now, for each of your prioritized care statements, go deeper. *Why* is this statement important to you? What is that *about* for you? For each answer, try to follow with another why question. This is like peeling an onion, as there are many layers of meaning that you can uncover. Your goal here is to try to get to the core value.

Example:

> I want my people to believe in me as their leader. (Why?)
>
> People won't follow a leader they don't trust. (Why?)
>
> If I don't trust you, I will always be afraid that you will lead in a way that could hurt me. (Why?)
>
> Because I will feel unsafe! At any moment the leader might do something destructive. I will go through my days not knowing what to expect, which is damaging to me and my students. (Why?)
>
> We all need some basic level of psychological safety to do our jobs and to learn.
>
> **Core Value:** Psychological safety

You will know when you are done when you can say and feel, "This one is about (a value or value statement) for me." Do this for each of the statements that you prioritized. Then add those core values to the center square of your 5-Square.

Now consider how your values relate to your identities—that complicated amalgam of how we see ourselves and how the world sees us. According to the idea of intersectionality (Crenshaw 1989),[2] we all have many identities, or facets of self, that make up who we are. Some of these include gender, race, sexuality, class, ability, place of origin, and religion, but the list is really only limited by the number of ways we make sense of ourselves and each other in the world. We know that multiple forms of discrimination accumulate across identity markers, marginalizing or privileging groups and individuals. Yet we also know that our identities are a source of our power. They weave together to create our cultures, from family culture to our many different group cultures. From all of these interwoven identity groups, we learn what matters to us in the world.

Re-read the list of values you just generated. Consider how your identities connect with and inform these values. How can an intentional anchoring in your identities empower you to shift your transactional leadership habits? Add identity notes to your 5-Square in a way that adds meaning to you.

You have just surfaced your power, or the values that can be your true north, in shifting your transactional leader mindsets and behaviors. Now you will think about how to harness that power in the moment.

Step 3: Building Self-Management Strategies

We cannot stop our triggers and our emotions. They are going to happen to us because they are hardwired. However, we *can* manage triggers and emotions when they happen, once we are aware of their patterns in our lives. Then we can rewrite our stories and shift our behavior. With awareness comes choice. Self-management is about choosing how we react to triggers and emotions and choosing new stories and behaviors.

In Chapter 2, you read about the three general strategies we use in our 5-Square coaching work. If you have any questions about them, please go back and re-read the chapter. I am now going to take you straight into the process of building three types of strategies: creating space, values-driven self-talk, and rewriting a noble story.

Creating Space Between Trigger and Response

Creating a few seconds of space between our perceived threat and what we actually do is a prerequisite to accessing any other strategies. Creating space begins in our bodies, managing our sensations to create a window of time for us to slow down and regain our ability to think. What can you do to create space between your triggers and your actions?

- Start by considering what you do you already that you could do more intentionally in a trigger moment. Do you already have meditative practices in your life, like yoga, prayer, or a mindfulness practice? If you do, you probably already have breathing strategies you can bring to bear.
- There may be other micromovements that you do already with your body that calm you down (from taking a sip of water to shifts in your posture). How could you more intentionally do those things in the moment? If it slows you down, then it works.

Write down at least one strategy to slow yourself down when triggered in your 5-Square.

Grounding in Your Standard with Self-Coaching

 Once you have slowed down and you are in your thinking brain, you can access your inner coach. This is when those values you identified earlier get activated.

- Which of the values you identified will serve you most when you are triggered and in danger of being hijacked by your emotions? Choose two that resonate the most.
- Now consider how these values can show up in the moment to anchor you in your true north. Imagine you have an angel on your shoulder whispering in your ear. What would that angel tell you that will be more powerful than the fear and self-limiting stories the devil on your other shoulder is yelling in your other ear?
- Crystallize what that angel—your inner coach—could say to you in the moment. Compose brief phrases that will be easy to access and powerful for you in the moment. Think bumper sticker or T-shirt message. Write up to three of these in your 5-Square.

Now take the final draft-thinking of your self-coaching and add it to the self-management box of your 5-Square.

Rewrite Noble Stories

Our stories become our reality. What stories do you need to tell yourself about the person or people in this context that will help you engage effectively as an adaptive leader? What do you need to tell yourself about *yourself* that will help you show up as the adaptive leader you want to be?

- Consider all of the self-limiting stories you recorded in your 5-Square when you were reflecting on your stuff. Which ones get in your way the most?
- Rewrite your stories about others. Connect with your empathy and compassion: What do you tell yourself is true about their best intentions? What do you respect about them? Where are they struggling as professionals or people that prompt compassion? What do you need to believe that *they* believe about *you*, or that they will believe about you if you mess up somehow? Write what resonates most to you in your 5-Square.
- Rewrite your stories about yourself. What do you need to believe that you can do, learn, or become? What do you need to believe about yourself if you struggle or make a mistake as an adaptive leader? Write what resonates most to you in your 5-Square.

Self-Work: Pause and Reflect

You have just generated your personal game plan for managing your stuff and harnessing your power. If you work these strategies deliberately over time, they should help you shift from self-limiting behaviors that have kept you from being the adaptive leader you want to become. Only intentional practice over time builds the new neural highways of habit. Before reading on, create a plan for following through on this practice. You will need to build structures into your daily life to remind you to practice and reflect. You will also need partners to help you stay focused and to provide feedback. Consider how you could enlist trusted people in both your personal and professional life to keep you focused.

You have now completed the self-work portion on the left side of the 5-Square. We will now move to the right side to begin building new awareness and strategies to see and engage others effectively as an adaptive leader.

Step 4: Build Social Awareness to Diagnose Needs and Set Targets

Self-work is a prerequisite, especially for you as a transactional leader, because your ability see others clearly has been clouded by your own baggage, or stuff. With new awareness and intention to self-manage, you are now prepared to see others through fresh eyes.

This first social awareness question for you to consider is a diagnostic one: *Where are they?* This simple question activates the muscle that you likely need to build the most as a transactional leader: empathy. Psychologist Paul Eckman explains that there are different kinds of empathy. The key to effective social awareness is cognitive empathy: knowing how others might be feeling and thinking without actually feeling it along with them, which Eckman calls emotional empathy (Eckman 2003).[3] As a transactional leader, you need to learn to appreciate emotions as a form of data that helps you diagnose where people are and what they need.

Take yourself back to the behavioral event you have been reflecting on throughout this chapter and focus on the person or people involved through the lens of the Green Line. Reflect on the following questions in your journal:

- How were they feeling? What emotions did they bring to the conversation, and how did their interaction with you affect their emotions? What might trigger their response to you?
- What stories do you think they were telling themselves about you, both before and then during the conversation?
- What stories do you think they believe about themselves? What core values drive them, based on your experience? What self-limiting beliefs might hold them back from reaching their potential?
- How does identity impact your interaction with them? What lines of difference and power between you might contribute to the challenge?
- What specific self-limiting behaviors do you believe are the result of all of the above? How are these behaviors preventing this person from being effective in their work and trusting in your relationship?

Once you have explored all these possibilities, record your best answers in the social awareness box of your 5-Square. If you have a manager, coach, or colleague you trust who is not involved in this dilemma (neutrality and confidentiality are very important here) but knows the other person or group, then share your theories and get additional perspective. When you do, reflect on how closely your analysis aligns to your colleague's. That answer will give you useful data about where you need to grow.

Where Do They Need to Be? (Defining Your Targets)

Now that you have deliberately considered where they are below the Green Line, you are ready to think adaptively about targets and objectives for your interaction with this person or group. Note that identifying strong targets is not possible without understanding the challenges and needs of the other person and the context. Your answers to the question "Where are they?" that you prioritized earlier should drive your targets. You should end up with a small number of targets that address challenges both above and below the Green Line. See my examples in Table 4.1.

In your 5-Square, generate a target for each of the where-they-are points you have prioritized.

Table 4.1: Sample targets.

Where they are (your diagnosis)		Where they need to be (your targets)
Above the Green Line		
Not completing a report on time	➡	Completing the report on time
Not communicating with me about the obstacles to completion	➡	Communicating with you about what is getting in the way
Below the Green Line		
Feeling like I am not invested in them as a professional or a human being	➡	Feeling like I am invested in them both professionally and personally
Not invested in the report as a practice because they do not see the value add	➡	Understand the value add and are invested in the report
Not willing to open up to me for fear of consequences	➡	Feeling safe to share their experience with me
Unhappy at work	➡	Happy and thriving in their work

Step 5: Manage Relationships to Meet Your Targets

Congratulations! You have stepped out of the self-limiting mindset of the transactional leader and exercised the core muscles of the adaptive leader: perspective-taking grounded in empathy and compassion. When this becomes habit, you will have outgrown your transactional mindset obstacle.

You are now prepared to consider relationship management: making decisions about how to engage people. To make the best choices, a leader should ask themselves the question, "What do they need from me to reach my targets?" As you learned in Chapter 2, we consider this question from the three emotional perspectives of connection, care, and challenge. Each person, group, and context will require its own blend of these three ingredients. When we get connection, care, and challenge right, we create the conditions for people to reach their full potential.

I recommend that you use your journal to think broadly about the following questions and then distill your thinking into the relationship management square of your 5-Square. Use your answers as a springboard for creative thinking about engagement. Consider connection, care, and challenge as an adaptive approach and write down what comes up. Do this thinking in the context of your behavioral moment case study, and in connection to the targets you have generated.

First return to your vision for success on the first page of your 5-Square plan to mine for strategies.

- To stir creative juices, re-read your aspirational vision from Step 1. If new ideas have emerged as you worked through this chapter, add them to the vision.
- Now read the vision again, pulling out the leadership actions that you might use to connect with, care for, and challenge your team. Add what seems important to the Relationship Management box of your 5-Square.

Now let's dig deeper into the concepts of connection, care, and challenge to deepen your engagement strategies.

What does the person or group in question need to feel truly *connected* with you as a human being? Consider these core behaviors of connection:

- *Authenticity*—How will you show up as *you*, the human being, with no persona or double-talk?

- *Vulnerability*—What do you need to share at a human emotional level (below your Green Line) that is relevant to this challenge? Consider how that will make it safe for others to share with you.
- *Listening*—What do you need to find out to confirm or revise your noble story and your theory about "where they are?" Consider the impact of *curious listening* on connection. There is nothing more effective you can do to make another person feel truly seen and heard.

What do they need from you to feel like you *care* about them?

- What can you say or do that will show your belief in their potential to grow?
- How can you show your investment in their growth and your relationship?
- How can you name the noble story that you hold for them with empathy and compassion?

How do they need you to *challenge* them to grow and meet your targets?

- How will you name their limiting behaviors and their impact with candor?
- How can you ground this conversation in your values and why you care? Your values are the source of your power when challenging.
- How and when will you name your targets (where you hope the conversation takes you both) for this person? How will you come back to them if the conversation veers off course?
- If the other person/people do not seem to be hearing your message, how will you increase your level of candor to "land the plane?" Consider crafting your most high-candor headline in advance.

Other Work: Pause and Reflect

You have just created a draft plan for engaging your stakeholders below and above the Green Line in adaptive leadership situations. It is important to understand that this plan is not a script that you will perform in a sequence. Engaging adaptively is inherently messy. You can influence it, but you cannot control it. You will need to use your self-management strategies to let go of your transactional-leader need for control and order. If you can lean into the mess, stay present and authentic, and meet people's needs where they are, then you will succeed. You must be ready to shift your criteria for what success looks like as an adaptive leader from a process perspective. This style of leadership is called adaptive because adapting to the needs of the moment is the ultimate measure of success.

Now the Real Work Begins

You have just done the reflective heavy lifting to shift your transactional leadership approach. If you intentionally hold this new awareness and exercise these new behavioral muscles over time, you will break out of your self-limiting rut, build relationships and trust, and start moving your people toward meeting their full potential.

That "if" means everything. We have all had epiphanies that felt like game changers for us, but which faded into the background of our consciousness over time. Intentional practice is the difference between a powerful but empty epiphany and transformational change. Remember the neuroscience behind this. We change when we build new neural pathways in our brains that replace the neural superhighways of our self-limiting mindsets and behaviors.

Your job now is to take this 5-Square plan and work it, intentionally, every day in your work. Print it out and post it somewhere in your workspace. You should be reading it over on a regular basis, especially when preparing for the kinds of interactions that you know are hard for you. You should revise and build on this 5-Square over time as you continue to build new awareness and come up with new strategies. This should be a living document that evolves as you evolve.

Chapter 11 will provide more guidance about how to keep your plan alive over time. In the next chapter, we will turn our attention to a self-limiting mindset that I often see working in tandem with transactional leadership: the unintended enabler.

Endnotes

1. Tema O. (2019). White Supremacy Culture. DRWorksBook, www.dismantlingracism .org/.
2. Crenshaw, K. (1989). Demarginalizing the intersection of race and sex: a Black feminist critique of antidiscrimination doctrine, feminist theory and antiracist politics. *University of Chicago Legal Forum* Vol. 1989, Iss. 1, Article 8. https://chicagounbound .uchicago.edu/cgi/viewcontent.cgi?article=1052&context=uclf.
3. Eckman, P. (2003). *Emotions Revealed: Recognizing Faces and Feelings to Improve Relationships Emotional Life*. New York: Time Books.

5 The Unintended Enabler

Unintended enablers are uncomfortable with conflict and are afraid of damaging relationships. When they sense emotional discomfort, enablers default to making people feel good. Consider Brian's story:

> Brian loves . . . most of his job. He loves that he can make his school a place where people love to come to work and to learn. He loves the people he works with, and they love him. Staff, families, and students all feel safe going to Brian with challenges they are facing. He makes people feel cared for and affirmed. But there is something that Brian knows is getting in his way. When he sees that someone's behavior or performance is not living up to his expectations, he gets stuck. In the moment he feels a sinking in his stomach that turns into a knot. Then he feels dread, self-doubt, and even frustration. Then an internal argument plays itself out in his head.
>
> > "But it's my job to name this. If I don't I'm a failure."
> > "But am I getting the facts right about this situation? What if I am wrong? Am I being unreasonable?"
> > "Is it even worth it? For this small issue, to risk losing influence and trust with this teacher?"
> > "And what if they tell their friends? Then I will lose trust with other staff too."
> > "And what if they leave? How can I replace them mid-year? And who will leave next?"
> > "And (if Brian gets really honest with himself) what if they don't like me anymore?"

As this internal conversation rages, Brian walks by the staff member and the moment passes. Later he does not bring it up in their one-on-one check-in. Or if he does, it sounds so caring and positive that the staff member is not even aware that they are receiving constructive feedback. Their behavior continues. Other staff see this playing out and receive these messages:

1. *That behavior is okay here.*
2. *Brian lets things slide. That means I have a free pass. That could also mean I may never know how Brian really feels about my performance.*

Does Brian's story resonate with you? Read this chapter if:

- ☐ The most common positive feedback you receive is about being caring and kind.
- ☐ The most common constructive feedback you receive is about people not feeling that they are growing, or successful, in their roles.
- ☐ Your staff do not consistently meet common expectations.
- ☐ Your most important student outcomes have not met expectations over time.
- ☐ You make excuses for people who do not meet your bar because they are working so hard.
- ☐ You are generally uncomfortable with conflict.
- ☐ You avoid "difficult conversations" involving constructive feedback and accountability, opting to leverage relationships instead.
- ☐ You believe, at some level, that having difficult conversations erodes trust and/or relationships.
- ☐ You have a negative view of positional power and use it only when you absolutely have to.
- ☐ Deep down, you are afraid of people not liking you.

Unintended Enabling in Learning Organizations

The negative impact that enabling leaders have on school culture and outcomes is unique because teaching and learning are what schools do. Enablers inadvertently communicate that they do not believe in teachers and students, which in turn erodes people's belief in their own capacity. Schools led by unintended enablers can be positive on the surface but may lack real investment in learning, and they are marked by underperformance in all substantive areas.

Further, enabling in schools historically plays out as a racial equity issue. Our American legacy of structural racism brings with it both visible and (to many) invisible ways in which educators lower expectations for Black and brown students. Enabling leaders reinforces this pattern by lowering expectations for adults.

If you know this mindset is getting in your way as a leader, keep reading. If you do not see yourself in the preceding checklist or case study, then maybe this chapter is not for you. Ask for feedback from your manager and a few trusted staff before making that decision. If others confirm your opinion, then skip ahead to the next chapter.

This chapter is a self-contained learning journey. If you take it on, you could spend several months focusing on changing deeply engrained habits and building new adaptive muscles. Download a 5-Square learning plan template from www.noblestorygroup.com to build your plan. You will also need a journal to explore new ideas.

Let's get started.

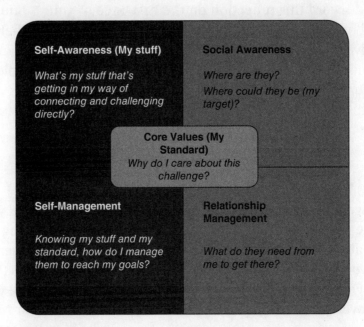

Figure 5.1: The EI 5-Square.

Step 1: Start with the End in Mind

This journey starts by thinking about what success will look like when you have outgrown your enabler beliefs and behaviors. Use your imagination to envision what you will be doing differently and how it will ideally feel to lead with connection *and* challenge. Pay particular attention to the situations you find most challenging (the preceding checklist might help you with that) but remember that your goal is to envision your *ideal* self in these situations. To help you drill down, consider the following questions. What will it look like and feel like to:

- Say the thing—the *real* thing—in the moment.
- Deliver direct, high-candor feedback when people do not meet expectations.
- Ensure your direct reports are clear where they stand on their performance and their growth areas.
- Make definitive decisions and stand by them.
- Challenge those who push back on expectations and decisions.
- Challenge and empower people to own their work and stay in their lanes.

You should record this reflection on the first page of your 5-Square learning plan. Journal first and then transfer to the 5-Square if journaling helps you think creatively. Give yourself uninterrupted time (at least 30 minutes) and emotional space to do this reflection. You might find it helpful to see an example vision from another 5-Square, and there is one in Appendix B. You will use this vision of success during this journey to generate awareness and strategies, and to measure your progress over time.

Step 2: Building Self-Awareness

When you have thought deeply about the leader you want to become, you are ready to hold up the mirror and build new awareness about what is getting in your way. As you think about this question at a high level, push yourself to remember specific times when you led as an unintended enabler that did not result in the outcomes you wanted. Once you have two or three examples in mind, choose one to use as a case study over the next few pages.

The real work of self-awareness building happens when we reflect on specific moments of our leadership as mini case studies. In coaching we call these case studies behavioral moments. When we zoom in on these moments of emotional cause and effect, decision, and behavior, we are able to identify the chain reaction of a self-limiting mindset.

What Are Your Triggers?

Identify the trigger moment of your case study. What happened that started you down the enabler path? Something triggered a feeling—another person's behavior, receiving a text or email, second hand reports of under-performance. For unintended enablers, triggers tend to be moments when we discover that others whom we care about (love, respect, empathize with, fear) do not live up to our standards in some way. What are those trigger moments for you? Be as clear as you can about the specific moment in your case study, then try to generalize to how this kind of trigger shows up regularly in challenging leadership moments. Write down what comes up in your 5-Square.

What Sensations and Emotions Do You Experience?

Our triggers start a self-limiting chain reaction that starts in our body. Neurological research shows that we process stress physiologically before we process it emotionally or intellectually. Our body is our early warning system—a fundamental aspect of self-awareness that most of us do not pay enough attention to. Think back again to your trigger moment. Where did you feel your reaction in your body? Note this reaction in your 5-Square.

Soon after the physical reaction comes an emotional reaction. Our emotional response to our trigger is more complicated than we might think. We often experience a contradictory blend of positive and dissonant emotions at the same time. When you are triggered and feeling the sensations you identified in your body, what emotions are you experiencing connected to yourself? What emotions are you experiencing connected to others? Write down the emotions you tend to experience in these moments. Push yourself to name as many as you can.

What Stories Get in Your Way?

Our stories—the inner narratives and assumptions about ourselves, others, and context that help us make sense of the world—come next. Right now, we are focusing specifically on the stories getting in your way. In the moment what were you telling yourself about yourself, others, and the situation? It might help you to connect your emotions with thoughts, as each emotion comes with a narrative. For example, our frustration could connect to the story "I can't believe this person is putting me in this situation" and it could also connect to the story "I can't believe I am letting myself be led down this path again." Write down all the self-limiting stories that came up in your case study moment and consider how they connect to other enabler moments.

As an unintended enabler, make sure that you are zeroing in on what you fear will happen if you *do* have the hard conversation when people do not meet your standard. I sometimes refer to these stories as the "monster under the bed" when I am coaching. Unpack those stories—these monsters—until they are all out in broad daylight so you can examine them without the emotion that comes with them in the moment. What do you notice? This should be an important awareness moment for you.

Our Stories and Our Identities

The deeper our stories, the more connected they are to our identities. Growing up in America, with our 400-year history of white male supremacy, it is inevitable that racism, sexism, and other forms of oppression impact the way we interact across lines of power, privilege, and identity. Becoming aware of how privilege or oppression plays a role in your enabler mindsets is key to overcoming them. Privileged groups, and especially white people, have been conditioned to avoid confronting or acknowledging our power, which can play out as enabling across lines of difference. Many who have been oppressed have developed self-defense strategies that serve in many ways but enable across lines of difference. Consider how your identities might connect to your enabling tendencies.

Write down all the self-limiting stories that come up in your case study moment and consider how they feed your enabler tendencies.

Then What Do You *Do*?

Your triggers, sensations and emotions, and self-limiting stories all lead you to *do* things that get in your way. These are your self-limiting behaviors. In the case study you have been unpacking, what did you do that got in your way? Consider the sequence of actions in that moment and in follow-up interactions. Consider not only your words but your tone, body language, and maybe even what you did *not* say or do that got in your way. Do not stop at your first or even second response either. Consider all of the relevant actions in a sequence related to this moment. Write it all down. We build deeper self-awareness when we really focus on all of our actions connected to one trigger moment.

What Is the Impact of Your Behaviors?

Now reflect on the full ripple effect of your actions. This effect likely goes much further than you have previously considered.

Wheatly's Green Line (see Chapter 1 and Figure 5.2) helps us reflect adaptively on our impact. Start by reflecting on the three circles above the line. Consider your intended leadership outcomes against your actual outcomes. Consider the ripple effect of these outcomes on your staff and students. What is the connection? Now focus on the three circles below the line and consider the social and emotional implications of your behavior. Again, start with self and follow the ripples out. How did your actions impact your self-perception? How did your behavior impact your relationships with others? How might it have impacted their ability to succeed?

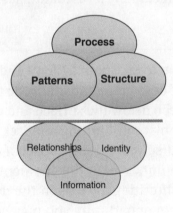

Figure 5.2: Wheatly's Six-Circle Model.
Source: Margaret Wheatly.

Unintended enablers can usually make the cause–effect link between lowering expectations for teachers and quality of instruction and student learning outcomes, but that is only the tip of the impact iceberg. At some level people know that we are lowering our expectations of them. When our bosses or teachers implicitly tell us through their actions that they do not believe we can do something, then we tend to doubt our abilities as well. This effect is particularly corrosive across lines of difference like race and gender. The effect is also contagious between different levels of learning; it can affect students as well as the teachers you supervise. Frankly, a leader who is a serial unintended enabler can undermine the conditions for learning across an entire organization.

Impact on reputation is another area we tend to not fully explore. Consider how this episode—and the pattern of similar episodes—affect your credibility with this person. What do they tell their colleagues, friends, and family who live and work in your community? What do others see and feel when you and this person are interacting in the hallway or in staff meetings? What are you implicitly giving your staff permission to do or not do, and what is the disconnect between what you say and what you allow? How does all of it affect your ability to achieve your leadership goals and, ultimately, your student outcomes?

Take a few minutes to journal on the impact of the earlier ripple effect, and any other ripples across your world you might have missed. When you think you have a pretty exhaustive list, consider sharing with a trusted colleague or manager to see if they can think of anything you might have missed or that might not be likely (we all have blind spots about our impact, especially when it comes to our reputation). Then return to your 5-Square and record the levels of impact that matter the most to you.

Pause and Reflect

At this point, I encourage you to take both a literal and metaphorical deep breath. Step back and offer yourself both grace and gratitude for the work you have done so far. You have just gone deep below the surface and explored the chain reaction behind your unintended enabler self-limiting mindset. It is painful to confront the ugly stories we are telling ourselves and the impact of our self-limiting behaviors. It is natural to feel down on ourselves at this moment. However, when we allow ourselves this clear-eyed self-critique, we open the door to change and growth. With self-awareness comes an opportunity you may not have known you had: to choose a different way of being.

This choosing begins with building new self-management strategies that shift your stories and behaviors.

Step 3: Build Self-Management Strategies ────────

We cannot stop our triggers and our emotions; they are hardwired. However, we *can* manage triggers and emotions once we become aware of them. Self-management is about choosing how we react to triggers and emotions and choosing new stories and behaviors.

In Chapter 2, you read about the three general strategies we use in our 5-Square coaching work. For a deeper explanation, go back and re-read. Here we will go straight into the process of building these strategies: creating space, values-driven self-talk, and rewriting a noble story.

Creating Space Between Trigger and Response

Creating a few seconds of space between a perceived threat and what we actually do is a prerequisite to accessing other strategies. Creating space begins in our bodies, managing our sensations to create a window of time for us to slow down and think. What can you do to create space between your triggers and your actions?

- Start by considering what you do already that you could do more intentionally in a trigger moment. Do you already have meditative practices in your life, like yoga, prayer, or a mindfulness practice? If you do, you probably already have breathing strategies you can bring to bear. A couple of deep breaths over a matter of seconds could be all you need to choose a different internal strategy and behavior.
- There may be other micromovements that you do already with your body that calm you down (from taking a sip of water to shifting in your posture). How could you more intentionally do those things in the moment? Consider the impact on your chain reaction of walking away from your computer for a glass of water, a walk around the block, or a moment with another person. If it slows you down, then it works.

Write down at least one strategy to slow down and interrupt the reaction to your trigger in the self-management box of your 5-Square.

Grounding in Your Standard with Self-Coaching

 Once you have slowed down and you are in your thinking brain, you can access your inner coach. This is when your values—your standard—gets activated.

To surface the values that matter most in this context, start by returning to the dissonance you felt about the stories, behaviors, and their impact that came up during your self-awareness building. Why do you care about *not* telling yourself the stories and acting out the behaviors of the unintended enabler anymore? Consider this question deeply. In your journal, list all of the reasons you care about changing your self-limiting stories and behaviors. Write whatever comes to mind so that you get all the possible reasons down on paper. Your list will likely range from how you want to feel about yourself and be perceived by others to why you chose to be an educator and leader.

When you think you have a relatively complete list, review and prioritize your top five. This should be an emotional exercise. You should feel in your gut what matters most to you. Now, for each of your prioritized care statements, go deeper. *Why* is this statement important to you? What is that *about* for you? For each answer, try to follow with another why question. It is like peeling an onion, as there are many layers of meaning that you will uncover. Your goal here is to try to get to the core value.

Example:

I want to be able to look myself in the mirror every day. (Why?)

I want to see someone in that mirror with self-respect. (Why?)

I want to live in alignment with who I know I can be. (Why?)

Core Value: This is about leading to reach my full potential.

You will know when you are done when you can say and feel, "This one is about (a value or value statement) for me." Do this for each of the statements that you prioritized. Then add those core values to the center square of your 5-Square.

Now consider how your values relate to your identities. According to the idea of intersectionality (Crenshaw 1989),[1] we all have many identities, or facets of self, that make up who we are. Some of these include gender, race, sexuality, class, ability, place of origin, and religion, but the list is really only limited by the number of ways we make sense of ourselves and each other in the world. We know that multiple forms of discrimination accumulate across identity markers, marginalizing or privileging groups and individuals. Yet we also know that our identities are a source of our power. They weave together to create our cultures, from family culture to our many different group cultures. From these interwoven identity groups, we learn what matters to us in the world.

Re-read the list of values you just generated. Consider how your identities connect with and inform these values. How can an intentional anchoring in your identities empower you to shift your enabler habits? Add identity notes in parentheses next to your values statements in your 5-Square.

You have just surfaced your power. Now think about how to harness that power in the moment with self-coaching. Take yourself back to that trigger moment and craft your "self-talk":

- Which of the values you identified will serve you most when you are triggered and in danger of being hijacked by your emotions? Choose one or two that resonate the most.
- Now consider how these values apply to this moment to orient you to your true north. Up to this point you have had an anti-coach whispering stories and advice that have mostly held you back. Now imagine that you have a new coach on your other shoulder. What can this new coach tell you that will be more powerful than the self-limiting stories that have held you back?
- Crystallize brief phrases your inner coach can bring to the moment that will be easy to access and resonant at a values level. Think bumper sticker or T-shirt. Write up to three of these in your 5-Square self-management box. Some examples from unintended enablers I have coached include:

This is not about me

This is my job

This is about growth and reaching potential

It's not fair for me to deny this opportunity for growth

Rewrite Noble Stories

Our stories become our reality. You have just written some new stories grounded in your power, or the values that you want to guide you in the moment. Now we shift to another powerful group of stories that need revising: what we tell ourselves about others' motives and opinions about us. These stories are largely based on perception and inference rather than on actual interpersonal data.

Go back to your self-limiting stories in your self-awareness square and pull out the ones about other people. If you know that this list is incomplete, add the rest of the self-limiting stories you tell about others in your moments of unintended enabling. Now, *flip them*. Replace them with alternative narratives that emphasize positive motives and/or opinions about you in the present context. Consider:

- What could you choose to believe about your students, families, colleagues, and staff that would help you be direct with and challenge them?
- What could you choose to believe about what they value that would support you to challenge?

Write what resonates most to you in your 5-Square.

An important piece of your noble story about others, especially as an unintended enabler, is what you choose to believe about other people's stories about *you*. Consider your self-limiting stories about other people's perceptions of you. You probably thought about these stories when you faced the monster under the bed. Now, rewrite those stories. What could you choose to believe that they think about *you*? What could you *choose* to believe that they will think about you if you challenge them? Write down the most relevant stories.

Finally, you need to consider the noble stories that you tell yourself *about yourself*. Rewrite your stories about yourself. What do you need to believe that you can do, learn, or become? What do you need to believe about yourself if you struggle or make a mistake as a leader? Add what matters most to your 5-Square.

Self-Work: Pause and Reflect

You have now completed the left side of the 5-Square and, in doing so, you have generated a game plan for managing your stuff and leveraging your power. If you work these strategies deliberately over time, they should help you shift from self-limiting behaviors that have kept you from becoming the leader you want to be. You will need to build structures into your daily life to remind you to practice and reflect, and you will need partners to help you stay focused and to provide feedback.

We will now move to the right side of the 5-Square to begin building new awareness and strategies to see and engage others.

Step 4: Build Social Awareness to Diagnose Needs and Set Targets

With your new self-awareness and intention to self-manage, you have prepared yourself to see others more clearly. As you shift your focus from self to others, the first question for you to consider is a diagnostic one: *Where are they?* This simple question activates a competency that may already be a strength for you as an unintended enabler: empathy and compassion. You are probably aware, however, that empathy is a double-edged sword for you. When you care too much about people you can experience what the Gestalt philosophy refers to as confluence—a dysfunctional closeness and blurred boundaries that causes us to join with others in ways that make us doubt our own judgment (Wyley 1989).[2] Your social awareness goal is to learn how to use your empathy strength to *accurately* perceive where others are below the Green Line. Psychologist Paul Eckman calls this cognitive empathy: knowing how others might be feeling and thinking without actually feeling it along with them, which Eckman calls emotional empathy (Eckman 2003).[3] As an unintended enabler, you need your self-management strategies to strengthen your cognitive empathy and manage your emotional empathy. Your goal is to keep yourself out of this analysis as you make the clearest diagnosis you can about the other person or group.

To begin this work, take yourself back to the same case study—or behavioral event—that you have been reflecting on throughout this chapter. Focus on the person or people involved through the lens of the Green Line. Reflect on the following questions in your journal:

■ How were they feeling? What emotions did they bring to the conversation, and how did their interaction with you affect their emotions? What might trigger their response to you?

- What stories do you think they were telling themselves about you, both before and then during the conversation? *Careful not to make this about you!* If you have something to own and fix, that's fine, but self-manage to put that to the side for now and stay in cognitive empathy. Look for their stories that might be misconceptions about you and evidence of their self-limiting mindsets.
- What stories do you think they believe about themselves? What core values drive them, based on your experience? What self-limiting beliefs might hold them back from reaching their potential?
- How does identity impact your interaction with them? What lines of difference and power between you might contribute to the challenge?
- What self-limiting behaviors does this person exhibit? How are these behaviors preventing them from growing, being effective in their work, and trusting your relationship?

These questions should look familiar to you, as they are the same below-the-surface questions you asked yourself on the other side of the 5-Square. Now you are picking up the magnifying glass—or the stethoscope—to diagnose someone else's standard and stuff.

Record your best answers to the preceding questions in the Social Awareness box of your 5-Square. As you do, try to stay in that cognitive empathy space of accurate perspective-taking. Notice and self-manage if you are pulled toward enabling empathy.

Where Do They Need to Be? (Defining Your Targets)

Now that you have a working diagnosis of where the other person is, you are ready to think about targets and objectives for engagement. Note that the strength of your targets depends on the strength of your diagnosis. Your goal here to is prioritize the behaviors and obstacles you diagnosed and to articulate intended outcomes, or changes, you hope to accomplish through your engagement. These targets tend to land in three basic categories: behaviors, mindsets, and relational conditions that you want to shift. Some examples are shown in Table 5.1. Note the alignment between diagnosis and the target.

Table 5.1: Sample targets.

Where they are (your diagnosis)		Where they need to be (your targets)
Above the Green Line		
Not meeting deadlines over time	➡	Meeting deadlines consistently
Not communicating with me about the obstacles to completion	➡	Communicating with me about what is getting in the way
Complaining about the report's lack of value with teammates	➡	Shifting to a solution-oriented approach to communication
Below the Green Line		
Not invested in our relationship, not feeling connected	➡	Feeling like I am invested in them both professionally and personally
Not invested in the report as a practice because they do not see its value	➡	Understand impact of not completing, and the value of completing, the report
Not aware of the impact they are having on team culture	➡	Aware of the impact on their reputation, team cohesion, and team morale when they complain
Unhappy at work	➡	Feeling challenged and like they are growing in their work

In your 5-Square, generate a target for each of the where-they-are points you have prioritized.

Step 5: Manage Relationships to Meet Your Targets

You have now done the internal work and perspective-taking to prepare yourself to engage. This is where the rubber hits the road for you as an unintended enabler. It is time for you to use all of your new awareness and strategies to choose new ways to connect, care, and challenge to reach your targets. For you, this likely looks like a rebalancing of your engagement toward more direct challenge. Each person, group, and context will require its own unique blend of these three ingredients to create the conditions for success, and the ingredient that you have been underusing has been challenge.

Use the following questions as a springboard for creative thinking about engagement. Do this thinking in the context of your behavioral moment case study, and in connection with the targets you have generated.

First return to your vision for success on the first page of your 5-Square plan:

- To get your creative juices flowing, re-read your aspirational vision from Step 1. If any new ideas have come up as you have worked through this chapter, add them to the vision.
- Read the vision again, pulling out the leadership actions that you might use to connect with, care for, or challenge the person or group in this context. As a reminder,
    - Connection = authentic human connection + accurate perspective on where they are below the Green Line
    - Care = authentic belief in others' potential + empathy (emotional understanding of where they are) + compassion (investment and desire to help)
    - Challenge = holding high expectations and pushing toward your targets with candor

Now call on your instincts and your social awareness of this context: What does the person or group in question need to feel truly *connected* with you as a human being? Make sure you are not confusing this question with what they might *want*. Connection does not always feel good, and your misconception about that has likely been a trap for you as an unintended enabler. Connection must feel *real*. Consider these core behaviors of connection:

- *Authenticity*—How will you show up as *you*, the human being, with no persona or double-talk?
- *Vulnerability*—What do you need to share at an emotional level (below your Green Line) that is relevant to this challenge? Do not shy away from sharing dissonant emotions! You must self-manage to allow yourself to put those real emotions out there without actually being in them in the moment. Consider how sharing your real self can be an invitation for others to share themselves with you.
- *Listening*—What do you need to find out to confirm or revise your noble story and your diagnosis about "where they are?" Consider the impact of asking *curious* questions and listening on connection. There is nothing more effective you can do to make another person feel truly seen and heard.

Now consider what they need from you to feel like you *care* about them? Remember that care in the 5-Square is not just about empathy, but also your belief in people's ability to grow and your investment in helping them grow. Expressing belief and investment will take you much further as an unintended enabler than empathy. For you, the challenge likely needs to be the main event and the care should ensure your listener that you are on their team.

- What can you say or do that will show your belief in their potential to grow in the context of the current challenge and your targets?
- How can you show your investment in their growth and your relationship without taking on all of the responsibility for both?
- How can you name the noble story that you hold for them as the counterpoint to your challenge of them?

And now for the main event. How will you *challenge* them to grow and meet your targets? *Everything you have done in this chapter has prepared you for this. Go for it!!!*

- How will you name their limiting behaviors and their impact with candor?
- How can you ground this conversation in your values and why you care? Your values are the source of your power when challenging.
- How and when will you name your targets (what you hope this conversation will achieve) for this person? How will you come back to them if the conversation veers off course?
- If the other person/people do not seem to be hearing your message, how will you increase your level of candor to turn up the volume. Consider crafting your most high-candor headline in advance.

Take some time to populate your relationships management box with all of the ways you might engage in the moment with connection, care, and challenge.

Other Work: Pause and Reflect

Congratulations! You have just created a draft plan for challenging your stakeholders while maintaining connection. It is important to understand that this plan is not a script you will perform in a sequence. Engaging adaptively is inherently messy. You will need to use your self-management strategies to push yourself to challenge when your old habits want you to make people comfortable. If you can lean into the mess, stay present and authentic, and say the real thing that needs to be said, then you will succeed. The most important question to ask yourself during and after an engagement will be, "Did I say what needed to be said?" If the answer is no, do not beat yourself up. Go back for another round. There will always be an opportunity to have another conversation.

Now the Real Work Begins

You have just done the reflective heavy lifting to shift your unintended enabler mindsets and behaviors. If you intentionally hold this new awareness and exercise these new behavioral muscles over time, you will break out of your self-limiting rut, hold high standards, change the trajectory of your organization's outcomes and culture, and start moving your people toward meeting their potential.

That "if" is a real caveat. We have all had epiphanies about what gets in our way that felt like game changers for us, but that faded into the background of our consciousness over time. Intentional practice is what connects an epiphany to transformational change. Remember the neuroscience behind this. We change when we build new neural pathways in our brains that replace the neural super-highways of our self-limiting mindsets and behaviors.

Your job now is to take your 5-Square plan and work it, intentionally, every day in your work. Print it out and post it somewhere in your workspace. You should be reading it over on a regular basis, especially when preparing for the kinds of interactions you know are hard for you. This should be a living document that evolves as you evolve. Chapter 11 will provide more guidance about how to keep your plan alive over time.

In the next chapter, we will turn our attention to an inner obstacle that is the Yang to the enabler's Yin: the negative controller mindset.

Endnotes

1. Crenshaw, K. (1989). Demarginalizing the intersection of race and sex: a Black feminist critique of antidiscrimination doctrine, feminist theory and antiracist politics." *University of Chicago Legal Forum*, Vol. 1989, Iss. 1, Article 8. https://chicagounbound.uchicago.edu/cgi/viewcontent.cgi?article=1052&context=uclf.

2. Wyley, C. (ed.). (1989). International Organization and Systems Development Program. From: Jochen Lohmeier, Baobab handout on Resistances in an Overview; Jonno Hanafin Associates, Handout on Resistance, and Petruska Clarkson, *Gestalt counselling in action*. 2nd ed. London: Sage, 1989. Chapter 4 on "Disfunctions and disturbances in the Cycle".

3. Eckman, P. (2003). *Emotions Revealed: Recognizing Faces and Feelings to Improve Relationships Emotional Life*. New York: Time Books.

6 The Negative Controller

The negative controller misdiagnoses leadership challenges by making the **fundamental attribution error**—the assumption that people themselves are the reason for their lack of growth rather than the lack of effective development opportunities in their work environment. Consider Alicia's story:

Alicia eats, sleeps, and breathes the mission of closing the opportunity gap for children. Her power as a leader comes from her commitment and passion. She has risen through the ranks because her unwavering bar of excellence and focus on outcomes has led to breakthrough achievement in every role . . . until now.

Some on her team love Alicia and would follow her anywhere. A good number, however, would describe their relationship with their leader as "toxic." Bring those team members up in conversation with Alicia and you will see and feel her energy shift. When problem solving with her manager, Alicia shares that these team members have skill gaps but she is much more concerned about their lack of commitment and negative outlook on kids and the work. In more candid moments behind closed doors, Alicia would say that these people are soft, lazy, and selfish. She doesn't understand or respect their constant need for empathy and affirmation, and the way they share their problems feels like complaining and excuse making. "Why should I have to teach adults how to be adults?!" she thinks to herself.

*When Alicia engages with these team members her energy shifts to
a chilly flatness. Her tone is formal and her words are clipped. When
these people fall short, her disgust is palpable. Exchanges become curt
at best and feel demeaning at their worst. It is more likely that Alicia
will disengage and then take on others' failed tasks herself so that "it will
get done right."*

*Alicia is a powerhouse, but the pace she is keeping is gradually deplet-
ing her reserves. Her school is moving, but her team is largely driven by
fear, and there is already talk about too many people leaving next year.*

Does Alicia's story resonate with you? Read this chapter if:

- ☐ You are regularly frustrated, disappointed in, and "done" with a number of your staff.
- ☐ Your underperformers were solid performers in previous jobs, or they go on to do better after they leave you.
- ☐ Your school's culture is driven by compliance and there is a lack of initiative to try new things.
- ☐ Some of your staff have gone to your manager to complain about your management
- ☐ Your staff attrition numbers over time are higher than the norm in your organization or sector. This may especially be true across lines of difference.

Negative Controllers in Learning Organizations

Ironically, negative controllers have the same negative impact on learning environments as unintended enablers. While enablers communicate a lack of belief in their
team by omission, negative controllers do so overtly with words, tone, and actions.
Their overt disappointment and frustration, micromanagement, or disregard lead
people to feel unsuccessful and unfairly treated. Those who struggle may internalize
these messages and get stuck or externalize their struggles and accuse their leaders of mistreatment and bias. Schools led by negative controllers may experience
high compliance and a sense of urgency, but they tend to be negative and unsafe
learning environments with high turnover.

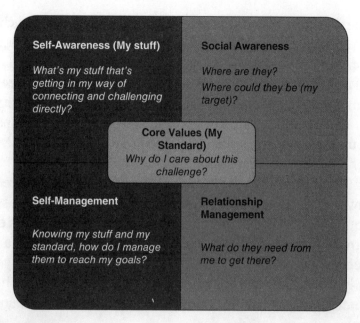

Figure 6.1: The EI 5-Square.

If you know that this mindset is getting in your way as a leader, keep reading. If you do not see yourself in the preceding checklist or case study then maybe this chapter is not for you. Ask for feedback from your manager and a few trusted staff before making that decision. If others confirm your opinion, then skip ahead to the next chapter.

This chapter is a self-contained learning journey. If you take it on, you could spend several months focusing on changing deeply engrained habits and building new adaptive muscles. Download a 5-Square learning plan template from www .noblestorygroup.com to build your personal plan. You will also need a journal to explore new ideas.

Let's get started.

Step 1: Start with the End in Mind

Before we analyze what is getting in your way, it helps to do some aspirational thinking about what success will look like when you have outgrown your negative controller habits. Use your imagination to envision what it is you will be doing and how it will ideally feel to lead with a balance of care and challenge. Pay particular attention to the situations you find most challenging (the preceding checklist might help you with that) but remember that your goal is to envision your *ideal* self in these situations.

You should record this reflection on the first page of your 5-Square. Journal first and then transfer to the 5-Square if journaling helps you think creatively. Give yourself uninterrupted time (at least 30 minutes) and emotional space to do this reflection. You might find it helpful to reference the vision from the sample negative controller 5-Square in Appendix C.

This aspirational thinking will become the vision of excellence that you use to generate awareness and strategies, and to measure your progress over time. I encourage you to put real effort into the feeling questions in this exercise. As a negative controller, your growth area is less about what you do than *how* you do it, or how it feels. Push yourself to name the specific emotions that you and others will feel ideally when engaging together in adaptive challenges. These emotions will be the outcomes that measure your growth in this mindset focus.

Step 2: Build Self-Awareness

When you have thought deeply about the leader you want to be, you are ready to hold up the mirror and build awareness about what is getting in your way. As you think about this, push yourself to remember specific times when you led as a negative controller that did not result in the outcomes you wanted. Once you have two or three examples in mind, choose one to use as a case study over the rest of this chapter. In coaching we call these case studies behavioral moments. When we zoom in on these moments of emotional cause and effect, decision, and behavior, we are able to identify the chain reaction of a self-limiting mindset.

What Are Your Triggers?

Identify the trigger moment of your case study. What happened that started you down the negative controller path? Something triggered a feeling—another person's behavior or maybe their outcomes. For negative controllers, triggers tend to be moments when they discover that people do not live up to their standards in some way. What are those trigger moments for you? Be as clear as you can about the specific moment in your case study, then think more broadly about how this kind of trigger shows up regularly in challenging leadership moments. Write down what comes up in the self-awareness box of your 5-Square.

What Sensations and Emotions Do You Experience?

Our triggers start a self-limiting chain reaction that starts in our body. Neurological research shows that we process stress physiologically before we process it emotionally or intellectually. Our body is our early warning system—a fundamental aspect of self-awareness that most of us do not pay enough attention to. Think back again to your trigger moment. Where did you feel your reaction in your body? Was it pressure in the chest, burning ears, or clenching hands? Note your reaction in your 5-Square.

Soon after the physical reaction comes an emotional reaction. Our emotional response to trigger moments is more complicated than we might think. We often experience a contradictory blend of positive and dissonant emotions at the same time. As negative controllers, the emotions we are most aware of when triggered are the ones associated with others (disappointment, disgust, frustration). However, you are likely experiencing other more subtle emotions connected to yourself (self-doubt, confusion). Write down all the emotions you tend to experience in these moments. Push yourself to name as many as you can.

What Stories Get in Your Way?

Our stories—the inner narratives and assumptions about ourselves, others, and context that help us make sense of the world—come next. Here we specifically focus on the stories that feed your self-limiting behaviors. In your case study, what were you telling yourself about others, yourself, and the situation that got in your way? It might help to connect each emotion with the thoughts that accompanied it. For example, a feeling of frustration could connect to the story "Why do I have to teach this person how to be an adult!" and it could also connect to the story "Somehow I think this is my fault." Write down all the self-limiting stories that came up in your case study moment and consider how they connect to other negative-controller moments.

As a negative controller, make sure you are zeroing in on two levels of story. The first and loudest are the ones you tell yourself about the people who let you down. Make sure you capture these stories in detail so you can see the themes in your judgment of others. The second more subtle level of stories are the ones you tell yourself about *you*. What do you tell yourself to do and think in these micromoments? What stories of self-judgment might you tell yourself about your abilities and character in these moments of failure? Include these stories in your 5-Square as well.

Our Stories and Our Identities

The deeper our stories, the more connected they are to our identities. Growing up in America, with our 400-year history of white male supremacy, it is inevitable that racism and sexism impact our perceptions of self and others. Becoming more aware of how unconscious bias shows up in your stories is a key step in building self-awareness as a negative controller. This is deep work that may take additional learning and support, as the effects of privilege and oppression are deeply rooted, hard to see, and painful to confront. But it's worth it. It is highly unlikely that you will make transformative growth as a negative controller without understanding and managing the implicit bias in your identity-related stories.

Add all of the self-limiting stories that have come up to your 5-Square.

Then What Do You *Do*?

Your triggers, sensations and emotions, and self-limiting stories all lead you to *do* things that get in your way. These are your self-limiting behaviors. In the case study you have been unpacking, what did you do that got in your way? Consider the sequence of actions in the moment and in follow-up interactions. Examine not only your words but your tone, body language, and maybe even what you did *not* say or do that got in your way. Do not stop at your first or even second response. Consider all of the relevant actions in a sequence related to this moment. Write it all down. We build deeper self-awareness when we really focus on all of our actions connected to one trigger moment.

What Is the Impact of Your Behaviors?

Now reflect on the full ripple effect of your actions. The impact likely goes much further than you have previously considered.

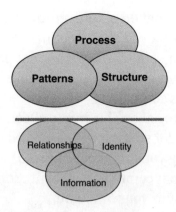

Figure 6.2: Wheatly's Six-Circle Model.
Source: Margaret Wheatly.

Wheatly's Green Line (see Chapter 1 and Figure 6.2) provides a helpful framework for considering impact. Start with the three circles above the line. Consider your intended leadership outcomes in your case study against your actual outcomes. Consider the ripple effect of this one-to-one engagement on the outcomes of your staff and students.

Now focus on the three circles below the line and consider the social and emotional implications of your behavior. Again, start with self and follow the ripples out. How did your actions affect your self-perception? How did your actions affect your relationships with others? How might it have impacted their ability to succeed?

Negative controllers can usually make the cause–effect link between the way they engage struggling staff and how those people feel about them, but that is only the tip of the iceberg. Negative emotions (disappointment, frustration) and behaviors (disengagement, micromanagement) from the leader limit growth. When our bosses or teachers implicitly tell us through their actions that they do not believe we can do something, then we tend to doubt our abilities as well. This effect is particularly corrosive across lines of difference like race and gender. The effect is also contagious from one level of learning space to the next. In this way, the negative controller can undermine the conditions for learning across an entire organization.

We tend not to consider the impact on reputation. Think about how your case study—and your pattern across similar episodes—likely impacts your credibility with this person. What do they tell their colleagues, friends, and family who live and work in your community? What do others see and feel when you and this person are interacting in the hallway or in staff meetings? For one, you are broadcasting what is unsafe to do in your school. How you treat people becomes ingrained in your school culture. All of this filters down to students, whose conditions for learning and academic outcomes suffer.

Take a few minutes to journal on this ripple effect. When you think you have a pretty exhaustive list, consider sharing with a trusted colleague or manager to see if they can think of anything you might have missed (we all have blind spots about our impact, especially when it comes to our reputation). Then record the levels of impact that matter the most in your 5-Square.

Pause and Reflect

At this point, I encourage you to take both a literal and metaphorical deep breath. Step back and offer yourself both grace and gratitude for the work you have done so far. You have just gone deep below the surface and explored the chain reaction behind your negative controller self-limiting mindset. It is painful to confront the self-limiting stories we tell ourselves and the impact that self-limiting behaviors have on ourselves and those around us. It is natural to feel down on ourselves at this moment. However, when we confront deep and personal obstacles, we open the door to change and growth. With self-awareness comes an opportunity you may not have known you had: to choose a more positive and effective way of being.

This choosing begins with building new self-management strategies that can shift your stories and behaviors.

Step 3: Build Self-Management Strategies ───────

 We cannot stop our triggers and our emotions; they are hardwired. However, we *can* manage triggers and emotions once we become aware of them. Self-management is about choosing how we react to triggers by emotions and choosing new stories and behaviors.

In Chapter 2 you read about the three basic self-management strategies we use in our 5-Square coaching: creating space, values-driven self-talk, and rewriting a noble story. For a deeper explanation, go back and re-read. Now we will go straight into the process of building these strategies.

Creating Space Between Trigger and Response

Creating a few seconds of space between our triggers and what we actually do is a prerequisite to accessing other strategies. This begins in our bodies, managing our sensations to create a window of time for us to slow down and think. What can you do to create space between your triggers and your actions?

- Start by considering what you already do that might serve you in trigger moments. Do you already have meditative practices in your life, like yoga, prayer, or a mindfulness practice? If you do, you probably already have breathing strategies you can bring to bear. A couple of deep breaths over a matter of seconds could be all you need to regain your ability to think clearly.
- There may be other micromovements that you do already with your body that calm you down (from taking a sip of water to shifting in your posture). How could you more intentionally do those things in the moment? Consider the impact on your chain reaction of walking away from your computer for a glass of water, a walk around the block, or a moment with another person or a pet. If it slows you down, then it works.

Write down at least one strategy to slow down and interrupt the reaction to your trigger in the self-management box of your 5-Square

Grounding in Your Standard with Self-Coaching

Once you have slowed down and returned to your thinking brain, access your inner coach. This is when your values—your standard—gets activated.

To mine the values that matter most in this context, start by returning to the dissonance you felt about the stories, behaviors, and their impact that came up during your self-awareness building. Why do you care about avoiding the stories and acting out the behaviors of the negative controller anymore? The answers likely connect to who you want to be, how you want to be perceived and experienced by others, what you want to accomplish, and why you do this work. In your journal, start listing all the reasons that come up. When you think you have a relatively complete list, review and prioritize your top five. This should be an emotional exercise. You should feel in your gut what matters most to you.

Now, for each of your prioritized care statements, go deeper. *Why* is this statement important to you? What is that *about* for you? For each answer, try to follow with another why question. It is like peeling an onion, as there are many layers of meaning that you can uncover. Your goal here is to try to get to a value.

Example:

I want the kids we serve to get a quality education that changes their life trajectory. (Why?)

They are at a disadvantage because of structural racism and economic inequality. (Why?)

I was able to succeed because others made it possible for me, and it is my responsibility to do the same for my people. (Why?)

Core Value: My life's purpose

You will know when you are done when you can say and feel, "This one is about (a value or value statement) for me." Do this for each of the statements that you prioritized. Then add those core values to the center square of your 5-Square.

Now consider how your values relate to your identities. According to the idea of intersectionality (Crenshaw 1989),[1] we all have many identities, or facets of self, that make up who we are. Some of these include gender, race, sexuality, class, ability, place of origin, and religion, but the list is really only limited by the number of ways we make sense of ourselves and each other in the world. We know that multiple forms of discrimination accumulate across identity markers, marginalizing or privileging groups and individuals. Yet we also know that our identities are a source of our power. They weave together to create our cultures, from family culture to our many different group cultures. From these interwoven identity groups, we learn what matters to us in the world.

Re-read the list of values you just generated. Consider how your identities connect with and inform these values. How can an intentional anchoring in your identities empower you to shift your negative controller habits? Add identity notes in parentheses next to your values statements in your 5-Square.

You have just surfaced your power. Now think about how to harness that power in the moment with self-coaching. Take yourself back to the trigger moment. With that in mind, craft your coaching "self-talk":

- Which of the values you identified will serve you most when you are triggered and in danger of being hijacked by your emotions? Choose one or two that resonate the most.
- Now consider how these values apply to this moment to orient you to your true north. Up to this point you have had an anti-coach whispering stories and advice that have mostly held you back. Now imagine that you have a new coach on your other shoulder. What can this new coach tell you about who you are and what you value that will be more powerful than your self-limiting stories?
- Crystallize brief phrases your inner coach can bring to the moment that will be easy to access and resonant at a values level. Think bumper sticker or T-shirt. Write up to three of these in your 5-Square self-management box. Some examples from negative controllers I have coached include:

> *This is about the behavior, not the person*
> *If they don't grow, our kids won't get what they need*
> *It's my job to find the way for this person to grow for our kids*

Rewrite Noble Stories

You just wrote some new stories grounded in your power. Now we shift to some other stories that need revising: what you tell yourself about others.

As a negative controller, rewriting these stories will probably be the most important learning you take from this chapter. This is because negative assumptions about others are at the core of your self-limiting beliefs. Your habit of defaulting to these stories amounts to deficit-based confirmation bias—the tendency to only look for and see what confirms your current stories about people for whom you already hold strong negative opinions. Their redeeming behaviors and qualities are there, but you subconsciously choose not to see them.

Go back to your self-limiting stories in your self-awareness square and pull out the ones about other people. If you know that this list is incomplete, add the rest of the self-limiting stories you tell about others. Now, *flip them*. Replace them with alternative narratives that emphasize positive motives and/or opinions in your case study context. Consider:

- What could you choose to believe about your students, families, colleagues, and staff that would help you choose more noble stories?
- What could you choose to believe about what they value and what they might be struggling with? Exercise empathy and compassion.
- What do you respect about them that you have omitted from your story?
- What stories do you need to tell yourself about the person or people in this context that will help you care about them and connect with them?

Rewriting noble stories is not just about others. You may also need to consider the stories you tell yourself *about* yourself. What stories do you need to rewrite about yourself? What do you need to believe you can do, learn, or become? What do you need to believe about yourself if you struggle or make a mistake as a leader?

Write what resonates most to you in the self-management box of your 5-Square.

Self-Work: Pause and Reflect

You have now completed the left side of the 5-Square and, in doing so, you have generated a game plan for managing your stuff and harnessing your standard. If you work these strategies deliberately over time, they should help you shift from self-limiting behaviors that have kept you from becoming the leader you want to be. You will need to build structures into your daily life to remind you to practice and reflect, and you will need partners to help you stay focused and to provide feedback.

We will now move to the right side of the 5-Square to begin building new aware-ness and strategies to see and engage others.

Step 4: Build Social Awareness to Diagnose Needs and Set Targets

With your new self-awareness and intention to self-manage, you are prepared to see others more clearly. As you shift your focus from self to others, the first question for you to consider is a diagnostic one: *Where are they?* This simple question should activate your Emotional Intelligence (EI) muscles of empathy (the ability to accurately read other people's emotional state and needs) and compassion (the desire to help).

Some leaders have a negative view of empathy because they believe that detouring into emotions leads to lowering standards. This is a misconception about what empathy is and its purpose in leadership. Psychologist Paul Eckman explains that there are different kinds of empathy. The key to effective social awareness is cognitive empathy: knowing how others might be feeling and thinking without actually feeling it along with them, which Eckman calls emotional empathy (Eckman 2003).[2] Leaders must understand that emotions are data that help them diagnose where people are and what they need. As a negative controller, you need to strengthen your cognitive empathy to diagnose developmental needs rather than judging and writing people off.

Most negative controlling school leaders I have worked with struggle to effectively bring empathy and compassion to adult challenges. Interestingly, these same leaders tend to practice strong empathy and compassion with their students. They clearly possess the competencies, but need to learn to apply them to adults in the same way they apply them to students. The first and most important step to doing so is a willingness to shift your story about adults. Hopefully, you have made progress there with your new noble stories.

The next step is to apply a diagnostic (rather than judgmental) lens to the person and the challenge. Take yourself back to the same case study—or behavioral event—you have been reflecting on throughout this chapter. Consider the person or people involved both above and below the Green Line. Reflect on the following questions in your journal:

- What self-limiting behaviors does this person exhibit? How are these behaviors preventing them from being effective in their work and trusting your relationship?

- What triggers and emotions do they bring that are getting in their way from being effective?
- What stories do you think they believe about themselves? What core values drive them, based on your experience? What self-limiting beliefs might hold them back from reaching their potential?
- What stories do you think they are telling themselves about you, both before and during the conversation?
- How does identity impact your interaction with them? What lines of difference and power between you might contribute to the challenge?

These questions should look familiar to you, as they are the same below-the-surface questions you applied to *yourself* on the other side of the 5-Square. Now you are picking up the magnifying glass—or the stethoscope—to examine someone else's standard and stuff.

Record your best answers to the preceding questions in the social awareness box of your 5-Square. As you do, try to stay in that space of empathy and compassion that you hold for students. Notice and self-manage if you are pulled toward judgment and rejection.

Where Do They Need to Be? (Defining Your Targets)

Now that you have a working diagnosis of where the other person is, you are ready to think about targets and objectives for engagement. Note that the accuracy of your targets depends on the strength of your diagnosis. Your goal here to is prioritize the behaviors and obstacles you diagnosed and articulate intended outcomes, or changes, you hope to accomplish through your engagement. These targets tend to land in three basic categories: behaviors, mindsets, and relational conditions that you want to shift. See some examples in Table 6.1. Note the alignment between diagnosis and the target.

In your 5-Square, generate a target for each of the where-they-are points you have prioritized.

Table 6.1: Sample targets.

Where they are (your diagnosis)		Where they need to be (your targets)
Above the Green Line		
Not completing a report on time	➡	Completing the report on time
Not communicating with me about the obstacles to completion	➡	Communicating with me about what is getting in the way
Complaining about the report's lack of value with teammates	➡	Shifting to a solution-oriented approach to communication
Below the Green Line		
They do not trust me		Believe that I am being fully transparent and that I am invested in their success
Believe that I think they are incompetent	➡	Believe that I see their strengths and that I think they are capable of growing
Not invested in the report as a practice because they do not see its value	➡	Understand impact of not completing the report and the value when the report is completed
Unhappy at work	➡	Happy and thriving in their work

Step 5: Manage Relationships to Meet Your Targets

You have now done the internal work and perspective-taking to prepare yourself to engage. It is time for you to use all of your new awareness and strategies to choose better ways to connect, care, and challenge to reach your targets. As a negative controller, this likely looks like a rebalancing of your engagement toward more authentic care. Each person, group, and context will require a unique blend of these three ingredients to create the conditions for success, and the ingredient you have been underusing has been care.

Use the following questions as a springboard for creative thinking about engagement. Do this thinking in the context of your behavioral moment case study, and in connection with the targets you have generated.

First return to your vision for success on the first page of your 5-Square plan:

- To get your creative juices flowing, re-read your aspirational vision from Step 1. If any new ideas have come up as you have worked through this chapter, add them to the vision.

- Now read the vision again, pulling out the leadership actions that you might use to connect with, care for, and challenge the person or group in this context. As a reminder,

  - Connection = authentic human connection + accurate perspective on where they are below the Green Line
  - Care = authentic belief in others' potential + empathy (emotional understanding of where they are) + compassion (investment and desire to help)
  - Challenge = holding high expectations and pushing toward your targets with candor

Now call on your instincts and the "where are they" diagnosis you made in the previous section: What does the person or group in question need from you to feel *connected* as a human being? Make sure you are not confusing this question with what they might *want*. Connection does not always feel good, but it must feel *real*. Consider these core behaviors of connection:

- *Authenticity*—How will you show up as *you*, the human being, with no persona or double talk?
- *Vulnerability*—What do you need to share at an emotional level (below your Green Line) that is relevant to this challenge? Consider how that will make it safe for others to share with you. Do not shy away from sharing dissonant emotions, but make sure they are coming from your standard and not your stuff. Also, make sure you self-manage to describe those real emotions without actually being *in* them in the moment.
- *Listening*—What do you need to find out to confirm or revise your noble story and your diagnosis about "where they are?" Consider the effect of asking *curious* questions and listening on connection. There is nothing more effective you can do to make another person feel truly seen and heard. Listening is the core competency of connection.

What do they need from you to feel like you *care* about them? *Everything you have done in this chapter has prepared you for this! Caring is key to conquering your negative controller mindset. Lean in here!*

- How can you more deliberately and consistently affirm their wins, strengths, and values? Especially when you are challenging them?

- What can you say or do that will show your belief in their potential to grow (like you do for students)?
- How can you show your investment in their growth and your relationship (like you do for students)?
- How can you name the noble story that you hold for them with appreciation, empathy, and compassion? You cannot fake this! Your self-management task is to build authentic noble story before you engage and hold it over time.

How do they need you to *challenge* them to grow and meet your targets?

- How will you name their limiting behaviors and their impact with candor, while holding the noble story?
- How can you ground this conversation in your values and why you care? Your values are the source of your power when challenging.
- How and when will you name your targets (what you hope this conversation will achieve) for this person? How will you come back to them if the conversation veers off course?
- If the other person does not seem to be hearing your message, how will you increase your level of candor while also increasing care? Consider crafting your most high-candor and high-care headlines in advance.

Make sure you have added your new engagement strategies to your 5-Square.

Other Work: Pause and Reflect

You have just created a draft plan for challenging your stakeholders while maintaining connection. It is important to understand that this plan is not a script you will perform in a sequence. Engaging adaptively is inherently messy. You will need to use your self-management strategies to push yourself to care and connect when your old habits want you to judge and reject. If you can lean into the mess, stay present and authentic, and hold an authentic noble story, then you will succeed. The most important question to ask yourself during and after an engagement will be, "Do I feel connected to this person, and do they feel connected to me?" If the answer is no, do not beat yourself up. Go back for another round. There can always be another conversation.

Now the Real Work Begins

You have just done the reflective heavy lifting to shift your negative controller mindsets and behaviors. If you intentionally hold this new awareness and exercise these new behavioral muscles over time, you will break out of your self-limiting rut, see your people through a developmental lens, build the connection necessary for them to grow, and ultimately change the trajectory of your organization's outcomes and culture.

That "if" carries a caveat. We have all had epiphanies about what gets in our way that felt like game changers for us, but that faded into the background of our consciousness over time. Intentional practice is what connects an epiphany to transformational change. Remember the neuroscience behind this. We change when we build new neural pathways that replace the neural superhighways of our self-limiting habits.

Your job now is to take your 5-Square plan and work it, intentionally, every day in your work. Print it out and post it somewhere in your workspace. Keep it open on your desktop. You should be re-reading it regularly, especially when preparing for the kinds of interactions you know are hard for you. This should be a living document that evolves as you evolve. Chapter 11 will provide more guidance about how to keep your plan alive over time.

In the next chapter, we will turn our attention to the inner obstacle most closely linked to the source of our power: the pacesetter mindset.

Endnotes

1. Crenshaw, K. (1989). Demarginalizing the intersection of race and sex: a Black feminist critique of antidiscrimination doctrine, feminist theory and antiracist politics. *University of Chicago Legal Forum*, Vol. 1989, Iss. 1, Article 8. https://chicagounbound.uchicago.edu/cgi/viewcontent.cgi?article=1052&context=uclf.
2. Eckman, P. (2003). *Emotions Revealed: Recognizing Faces and Feelings to Improve Relationships Emotional Life*. New York: Time Books.

7 The Pacesetter

High intensity, high standards, constant improvement and high performance characterize the pacesetter leadership style (Goleman 2001).[1] However, pacesetters also tend to work at unsustainable rates and nurture unsustainable work cultures in their organizations. In education pacesetters are usually driven by an admirable desire to promote excellence in the mission to maximize student achievement. While pacesetting may yield strong outcomes during short-term challenges, like start-up or turnaround, over time it erodes outcomes, culture, and stability. Pacesetting as a default leadership style leads to what McKee, Johnston, and Boyatzis (2008) call the sacrifice syndrome: "A vicious cycle of stress and sacrifice, resulting in mental and physical distress, burnout, and diminished effectiveness."[2] If the sacrifice syndrome becomes our way of being, we are destined to become a fraction of ourselves—our capacity, our presence, our passion and joy.

Consider Victor's story:

> *Victor has always worked harder than his peers. He was raised that way and his work ethic has served him well. In his choice of careers, Victor found a powerful purpose for channeling this ethic. His organization's culture of sacrifice for the mission—"education is the Civil Rights Movement of our time!"—resonated deeply with his desire to pay forward his own good fortune. So, Victor dove in with both feet and became a model of "whatever it takes." He quickly rose through the ranks from teacher to assistant principal to principal.*

Now in his second year as principal, the pace seems to be catching up with him. The twelve-hour days and working on weekends is getting harder to sustain. His exercise routine has all but disappeared. It has been weeks since he spoke to his siblings and months since he has reached out to most of his closest friends. He has developed chronic heartburn and is worried about the number of antacids he takes on a daily basis. He wants to move forward and start a family with his partner, but they are both unsure of how he could possibly raise kids with his job.

Victor feels stuck on a hamster wheel and he does not see a way off. The amount of work is not going to change. His organization, while talking a good game about sustainability, is run by leaders who work like Victor does. Most of his peers are new leaders like him, and the organization has a 30% attrition rate. As far as Victor can tell, this is just the nature of school leadership.

Victor is miserable and scared that he won't make it, literally. Further, his staff feel the same way. They are overwhelmed, burnt out, and, as a group, not sure how long they can stay in the work. While the school is a place where staff are committed and passionate about teaching and the mission, it is also a place that feels pushed to its limits.

Does Victor's story resonate with you? Read this chapter if:

- ☐ Your mental and/or physical health feels compromised by your work style.
- ☐ You feel you have no time to recover because of your workload.
- ☐ You can't stop thinking about work when you are not there.
- ☐ You feel numb or disconnected from others much of the time.
- ☐ Your most important personal relationships have suffered because work has crowded them out.
- ☐ You believe it is the expectation of your organization to work like you do.
- ☐ The prevailing story among the people you lead is that they are devoted to the work but are not sure how long they can keep doing it.
- ☐ You have experienced, or expect to experience, significant staff turnover over time.

This Is Not Just About You

Before going any further in this chapter, we need to talk about locus of control. Your pacesetter leadership style is not just about you. Your personal inclination to this approach is likely nurtured by the culture you work in and the organizational structures that have built up around that culture. Educators as a group are mission-driven people who self-select into a culture of sacrifice. We choose this work because we see an emergency—structural inequality, the opportunity gap, insufficient schools for all children—and we sign up *expecting* to make personal sacrifices. Many see this sacrifice as a badge of honor, and taking time for self-care as selfish. We dedicate our lives to the work and we tend to neglect physical or social–emotional health.

This educator culture of sacrifice rests in our larger national (and increasingly global) culture of workism: the belief that work should be at the center of our identity, our lives, and our society. Among professionals in our country, we increasingly believe that the meaning of life should be found in work (Thompson 2019).[3] We live in a culture that tells us we should be working all the time, and that if we are not doing something for work then it is not worth doing.

The structures of our society and our schools reinforce this workism. Access to technology keeps work at our fingertips 24/7. The evolution of data-driven practices, school systems, and teacher coaching models have created complex and time-intensive new layers of work. Somehow, the more we strive to increase our efficiency, the more work we have to do. We always feel behind and in need of catching up, and so we feel stuck in a hamster wheel of work that we cannot escape.

So, your pacesetter leadership challenge is not just about you. Yes, you do have self-limiting mindsets and behaviors to work on that are in your locus of control. But you have some obstacles that are outside of your locus of control that get in the way of your making personal change. In this chapter, we will focus on both what you can shift in yourself and how you can influence the culture and systems around you to move beyond the pacesetter style.

Pacesetting, the Sacrifice Syndrome, and Schools

The most obvious and increasingly dire impact of pacesetting in schools is on leader and teacher attrition. Sustainable work conditions and behaviors have long been a challenge in schools. We have over the last decade become painfully aware of escalating teacher and school leader attrition and the impact that has on school culture and quality of instruction. In our current Covid moment, unfilled teacher and staff positions and teacher absenteeism are disrupting many schools' ability to maintain basic safety, let alone create the conditions needed for learning. A recent study by the Rand American Teacher Panel shows that more than 40% of teachers are considering leaving or retiring and over half of those surveyed said this was due to the pandemic (Zamarro et al. 2021).[4] Attrition is becoming the biggest challenge for our sector, and yet we haven't paid much attention to pacesetting as a root cause.

In schools, pacesetting has a uniquely damaging effect because pacesetting and the sacrifice syndrome are contagious. We have what scientists call mirror neurons that react to the emotions of those around us. These neurons dance with each other in our separate heads and hearts. The same research shows that the emotions of the person with the most power in the room are significantly more contagious than those of others (Goleman and Boyatzis 2008).[5]

These findings prove what most of us already know: learning environments are petri dishes of emotional contagion. Teachers react to the emotional energy of their leaders and students react to their teachers. If a leader is experiencing chronic stress, then so will their teachers and their students. If a leader does not prioritize effective self-care to manage their workload and stress, then their teachers and students will be less likely to do so.

I write this chapter in the midst of the Delta variant wave of the global coronavirus pandemic. Here in the U.S., we have passed 700,000 deaths and many of our students' learning continues to be disrupted by the pandemic after having been in remote learning for over a year. This phenomenon of emotional contagion feels particularly important when we consider that how we cope with our stress and trauma affects student as they attempt to cope with theirs. I am hopeful that the pandemic has raised awareness that, if we continue to live and work like we can ignore our wellness, we will fail to meet our teachers' and our students' most urgent needs. Serving our students must include interrupting our unhealthy patterns and modeling effective self-care. If we do not, our stress magnifies their stress and our disregard for self-care impacts their ability to care for themselves.

The severity of Covid conditions is also making us increasingly aware that sustainability is an equity issue. Sustainability's greatest enemy in our sector is urgency—the white cultural norm that dominates many mission-driven learning organizations. Urgency in itself can be a healthy driver in the right quantities.

However, as a default norm and when overplayed, it has done real harm to both organizations and the communities that they serve. Tema Okun wrote in 2019 about how urgency causes us to rush to solutions to short-term challenges without building the awareness of long-term unintended consequences across the complex systems in which we work and live. Urgency makes it difficult to take time to be inclusive and frequently results in sacrificing the interests of communities of color.[6] The result, as one of my wise colleagues puts it, is that "urgency eats equity for breakfast."

The Work Ahead

This chapter is a self-contained learning journey. If you take it on, you could spend several months focusing on changing deeply ingrained habits and building new adaptive muscles. Download a 5-Square learning plan template from www .noblestorygroup.com to build your plan. You will also need a journal to explore new ideas.

Let's get started.

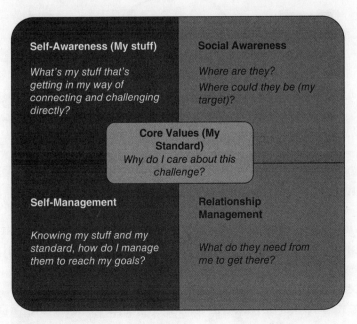

Figure 7.1: The EI 5-Square.

Step 1: Start with the End in Mind

Before focusing on what is getting in your way, it helps to do some thinking about what success will look like when you have grown out of your pacesetter habits. Unlike previous chapters, I will begin this section by sharing my learning about what we should be aiming for.

I used to think "life balance" was the opposite of the sacrifice syndrome. I now believe that life balance may be an unrealistic and a dangerous goal for school leaders because our work will always be marked by periods of sacrifice. If our goal is balance every day, then we risk thinking about these times of sacrifice as a personal failure. What is realistic, however, is a cycle of sacrifice and *renewal*, illustrated in Figure 7.2. Leaders can create deliberate periods of renewal (practicing self-care and recharging their reserves of hope and compassion) after being called on to react to deeply adaptive crises and threats (McKee, Johnston, and Boyatzis 2008).[7]

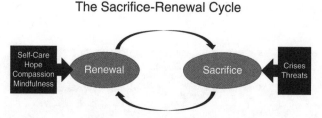

Figure 7.2: The Sacrifice-Renewal Cycle.

Source: Annie McKee, Richard Boyatzis, and Fran Johnston. (2008). *Becoming a Resonant Leader.* Cambridge, MA: Harvard Business Review Press.

I know school leaders who have learned to make the job sustainable through sacrifice and renewal cycles. As a group:

- They prioritize themselves as much or more than they prioritize the work.
- They build healthy baseline routines of self-care and elevate them to sacred priorities.
- They are able to turn the work off when it is time for self.
- They create periods of renewal to restart healthy habits after making deliberate choices to sacrifice during periods of challenge.

- They plan deliberate renewal periods around the predictable cycles of a school year.
- They don't do other people's work. They are clear about roles and responsibilities and they effectively direct work to the right people.
- They manage up to right-size the work for themselves and their teams.
- They play the long game. For example, if they are in prolonged times of sacrifice—like leading through turnaround or a pandemic—then they build even stronger boundaries around sacred time for self-care.
- They understand that the work is never done, so the goal is strong prioritization. They are constantly making proactive and game-time decisions about what deserves their time and what will have to wait, get delegated, or not get done at all.
- They don't let short-term urgency cloud their long-term lens, and they help their teams to do the same. They create a collective value of taking time and creating space for the important work that requires it.

Now, with the preceding list in mind, consider what a sustainable life as a school leader could look like for you. In your ideal world, what would you be doing and how would it feel to effectively balance sacrifice and renewal in your life and work. Pay particular attention to the situations you find most challenging (the preceding checklist might help you with that) but remember that your goal is to envision your *ideal* self in these situations.

You should record this reflection on the first page of your 5-Square. Journal first and then transfer to the 5-Square if journaling helps you think creatively. Give yourself uninterrupted time (at least 30 minutes) and emotional space to do this reflection. You might find it helpful to see an example from another 5-Square, and there is one in Appendix D.

This aspirational thinking will become the vision you use to generate awareness and strategies, and to measure your progress over time. I encourage you to put real effort into the feeling questions in this exercise. As a pacesetter, your vision should be as much about your internal conversations as it is about your interpersonal and organizational conversations. Push yourself to name both actions and emotions that will define success.

Step 2: Build Self-Awareness

 When you have thought deeply about the leader you want to be and the life you want to lead, you are ready to hold up the mirror and build awareness about what is getting in your way.

Starting with Behavior

Unlike previous chapters where we started with triggers, we will start this self-awareness journey with behavior—what you are doing that's getting in your way. For pacesetters, the basics are pretty universal. You are likely doing one or more of the following:

- Choosing to work at times when you should be choosing self-care and renewal.
- Doing a poor job of prioritizing your tasks.
- Doing other people's work.
- Carrying the emotional loads of others.
- Perseverating about work at home (not being able to turn it off).

Take out your journal and consider which of these behaviors apply to you and what they look like in your life. For example, consider the moments of choice when you actually choose work over self-care. What sequence of actions leads to that choice, and then what do you do as a result of your choice? You should be considering actions you choose when alone as well as those that involve others. It is likely that the choices you make on your own—to work or rest, to engage or disengage—are more of an obstacle than those you make involving others. The exception to this is determining who takes on what tasks on your team (you or others). Write it all down in your journal, then transfer the actions that you care about shifting the most to the self-awareness box of your 5-Square.

When Your Standard Becomes Your Stuff

Now we consider the root cause of your self-limiting behaviors. In my experience, the pacesetter is stuck at the most fundamental cause: values. There are typically two values that are at war inside of them. In their 2019 book *Immunity to Change*,

Kegan and Lehey call this values tension "competing commitments."[8] Pacesetter educators tend to articulate their competing commitments in the following groups:

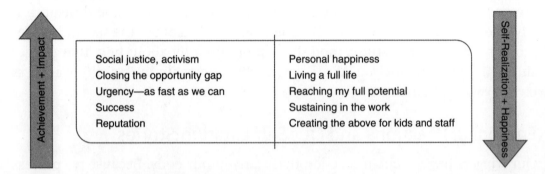

Figure 7.3: Common pacesetter competing commitments.

In the language of the 5-Square, leaders experience tension between these two groups of values, or standards, at both an existential level and in the micromoments of day-to-day leadership. The fundamental question to consider: *When does your standard become your stuff?* (See Figure 7.3.) In other words, in what contexts do some of your values become self-limiting? The answer to that question can be found in *behavior and impact.* When our standard dictates behaviors that do not achieve our goals, then they become our stuff.

In your 5-Square, add two lists of values. The first should answer the question, "Why have you chosen to do this work?" The second should answer the question, "Why do you care about overcoming your pacesetter leadership habits?" In these two lists, you will likely find your competing commitments. We will come back to these lists when you start to build your self-management strategies.

Competing Commitments in Context

To understand how you are getting stuck in your competing commitments, you must build deeper awareness about your emotions and the limiting stories you tell yourself in key choice moments. In preparation, try to remember recent pacesetting moments that did not result in the outcomes you wanted (for yourself and for your school). Once you have two or three examples in mind, choose one to use as a case study over the rest of this chapter.

Now, identify the trigger moment of your study. Something happened that triggered an emotional reaction in you, compelling you to take on work or emotional weight at the expense of your personal health and boundaries. Victor in our case study gets triggered by urgent requests, a full in-box, and his unfinished to-do list. What are yours? Be as clear as you can about the specific trigger moment in your case study, then think more broadly about how that trigger shows up regularly for you. Write down what comes up in the self-awareness box of your 5-Square.

Emotional Reactions and Our Self-Limiting Stories

Our triggers begin a chain reaction that starts in our body. Because we process stress physiologically before we process it emotionally or intellectually, our bodies are our early warning system. Where did you feel your reaction in your body when you were triggered? Was it pressure in the chest, burning ears, or clenching hands? Note your reaction in your 5-Square.

Our emotional reactions follow our physical reactions. As a pacesetter, you are likely to experience a complex range of emotions that focus inward as well as outward, and that range from very dissonant to positive.

In their work on competing commitments, Kegan and Lehey focus on fear in this moment of choice. They ask the ingenious question, "What are you afraid will happen if you *do* choose the new behavior you aspire to?" Given our focus, the question to ask yourself is, "What are you afraid will happen if you *do* choose self-care, renewal, or delegating work?" One response might be, "If I *do* prioritize self-care, then my colleagues will see me as selfish and lazy." This is an example of a self-limiting story. Write the limiting stories that come up for you in the self-awareness box of your 5-Square. Consider how these stories shed light on how your values can become your obstacles (your standard becomes your stuff).

Your pacesetter stories and behaviors serve you by protecting you from the fears that you just surfaced. While it may seem illogical to you, consider how some of your pacesetter choices might be making you feel good in the short term. For example, we can feel energized or effective in the moment when facing challenges or tasks that we know we have the ability to complete. When I was a principal, all school leaders were expected to teach a class. My first two years I chose to teach

8th grade literature—a very heavy prep. I poured myself into that work because it was the time every day that I felt most successful and impactful.

Consider how jumping into reactive challenges, doing work outside of your role, or even retreating to your office to answer email might help you feel a short-term positive. As you do, try to write down the stories you tell yourself in the moment (Saving the day! Getting to inbox zero!) that connect with those emotions. What are you telling yourself about pacesetting in the moment that makes you feel effective or affirmed? What stories are you telling yourself about being a leader, or a change agent, or just being effective? How might these stories be getting in your way? Being aware of how these positive emotions and stories serve you, and how they do not, plays an important role in shifting your habits.

Identity and Our Stories

The deeper our stories, the more connected they are to our identities. Growing up in America with our 400-year history of white male supremacy, it is inevitable that racism and sexism impact our mindsets and behaviors. Becoming aware of how white cultural norms play a role in your pacesetter tendencies is key to overcoming them. I wrote about urgency at the beginning of this chapter. Tema Okun also writes about the norm of "quantity over quality" that is a hallmark of pacesetter leadership style. She defines these norms as follows:

- Urgency—*fast, highly visible results are more important than building collaboration, allies, and the interests of communities.*
- Quantity over quality—*valuing and directing resources to what can be measured, while devaluing things that are hard to measure like process and relationships.*

The stronger and more exclusive the dominant culture is in your organization, the more likely it becomes that your pacesetter tendencies will manifest themselves. Consider how these white cultural norms and other narratives of privilege or oppression may be at play for you.

Add all of the important sensations, emotions, and stories you surfaced in this section to the self-awareness box of your 5-Square.

The Deep and Broad Impact of Pacesetting

Now reflect on the ripple effect of your actions. The impact likely goes much further than you have previously considered. Pacesetters can usually make the cause–effect link between the way their choices impact their lifestyle, but they tend to only see the tip of the iceberg of their impact on their staff students, and outcomes.

Wheatly's Green Line (see Chapter 1 and Figure 7.4) provides a helpful framework for considering impact. Start with the three circles above the line. Consider your intended leadership outcomes of your leadership approach above the Green Line as well as the social and emotional ripple effect below the Green Line.

Start with yourself. What are the ways your pacesetter work choices have impacted your effectiveness? Consider the impact of the sacrifice syndrome on your self- and social awareness, and on the accuracy of your perspective. Consider the effect on your overall capacity to do your best work, and to show up as your most effective and powerful self in adaptive situations.

Now let's go to the three circles below the line. What are the many ways that pacesetting has affected your well-being? How about your physical health? Consider your relationship with your work: how you feel walking into your building every day. Now consider your relationships. What is the current state of your connections with the people you care about most in the world? Have your work choices harmed them? How do they feel about you?

Now consider the effect of pacesetter leadership on staff and students. At the beginning of this chapter we discussed emotions being contagious, and how a

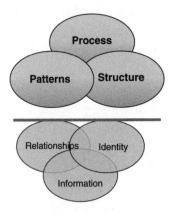

Figure 7.4: Wheatly's six-circle model.

leader's absence of self-care behaviors rubs off on staff and students. Think about the many ways you create a dysfunctional culture around self-care. What behaviors—from the times you arrive and leave to the hours you send email—become the unwritten expectations for others? What is the collective perception of what effective leadership looks like? How do your emotions affect how others feel walking into the building every day? How do your behaviors and emotions influence their feelings about their work and about learning? How does it hinder staff and student's ability to achieve (especially our most vulnerable learners)?

Start with the lens of race, equity, diversity, and identity. Consider how pacesetter leadership could be a destructive force related to equity and belonging in your organizational culture. Pacesetter leaders likely reinforce Okun's white cultural norms of urgency and quantity vs. quality while excluding others' ways of working across lines of cultural difference. How do these exclusive conditions have a particularly damaging impact on learning environments for staff and students who experience schools imposing these cultural norms on them?

Next, consider pacesetter leadership's impact on attrition in your organization. We rarely consider the disastrous long-term impact of pacesetter leadership on teacher and leader skill related to attrition. While senior education leaders and policy makers know attrition is an emergency in our sector, they seldom connect the dots to pacesetter leadership. It costs education organizations tens of thousands of dollars to train new teachers and, on average, $75,000 to hire and prepare new school leaders (Learning Policy Institute 2017; School Leader Network 2014).[9] In addition to these costs, it takes years for new teachers to reach levels of high performance, and this growth curve significantly impacts student achievement outcomes (Kini and Podolsky 2016).[10] The research on principals shows that it takes five years for principals to really put their visions in place and change the school's performance (Superville 2014).[11] In my opinion, the worst outcome of the pacesetter leadership style is the loss of veteran teachers, as teacher tenure is one of the most significant indicators of increased student achievement.

Further, high turnover creates a vicious self-sustaining cycle. When teachers and leaders leave, those who remain spend a significant amount of time and energy finding and training new people. Below the Green Line, as relationships disappear and new relational trust must be built, leaders, teachers, and students also carry an additional emotional burden. The workload—and emotional load—grows exponentially when a large number of people come and go in a given school year. In this way, turnover creates the pressure for even more pacesetter leadership decisions, which are likely to lead to even more attrition.

Take a few minutes to journal about the ripple effect of your pacesetter leadership on yourself, your staff and students, and your outcomes. When you think you have a pretty exhaustive list, record the levels of impact that matter the most in your 5-Square.

Pause and Reflect

At this point, I encourage you to take both a literal and metaphorical deep breath. Step back and offer yourself both grace and gratitude for the work you have done so far. This all sounds horrible, and it is painful to confront the self-limiting stories we tell ourselves and the impact that self-limiting behaviors have on ourselves and those around us. It is natural to feel down on ourselves at this moment. However, when we confront deep and personal obstacles, we open the door to change and growth. With self-awareness comes an opportunity you may not have known you had: to choose a more positive and effective way of being.

This choosing begins with building new self-management strategies that can shift your stories and behaviors.

Step 3: Build Self-Management Strategies

 We cannot stop our triggers and our emotions; they are hardwired. However, we *can* manage triggers and emotions once we become aware of them. More importantly, we can choose the stories we tell ourselves in response to our emotional reactions. Self-management is about derailing the chain reaction of ineffective habits at the level of emotion and stories so that we can choose new behaviors.

Plan Ahead

For pacesetters, the foundation for self-management is a strong self-care plan. Like so many things in life (solo work time, challenging conversations, vacations), self-care is hard to pull off if you do not plan for it in advance. Hopefully, this self-management strategy allows you to apply some planning and execution strengths that serve you in your work.

If you read and completed the self-work in Chapter 3, then you already created most of your plan. Take that work back out, review it, and add any self-care actions from your aspirational vision in this chapter. With this plan you are ready to prioritize and commit to trying some new things. Put your goal setting and execution skills to work. Don't over-commit to too much at once. Make your goals as *smart* as you can. Take out your calendar and schedule some lunches with your partner. Your job at this point is to deliberately start building your baseline self-care practices. Planning is of course the easy part. Prioritizing yourself first and following through is the real challenge. You will need the following self-management strategies to make that happen.

Creating Space Between Trigger and Response

Now that you have a proactive self-care plan, you need in-the-moment strategies to support effective decision-making. Creating a few seconds of space between your triggers and what you actually do is the lead factor and the prerequisite to accessing other in-the-moment strategies. This pause is the strategy that interrupts the cycle. It makes time for us to slow down and think. What can you do to create space between your triggers and your actions?

- Start by considering what you already do that might serve you in trigger moments. Do you already have meditative practices in your life like yoga, prayer, or a mindfulness practice? If you do, you probably already have breathing strategies you can bring to bear. A couple of deep breaths over a matter of seconds could be all you need to regain your ability to think clearly.
- There may be other micromovements that you do already with your body that calm you down (from taking a sip of water to shifting your posture). How could you more intentionally do those things in your moments of choice? Consider the impact in the trigger moment of walking away from your computer for a glass of water, doing some stretches, or simply sitting down or standing up. If it slows you down, then it works.

Write down at least one strategy in the self-management box of your 5-Square

Grounding in Your Standard with Self-Coaching

 Once you have slowed down and returned to your thinking brain, access your inner coach. This is when your values—your standard—gets activated. For you, this is about winning the battle between your competing commitments. Effective self-coaching will help you choose your standard and not your stuff in the challenge moment.

Re-read the values you added to the center square of your 5-Square (your standard square). Now take yourself back to the trigger moment in your case study. With that in mind, craft your coaching "self-talk":

- Which of the values you identified will best serve you when triggered and in danger of defaulting to self-limiting pacesetter behavior? Choose one or two.
- Now consider how these values can orient you to your True North at this moment. Up to this point you have had an anti-coach whispering stories and advice that have mostly held you back. Now imagine that you have a new coach on your other shoulder. What can this new coach tell you that will be more powerful than your self-limiting stories?
- Crystallize brief phrases your inner coach can bring to the moment. Think bumper sticker or T-shirt. Write up to three of these in your 5-Square self-management box. Some examples from pacesetters I have coached include:

> *The work will never be done. It's okay to give myself this time.*
> *What is really most important right now? Is this task really more important than my wellness?*
> *I create the culture of self-care. If I don't, then they won't.*
> *If I do this task for them, then I'm enabling and withholding a growth opportunity*
> *Healthy leaders and teachers create better outcomes for kids*

Now consider how your values relate to your identities. According to the idea of intersectionality (Crenshaw 1989),[12] we all have many identities, or facets of self, that make up who we are. Some of these include gender, race, sexuality, class, ability, place of origin, and religion, but the list is really only limited by the number of ways we make sense of ourselves and each other in the world. We know that identity markers can be used to marginalize or privilege groups and individuals. Yet we also know that our identities are a source of our personal power. They weave together to create our cultures, from family culture to our many different group cultures. From these interwoven identity groups, we learn what matters to us in the world.

Re-read the list of values and inner-coach statements you just generated. Consider how your identities connect with and inform them. How can an intentional anchoring in your identities empower you to shift your pacesetter habits? Weave your identity narratives into the inner-coach statements you just wrote.

Once you feel you have two or three strong coaching statements that will empower you to interrupt your pacesetter behaviors, add them to the self-management box of your 5-Square.

Rewrite Noble Stories

You just wrote some new stories grounded in your power. Now we shift to some other stories that need revising: what you tell yourself about others.

Go back to the self-limiting stories in your self-awareness square and pull out the ones about what other people think and do that feed your pacesetting. If you know that this list is incomplete, add other stories about them that get in your way. Now, *flip your stories*. Replace them with alternative narratives that emphasize positive motives, opinions, or actions in your case study context. Consider:

- What could you choose to believe about your students, families, colleagues, and staff that would help you shift your actions? (Example: *My manager is just as stuck as I am and wants to find solutions, too.*)
- What could you choose to believe about what they value and what they might be struggling with that supports your aspiration to change? (Example: *My teachers want to grow. They want me to empower them to do their work, not do it for them.*)

Rewriting noble stories is not just about others. You likely need to consider the stories that you tell yourself *about* yourself. What stories of judgment do you need to rewrite about *yourself* that will allow you to choose self-care? (Example: *I am actually a* better *leader—and not a slacker—if I model self-care.*) These stories may be the at the heart of what it will take for you to give yourself permission to change.

Write the noble stories that will most empower you to change in the self-management box of your 5-Square.

Self-Work: Pause and Reflect

You have now completed the left side of the 5-Square and, in doing so, you have generated a game plan for managing your stuff and harnessing your standard to support making new choices. If you work these strategies over time, these choices will become your habits. You will need to build structures into your daily life to remind you to practice and reflect, and you will need partners to help you stay focused and to provide feedback.

We will now move to the right side of the 5-Square to begin building new awareness and strategies to see and engage others.

Step 4: Build Social Awareness to Diagnose Needs and Set Targets

 Unlike most other self-limiting mindsets, your efforts to change your pacesetter habits are inextricably linked to others. As I explained at the beginning of this chapter, pacesetting and the sacrifice syndrome may be influenced by culture and systems as much as they are the result of personal habits. You may live in a work world that encourages or implicitly expects some of the behaviors you are trying to change. These cultural forces may be invisible to you and to others until you start looking for them. The same is true of organizational structures, which may also be perceived as responsible for many of your collective successes. Your colleagues probably feel the tension between their competing commitments and feel stuck on the hamster wheel themselves.

These cultural and structural variables make the right-side 5-Square work in this chapter particularly challenging. To make your personal change you not only need to understand and engage individuals and teams, but also understand and possibly engage at a systemic level.

Take the first Social Awareness question, *"Where are they?"* You can consider that question at five different levels of system:

- How have *I* caused the pacesetter problem for myself and others? How have my mindsets and actions created a pacesetter culture and structures that reinforce it?
- Where is this *person*—my direct report, my boss, this parent—in their awareness of the pacesetter problem, their motivation to support my change, and their motivation to make personal change?
- Where is my *team*—my staff as a group—in their awareness of the problem, their motivation to support my change, and their motivation to make changes in our school?
- Where is the *organization*—senior leadership, the board, or maybe the district or the network as a whole—in their awareness of the problem, their motivation to support my change, and their motivation to shift culture and structures to support change?
- Where are the *external influencers*—the governing bodies, politicians, interest groups, and others related to the sector that hold influence over my ability to effect change?

To effectively advocate for your personal leadership change, you will need to consider the "where are they" question at every level of your system.

There is, however, another layer of complexity. Within each level of system, you must also determine how the obstacles connect to self, culture, and structure. Table 7.1 seeks to simplify this complexity.

As you shift from pacesetter to a leader who practices and promotes self-care, you will confront obstacles at each level of the system and you will have to diagnose each obstacle along the way. To change yourself you will also have to manage change with others. The upside to that challenge is that, in doing so, you will be helping others grow, shifting culture, and dismantling structures that reinforce the sacrifice syndrome at different levels of your organization along the way.

But be realistic! An important social awareness follow-up question is to consider the extent of your power to influence different levels of the system. Your role (formal power) and reputation (relational power) in relation to the answers to your "where are they" questions should dictate the scope of your targets.

Table 7.1: A systems analysis for organizational change.

Root Cause →		Self (my mindsets, actions, emotional contagion)	Culture (what's invisible in our daily interactions)	Structures (layers of protocols and internal systems)
Level of System →	Myself			
	Individual Others (staff, my manager, parents, students)			
	Teams (my school team or cohort team)			
	Organization (C-level leadership, board, families, community groups)			
	External Influencers (Governing entities, sector stakeholders, politicians)			

Defining Your Targets (Where You Need Them to Be)

Your targets are the intended outcomes, or changes, you hope to accomplish through your engagement with others. They land in three basic categories: behaviors, mindsets, and relational conditions that you want to shift.

The one target that is a given is your desire to shift your own unhealthy patterns of pacesetting and sacrifice syndrome. Your additional targets depend on the answers to the preceding questions, aligning to the levels of system and root causes in the following ways:

■ Your boss(es): How will you manage up to right-size your load and advocate for shifts in structures and/or culture?

- Your staff: How do you want to empower your people individually to work on their own sacrifice syndrome and more effectively carry their own loads?
- Your team: How do you want to raise group awareness to leverage your team to build culture and structures aligned to healthy sacrifice and renewal cycles?
- Your organization: To what extent do you want to raise awareness across your organization about the culture and structures reinforcing pacesetting and sacrifice syndrome? What role do you want to play in leading change?
- External influencers: In what ways can you raise awareness and intentionally develop and organize allies to effect changes in policy and the greater culture of the sector?

Give these questions some thought. If you can, engage friends who are wise about organizational change and who know enough about your organization and your place in it to offer advice. Then add the list of targets you want to take on to your 5-Square.

Step 5: Manage Relationships to Meet Your Targets

Now that you have taken perspective and planned your targets, you are ready to consider the most effective ways to connect, care, and challenge to reach them. Each person, group. and context will require a unique blend of these three ingredients.

Use the following questions as a springboard for creative thinking about engagement. It will help to do this thinking in context and in connection with the targets you have generated.

To get your creative juices flowing, re-read what you wrote about engaging others in your aspirational vision (Step 1 in this chapter). If any new ideas have come up as you have worked through this chapter, add them to the vision. Now read the vision again. Pull out the actions you might use to connect with, care for, and challenge the people or groups in your case study. Add them to the relationship management box of your 5-Square.

Now draw on your analysis of system and root causes to get even more strategic.

What does the person or group in question need from you to feel *connected* as a human being in the context of your pacesetter targets? Make sure you are not confusing this question with what they might *want*. Connection does not always feel good, but it must feel *real*. Consider these core behaviors of connection:

- *Authenticity and Vulnerability*—How will you show up as *you*, the human being, who is struggling with pacesetting and sacrifice syndrome? What will you share below your Green Line about your struggles and your aspirations for self-care and effective sacrifice-renewal cycles? How could your story make it safe for others to share their challenges with you? Do not shy away from sharing dissonant emotions, but make sure they are coming from your standard and not your stuff.
- *Listening*—What do you need to find out to confirm or revise your noble story and your diagnosis about "where they are" on the pacesetter issue? Consider how being curious, asking questions, and then listening builds connection. There is nothing more effective you can do to make another person feel seen and heard.
- How could you ground everything you hear in common values while raising your team's awareness about competing commitments?

What do they need from you to believe that you *care* about them?

- How can you *affirm* others' fears and competing commitments while also naming that those fears and values might be getting in their way?
- How can you show your *belief* in their potential to grow, and their commitment to shared values? How can you paint a picture of hope? Of a both/and solution?
- How can you show your *investment* in their (or the organization's) growth and in your relationship? How can you name the noble story you hold for them with empathy and compassion?
- How can you begin to create a path by creating clarity on roles, responsibilities, and goals?

How do they need you to *challenge* them to grow and meet your targets?

- How can you call out the competing commitments at the heart of the problem to surface fears and address them.

- How can you challenge stories that underplay or omit the negative impact of pacesetter behaviors, culture, and systems on student outcomes?
- How can you push people beyond short-term impact and outcomes to consider long-term impact and outcomes when analyzing current practice, structures, and culture?
- How can you name this short-term vs. long-term tension as an equity issue connected to the white cultural norm of urgency?
- How and when will you name your targets? How will you come back to them if the conversation veers off course?
- If the other person does not seem to be hearing your message, how will you increase your level of candor while also increasing care? Consider crafting your most high-candor and high-care headlines in advance.

Add the engagement strategies you craft to the Relationship Management box in your 5-Square.

Other Work: Pause and Reflect

You have just created a draft plan for challenging your stakeholders while maintaining connection. It is important to understand that this plan is not a script you will perform in a sequence. Engaging adaptively is inherently messy. With this issue of sustainability, adaptive engagement is made exponentially more complicated by the levels of system—and power dynamics—you potentially will be managing. You will need to use your social awareness not only to choose the most effective way to influence others to reach your targets, but also to assess risk and determine how much to engage different stakeholders in the first place. Only you can make that assessment about the personal opportunity cost of engagement across levels of system and power in your context. If and when you do decide to engage, you are now clear about what your targets and tactics will be.

Now the Real Work Begins

Congratulations! You have just created a draft plan for engaging others to support your—and potentially your team's—shift from pacesetter leadership to healthy sacrifice and renewal. If you work this plan, you will shift your personal leadership and likely the culture and structures that determine others' ability to sustain as well.

That "if" carries a caveat. We have all had epiphanies that felt like game changers for us, but that faded into the background of our consciousness over time. Intentional practice is what connects an epiphany to transformational change. We change when we build new neural pathways that replace the neural superhighways of our self-limiting habits. With pacesetting, the if also depends on effectively managing your stakeholders to support your new habits.

Your job now is to take your 5-Square plan and work it, intentionally, every day. Print it out and post it somewhere in your workspace. Keep it open on your desktop. You should re-read it regularly, especially when preparing for the kinds of interactions you know are hard for you. This should be a living document that evolves as you evolve. Chapter 11 will provide more guidance about how to keep your plan alive over time.

In the next chapter, we will turn our attention to a self-limiting mindset that often exacerbates pace setting and the sacrifice syndrome: the doer.

Endnotes

1. Goleman, D, Boyatzis, R., and McKee, A. (2001). *Primal Leadership: Unleashing the Power of Emotional Potential.* Cambridge, MA: Harvard Business Review Press.
2. McKee, A., Johnston, F., and Boyatzis, R. (2008). *Becoming a Resonant Leader: Develop Your Emotional Intelligence, Renew Your Relationships, Sustain Your Effectiveness.* Cambridge, MA: Harvard Business Review Press.
3. Thompson, D. (2019). Workism is making Americans miserable. *The Atlantic* (24 February).
4. Zamarro, G., Camp, A., Fuchsman, D., and McGee, J. (2021). American schools are at risk of their own Great Resignation. Quartz (20 September). https://qz.com/2060734/is-there-a-shortage-of-teachers/.
5. Goleman, D. and Boyatzis, R. (2008). Social intelligence and the biology of leadership. *Harvard Business Review* magazine (September).
6. Okun, T. (2019). White Supremacy Culture. DRWorksBook. www.dismantlingracism.org/.
7. McKee, A., Boyatzis, R., and Johnston, F. (2008). *Becoming a Resonant Leader.* Cambridge, MA: Harvard Business review Press.

8. Kegan, R., and Lehey, L.L. (2009). *Immunity to Change: How to Overcome It and Unlock the Potential in Yourself and Your Organization.* Cambridge, MA: Harvard Business School Press.

9. Learning Policy Institute. (2017). What's the cost of teacher turnover? (13 September). https://learningpolicyinstitute.org/product/the-cost-of-teacher-turnover; School Leader Network. (2014). Churn: the high cost of principal turnover. https://newteachercenter.org/wp-content/uploads/2021/07/Churn-The-High-Cost-of-Principal-Turnover_RB21.pdf.

10. Kini, T. and Podolsky, A. (2016). Does teacher experience increase teacher effectiveness? A review of the research. Learning Policy Institute (3 June). https://learningpolicyinstitute.org/product/does-teaching-experience-increase-teacher-effectiveness-review-research.

11. Superville, D.R. (2014). "Principal turnover takes costly toll on students and districts, report says." *Education Week* (5 November). https://www.edweek.org/leadership/principal-turnover-takes-costly-toll-on-students-and-districts-report-says/2014/11.

12. Crenshaw, K. (1989). Demarginalizing the intersection of race and sex: a Black feminist critique of antidiscrimination doctrine, feminist theory and antiracist politics." *University of Chicago Legal Forum* Vol. 1989, Iss. 1, Article 8. https://chicagounbound.uchicago.edu/cgi/viewcontent.cgi?article=1052&context=uclf.

8 The Doer

Doers believe that their job is to the be the #1 performer. They are usually promoted to their new roles in part *because* they were great doers in their previous roles, so the mindset and behaviors are deeply engrained. In their new roles, they struggle to shift from doing to directing, which leads them to take on others' work at the expense of their own (which they are uniquely qualified or tasked to do).

Consider Brooke's story:

> Brooke became a rising star very early on in her organization. She was a strong teacher, but she particularly distinguished herself in her ability to plan and execute projects and systems. When she became an assistant principal, she turned every initiative that she owned to gold. Meal transitions, dismissal, class schedules, testing, teacher observations, and evaluation—they all ran more smoothly when Brooke took them over. The team loved the way Brooke "cleared the runway" so they could focus on teaching and learning. No one was surprised when she was chosen to succeed her principal.
>
> Things start smoothly with Brook at the helm. She feels good about working incredibly hard and solving problems for people, and her staff notice and appreciate the hard work. Brooke spends her days taking on tasks as they come. She does not hesitate to jump in to help with a struggling student in the hallway or as she passes by a classroom. When her leaders struggle, she jumps right in to take over. It feels good to help and it feels good to be effective. At first.

Gradually, the job seems to get bigger and bigger. Brooke works all the time, and there always seems to be more work to do. She can't find any time during the day to do the core pieces of her job. For the first time in her career she starts dropping balls, making last-minute reactive decisions, and communicates reactively with her team.

Perceptions shift. Brooke's leadership team become increasingly unclear about their roles and responsibilities because Brooke takes on pieces of their work. Sometimes Brooke takes on tasks they struggle with in a way that seems that she does not trust them. Her leaders learn to hold back and wait for her to take the lead or tell them what to do. They lose confidence in themselves and feel like their development is stagnating.

Teachers observe this dynamic. They, too, feel unclear about who owns what on the leadership team. They learn pretty quickly to just go to Brooke with everything. Over time, however, Brooke's lack of follow-through increasingly frustrates staff. Between the lack of clarity, inconsistency in follow-through, and increasingly reactive communication, the team begins to lose their confidence in Brooke.

Read this chapter if:

- You feel stuck in a reactive loop of task completion.
- People regularly come to you to complete tasks that others should own.
- You have a habit of jumping into reactive challenges when you see them.
- You tell yourself that it is easier to complete a task yourself than to support someone else to do it.
- You hesitate to delegate when you should.
- You get constructive feedback about the clarity and timeliness of your communication and the consistency of your follow-through.
- You and your team are often unclear about roles and responsibilities and who should take on tasks as they arise.

Doers in Education Organizations

The doer is one of the more common self-limiting mindsets that leaders experience when transitioning from one level of leadership to the next (Leadership Pipeline). Mid-level leaders can also be easily sucked into this mindset when their managers are doers.

The doer leader sinks into an unsustainable work life that can lead to the sacrifice syndrome (see Chapter 7). It can be experienced by their teams as pacesetting, which is contagious (also Chapter 7). And because doers struggle to get to the proactive directing part of their job, their organizations tend to lack clarity of roles and direction, eroding psychological safety. Further, because leaders are doing other people's work rather than developing them to do it themselves, they clog the leadership pipeline.

Doer leadership behaviors also have an excluding effect on teams because they tend to embody white supremacist culture norms. In her 2019 article "White Supremacy Culture,"[1] Tema Okun names several white cultural norms that reinforce doer mindsets and behaviors, including:

- Perfectionism—*Our work must be perfect, we focus mostly on what isn't perfect, and we make it personal.*
- Only one right way—*My way is the right way and if you don't do it my way there is something wrong with you.*
- Power hoarding—*I should control this because I'm the leader and have the best interests of the school at heart.*
- Individualism—*We are individual actors who solve problems alone. In a challenge, I turn inward to solve it.*
- I'm the only one—*If something is going to get done right, I have to do it myself.*

Doer leaders inadvertently reinforce these white cultural norms and exclude others' norms across lines of cultural difference. These exclusive conditions have a particularly damaging impact on learning environments. Because emotions are contagious and learning is emotional work, adult development affects student development. Doers remove learning opportunities from the people they lead in ways that make people question their own abilities and belonging. This promotes fixed mindset and a hesitance to innovate. This fixed mindset is the emotional contagion students experience that creates the conditions for their learning. These conditions are a significant barrier to learning, particularly across lines of difference and for our more under-resourced and learning-challenged students.

The Work Ahead

If you know that the doer mindset is getting in your way, keep reading. If you do not see yourself in the preceding checklist or case study, then maybe this chapter is not for you. Ask for feedback from your manager and a few trusted staff before making that decision. If others confirm your opinion, then skip ahead to the next chapter.

This chapter is a self-contained learning journey. If you take it on, you could spend several months focusing on changing deeply engrained habits and building new adaptive muscles. Download a 5-Square learning plan template from www .noblestorygroup.com to build your plan. You will also need a journal to explore new ideas.

Let's get started.

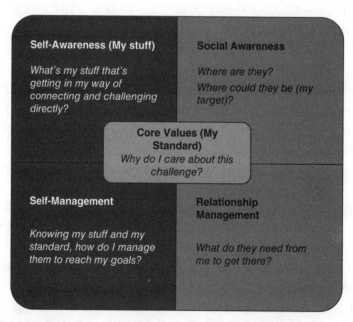

Figure 8.1: The EI 5-Square.

Step 1: Start with the End in Mind

It helps to start by doing some aspirational thinking about what success will look like when you have outgrown your doer habits. Use your imagination to envision what you will be doing and ideally how it will feel to right-size your work and be wildly effective. Pay particular attention to the situations you find most challenging (the preceding checklist might help you with that) but remember that your goal is to envision your *ideal* self in these situations. As a doer, you should think just as deeply about managing yourself in important independent decision-making moments as you do about managing others in collective moments. To help you drill down, consider the following list. What will it look like and feel like to:

- Get crystal clear about roles and responsibilities.
- Stay in your lane and not take on others' work.
- Prioritize time for proactive planning.
- Communicate time-sensitive information in advance.
- Manage up to right-size your work.
- Challenge and empower people to own their work and stay in their lanes.

This aspirational thinking will become the vision of excellence you use to generate awareness and strategies, and to measure your progress over time. You should record this reflection on the first page of your 5-Square. Journal first and then transfer to the 5-Square if journaling helps you think creatively. Give yourself uninterrupted time (at least 30 minutes) and emotional space to do this reflection. You might find it helpful to see an example vision from another 5-Square, and there is one in Appendix E.

Step 2: Build Self-Awareness

When you have thought deeply about the leader you want to be, you are ready to hold up the mirror and build awareness about what is getting in your way. As you think about this, push yourself to remember specific times when you led as a doer that did not result in the outcomes you wanted. It may help to revisit the checklist at the beginning of this chapter as you think of examples. Once you have two or three in mind, choose one example to use as a case study over the rest of this chapter.

In coaching we call these case studies behavioral moments. When we zoom in on these moments of emotional cause and effect, decision, and behavior, we are able to identify the chain reaction of a self-limiting mindset.

What Are Your Triggers?

Identify the trigger moment of your case study. What happened that started you down the doer path? Something—an email, the discovery of a dropped ball, a struggling staff member, a call for help—triggered a feeling. What are those trigger moments for you? Be as clear as you can about the specific moment in your case study, then think more broadly about how this kind of trigger shows up regularly in challenging leadership moments. Write down what comes up in the self-awareness box of your 5-Square.

What Sensations and Emotions Do You Experience?

Our triggers cause a self-limiting chain reaction that starts in our body. Neurological research shows that we process stress physiologically before we process it emotionally or intellectually. Our body is our early warning system—a fundamental aspect of self-awareness that most of us do not pay enough attention to. Think back again to your trigger moment. Where did you feel your reaction in your body? Was it pressure in the chest, burning ears, or clenching hands? Note your reaction in your 5-Square.

Soon after the physical reaction comes an emotional reaction. Our emotional response to trigger moments is more complicated than we might think. We often experience a contradictory blend of positive and dissonant emotions at the same time. As a doer you may feel frustrated about others' mistakes or your own bad habits. Simultaneously, you may feel excitement and competence as you swoop in to save the day or perform a task well. Being aware of how these positive emotions affect you is crucial to shifting your habits.

What Stories Get in Your Way?

Our stories—the inner narratives and assumptions about ourselves, others, and context that help us make sense of the world—come next. Here we specifically focus on the stories that feed your self-limiting behaviors. In your case study, what were you telling yourself about others, yourself, and the situation that got in your way? It might help to connect each emotion with the thoughts that accompanied it. For example, a feeling of hopelessness could connect to the story, "This job is totally unsustainable," which limits your motivation to find different ways of working. Or, a feeling of frustration could connect to the story, "If I want something done right, I have to do it myself," which leads you to jump in and do other people's work. Remember that your doer stories may also connect to positive emotions. When you see a student discipline challenge in your hallway you may feel excitement and anticipation, and you may be telling yourself some version of, "This student and teacher need me to save the day for them. I am good at this and I can help them."

Our Stories and Our Identities

The deeper our stories, the more connected they are to our identities. Growing up in America with our history of racism, we all have blind spots about how these beliefs connect to white supremacy. At the beginning of this chapter, I listed several deep stories that embody white cultural norms. Consider what stories you might be telling yourself about perfectionism, there being only one right way, hoarding power, individualism over collaboration, or being "the only one" who can solve problems. How do these stories reinforce your doer behaviors?

Write down all the self-limiting stories that came up in your case study moment and consider how they feed your doer behaviors.

Then What Do You *Do*?

Your triggers, sensations and emotions, and self-limiting stories all lead you to *do* things that get in your way. These are your self-limiting behaviors. In the case study you have been unpacking, what did you do that got in your way? Consider the sequence of actions in the moment and in follow-up interactions. Examine not only your words but your tone, body language, and maybe even what you did *not* say or do that got in your way. Do not stop at your first or even second response. Consider all of the relevant actions in a sequence related to this moment. Write it all down in your self-awareness box of your 5-Square. We build deeper self-awareness when we really focus on all of our actions connected to one trigger moment.

What Is the Impact of Your Behaviors?

Now reflect on the full ripple effect of your actions. The impact likely goes much further than you have considered previously.

Wheatly's Green Line (see Chapter 1 and Figure 8.2) provides a helpful framework for considering impact. Start with the three circles above the line. Consider your intended leadership outcomes in your case study against your actual outcomes. Consider the ripple effect of this one-to-one engagement on the outcomes of your staff and students.

Now focus on the three circles below the line and consider the social and emotional implications of your behavior. Again, start with self and follow the ripples out. How did your actions affect your self-perception? How did your actions affect your relationships with others? How might it have impacted their ability to succeed?

Doers can usually make the cause–effect link between their decisions and being overwhelmed with work, but that is only the tip of the iceberg. Consider how your doer mindsets and behaviors impact your staff and students. The beginning of this chapter listed several ways that doers impact learning organizations. What is your personal version of this story? List all the ripple effects of your self-limiting behaviors on the conditions for learning in your building.

We tend not to consider the effect of these personal leadership self-limiting behaviors on reputation. Think about how your case study—and your pattern across similar episodes—likely impacts your credibility. What do people tell their colleagues,

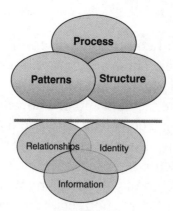

Figure 8.2: Wheatly's Six-Circle Model.

friends, and family who live and work in your community? What do others assume about you when your doer habits play out?

Take a few minutes to journal on this ripple effect. When you think you have a pretty exhaustive list, consider sharing with a trusted colleague or manager to see if they can think of anything you might have missed (we all have blind spots about our impact, especially when it comes to our reputation). Then record the levels of impact that matter the most in your 5-Square.

Pause and Reflect

At this point, I encourage you to take both a literal and metaphorical deep breath. Step back and offer yourself both grace and gratitude for the work you have done so far. You have just gone deep below the surface and explored the chain reaction behind your doer self-limiting mindset. It is painful to confront the stories we tell ourselves and the impact that our actions have on ourselves and those around us. It is natural to feel down on ourselves at this moment. However, when we confront deep and personal obstacles, we open the door to change and growth. With self-awareness comes an opportunity you may not have known you had: to choose a more positive and effective way of being.

This choosing begins with building new self-management strategies that can shift your stories and behaviors.

Step 3: Build Self-Management Strategies

We cannot stop our triggers and our emotions; they are hardwired. However, we *can* manage triggers and emotions once we become aware of them. Self-management is about choosing how we react to triggers and emotions by choosing new stories and behaviors.

In Chapter 2, you read about the three basic self-management strategies we use in our 5-Square coaching: creating space, values-driven self-talk, and rewriting a noble story. For a deeper explanation, go back and re-read. Now we will go straight into the process of building these strategies.

Creating Space Between Trigger and Response

Creating a few seconds of space between our triggers and what we actually do is a prerequisite to accessing other strategies. This begins in our bodies, managing our sensations to create a window of time for us to slow down and think. As a doer, you have some deeply ingrained patterns of choosing work as a default and jumping into other people's work when you should direct. What can you do to create space between your desire to do and the choices you make?

- Start by considering what you already do at other times in your life that might serve you in trigger moments. Do you already have meditative practices in your life, like yoga, prayer, or a mindfulness practice? If you do, you probably already have breathing strategies that help you slow down. A couple of deep breaths over a matter of seconds could be all you need to regain your ability to think clearly.
- There may be other micromovements that you do already with your body that calm you down (from taking a sip of water to shifting your posture). How could you more intentionally do those things in the moment? Consider the impact on your chain reaction of walking away from your computer for a glass of water, or stepping back and breathing when you see that student discipline challenge in the hallway. If it slows you down, then it works.

Write down at least one strategy to slow down and interrupt the cycle in the self-management box of your 5-Square

Grounding in Your Standard with Self-Coaching

Once you have slowed down and returned to your thinking brain, access your inner coach. This is when your values—your standard—gets activated.

Your job here is to identify your values that matter most in this context. Start by remembering the dissonance you felt when you surfaced your self-limiting stories and behaviors, and their impact on yourself and others. Why do you care about *not* being a doer anymore? Your answers likely connect to what you want to accomplish, what kind of leader you want to be, and what kind of life you want to live. In your journal, start listing all of the reasons that come up. When you think you have a relatively complete list, review and prioritize your top five. This should be an emotional exercise. You should feel in your gut what matters most to you.

Now, for each of your prioritized care statements, go deeper. *Why* is this statement important to you? What is that *about* for you? Each time you answer this question, try deepening your answer with another why question. It is like peeling an onion, as there are many layers of meaning that you can uncover. Your goal here is to try to get to a core value.

Example:

I don't want to work all the time. (Why?)

It's not good for me or my team. (Why?)

I believe that if I don't do this, then I won't create the conditions for my students and my staff to do this. (Why?)

When I prioritize self-care and right-size my work, so will my staff. (Why?)

I have to *walk the walk* to create the right conditions for others.

You will know when you are done when you can say and feel, "This one is about (a value or value statement) for me." Do this for each of the statements that you prioritized. Then add those core values—your standard—to the center square of your 5-Square.

Now that you have just surfaced your power, plan for how you can harness it in your trigger moments. Take yourself back to the trigger moment of your case study and use your standards to craft your "self-talk":

- Which of the values you identified will serve you most when you are triggered and in danger of being hijacked by your emotions? Choose one or two that resonate the most.
- Now consider how these values apply to this moment to orient you to your true north. Up to this point you have had an anti-coach whispering stories and advice that have mostly held you back. Now imagine that you have a new coach on your other shoulder. What can this new coach tell you that will be more powerful than your self-limiting stories?

■ Crystallize brief phrases your inner coach can bring to the moment that will be easy to access and resonant at a values level. Think bumper sticker or T-shirt. Write up to three of these in your 5-Square self-management box. Some examples from doers I have coached include:

> *Is this my work or someone else's work?*
> *Don't enable. Empower!*
> *The work will never be done. It's time to take some time for self.*

Finally, consider how your values relate to your identities. According to the idea of intersectionality (Crenshaw 1989),[2] we all have many identities, or facets of self, that make up who we are. Some of these include gender, race, sexuality, class, ability, place of origin, and religion, but the list is really only limited by the number of ways we make sense of ourselves and each other in the world. We know that identity markers can be used to marginalize or privilege groups. Yet we also know that our identities are a source of our personal power. They weave together to create our cultures, from family culture to our many different group cultures. From these interwoven identity groups, we learn what matters to us in the world.

Re-read the list of values and inner-coach statements you just generated. Consider how your identities connect with and inform them. How can an intentional anchoring in your identities empower you to shift your doer habits? Weave your identity narratives into the inner-coach statements you just wrote.

Rewrite Noble Stories

Now we shift to some other stories that need revising: the stories you tell yourself about others.

As a doer, you likely need to focus on two kinds of stories about others. The first are those that judge their abilities. Stories that assume others *can't do* often amount to deficit-based confirmation bias—the tendency to only look for what confirms your current negative stories. Their redeeming qualities and potential are there, but you subconsciously choose not to see them. Go back to your self-awareness square and pull out your self-limiting stories about others. If you know that this list is incomplete, add other relevant stories.

Now, *flip them*. Replace them with alternative narratives that emphasize positive motive and potential.

- What could you choose to believe about what your staff value and why they are struggling? Exercise empathy and compassion.
- What could you choose to believe about their potential and their desire to grow?

The second type of story you likely need to revise concern *their* stories about *you*. Consider the self-limiting stories you tell yourself about what your staff want and need from you. How could you flip these stories to emphasize the versions of what your staff need and want that reflect their noble desire to grow and feel empowered in their roles?

Write the noble stories that resonate most to you in the self-management box of your 5-Square.

Self-Work: Pause and Reflect

You have now completed the left side of the 5-Square and, in doing so, you have generated a game plan for managing your stuff and harnessing your standard. If you work these strategies deliberately over time, you will overcome the doer habits that live inside yourself.

Now we move to the right side of the 5-Square to tackle the doer habits at play between you and others.

Step 4: Build Social Awareness to Diagnose Needs and Set Targets

With your new self-awareness and intention to self-manage, you are prepared to see others more clearly. As you shift your focus from self to others, the first question for you to consider is a diagnostic one: *Where are they?* This simple question should activate your Emotional Intelligence (EI) muscles of empathy (the ability to accurately read other people's emotional state and needs) and compassion (the desire to help). Exercising the muscles together should help you diagnose needs while avoiding the blind spots that come with judgment.

You should consider where your team is as a result of your doer leadership style. Your analysis should focus on individuals, your school culture, and the structures you have created to get the work done. Be sure to reflect both above and below Wheatly's Green Line. You might start with your "impact" reflection in your self-awareness box. Following are some additional questions to consider:

- What self-limiting behaviors do your people exhibit that connect to your doer leadership style? How are these behaviors preventing them from being effective in their work and trusting your relationship?
- What stories do you think they believe about themselves related to this dynamic?
- What stories do you think they are telling themselves about your actions and what you believe about them?
- What cultural norms—assumptions about the way things work—have you created related to doing?
- What structures, or lack of structures, have you created that feed your doer approach?
- How does identity impact the doer dynamic here? What lines of difference and power between you and your team might contribute to the challenge?
- What values motivate your team to do this work? In their lives? What do they care about?

Record your best answers to the preceding questions in the Social Awareness box of your 5-Square.

Where Do They Need to Be? (Defining Your Targets)

Now that you have a working diagnosis of where the other person is, you are ready to think about targets and objectives for engagement. Note that the accuracy of your targets depends on the strength of your diagnosis. Your goal here is to prioritize the behaviors and obstacles you diagnosed and articulate intended outcomes, or changes, you hope to accomplish through your engagement. These targets tend be either behaviors, mindsets, or relational conditions that you want to shift. In your shift from doer to director, it may help you to think about engaging others through three phases:

1. Stepping back and building awareness about the doer dynamic.
2. Making new agreements about how to work together grounded in clarifying roles and responsibilities for all stakeholders.
3. Managing and coaching your team to stay in their new lanes and perform in what may feel like new roles.

Table 8.1 shows some examples. Note the alignment between diagnosis and the target.

In your 5-Square, generate a target for each of the where-they-are points you have prioritized.

Table 8.1: Sample targets.

Where they are (your diagnosis)	Where they need to be (your targets)
Above the Green Line	
Coming to me to solve problems and make decisions that they should be owning independently	Independently making day-to-day decisions, executing, and coming to me afterwards to debrief
Not clear about who should be doing what Roles are not well-defined	Define clear roles and responsibilities and stay in our lanes
Below the Green Line	
Unaware of the impact my doing has on their outcomes and growth trajectory	Aware of this dynamic and its impact on us and our students
Lacking confidence in their ability because I have been doing their work for them when they struggle	Empowered, motivated, and confident to own the parts of their job that I have been doing
Frustrated with me for disempowering them	Feeling that I believe in them and that I am investing in their growth
Wanting to grow, reach their potential, and be successful	Seeing delegation and reshuffling of tasks as opportunities to grow, reach potential, and improve outcomes

Step 5: Manage Relationships to Meet Your Targets

You have now done the internal work and perspective-taking to prepare yourself to engage others as a director rather than a doer. This is where the rubber meets the road. It is time for you to use all of your new awareness and strategies to choose better ways to connect, care, and challenge to reach your targets. Each person, group, and context will require a unique blend of these three ingredients to create the conditions for success.

Use the following questions as a springboard for creative thinking about engagement. Do this thinking in the context of your personal case study, and in connection with the targets that you have generated.

First return to your vision for success on the first page of your 5-Square plan:

- To get your creative juices flowing, re-read your aspirational vision from Step 1. If any new ideas have come up as you have worked through this chapter, add them to the vision.
- Now read the vision again, pulling out the leadership actions that you might use to connect with, care for, and challenge the person or group in this context. Add what resonates most to the Relationship Management box of your 5-Square

Now call on your instincts and the "where are they" diagnosis you made in the previous section:

What does the person or group in question need from you to feel *connected* as a human being? Make sure you are not confusing this question with what they might *want*. Connection does not always feel good, but it must feel *real*. Consider these core behaviors of connection:

- *Authenticity*—How will you show up as *you*, the human being, with no persona?
- *Vulnerability*—What do you need to share at an emotional level (below your Green Line) about your doer self-limiting mindsets and behaviors? Consider how that will make it safe for others to share with you. Make sure you self-manage to describe those real emotions without actually being *in* them in the moment.

■ *Listening*—What do you need to find out to confirm or revise your diagnosis about "where they are?" in this doer dynamic. Consider the effect of asking *curious* questions and listening on connection. There is nothing more effective you can do to make another person feel truly seen and heard.

What do they need from you to feel like you *care* about them?

■ What can you say or do that will show your belief in their potential to grow? How can you paint a hopeful picture of this person thriving through this change?

■ How can you show your investment in their growth and your relationship? How can you name the noble story that you hold for them with empathy and compassion?

■ It may be a stretch, but consider how *clarity* about roles and responsibility shows care. This shift from doer to director won't work for your team unless everyone is crystal clear about who owns what. This may be a heavy lift, but creating a teamwide roles and responsibilities chart that you all consult regularly will be essential for making this shift.

How do they need you to *challenge* them to grow and meet your targets?

■ How can you ground this conversation in your values and why you care? Your values are the source of your power when challenging.

■ How and when will you name your targets (the specific shifts you want you and your team to make)? How will you come back to them if the conversation veers off course?

■ How will you directly and clearly delegate tasks, even when they are last-minute or when the other person already has a lot on their plate?

■ How will you directly name it when people are asking you do to their work, or when they are doing others' work?

■ If the other person does not change their behavior, how will you increase your level of candor while also increasing care? Consider crafting your most high-candor and high-care headlines in advance.

■ Beyond accountability, how will you build your team's mindsets and skills if they struggle to make the shift to more independence in their work?

Make sure you have added your new engagement strategies to your 5-Square.

Other Work: Pause and Reflect

You have just created a draft plan for shifting your team from being victims of your doer approach to empowered individual contributors and leaders. It is important to understand that this plan is not a script you will perform in a sequence. Engaging adaptively is inherently messy. You will need to use your self-management strategies to avoid your inevitable desire to do the work when your triggers arise. If you can stay positive, consistent with expectations, and keep investing in others' growth along the way, then you will be successful.

Now the Real Work Begins

That "if" in the last sentence is a real caveat. We have all had epiphanies about our leadership that felt like game changers, but that faded into the background of our consciousness over time. Intentional practice is what connects an epiphany to transformational change. Remember the neuroscience behind this. We change when we build new neural pathways that replace the neural superhighways of our self-limiting habits.

Your job now is to take your 5-Square plan and work it, intentionally, every day in your work. Print it out and post it somewhere in your workspace. Keep it open on your desktop. You should be re-reading it regularly, especially when preparing for the kinds of interactions you know are hard for you. This should be a living document that evolves as you evolve. Chapter 11 will provide more guidance about how to keep your plan alive over time.

In the next chapter, we will turn our attention to an inner obstacle that can show up as an enabler of any of the other self-limiting mindsets in this book: imposter syndrome.

Endnotes

1. Okun, T. (2019). White Supremacy Culture. DRworksBook. https://www.dismantlingracism .org/uploads/4/3/5/7/43579015/okun_-_white_sup_culture.pdf.
2. Crenshaw, K. (1989). Demarginalizing the intersection of race and sex: a Black feminist critique of antidiscrimination doctrine, feminist theory and antiracist politics." *University of Chicago Legal Forum* Vol. 1989, Iss. 1, Article 8. https://chicagounbound. uchicago.edu/cgi/viewcontent.cgi?article=1052&context=uclf.

9 The Imposter

Leaders experiencing imposter phenomenon (also known as imposter syndrome) fear that they are not really qualified for their job, that others believe this too, and that sooner or later they will be confronted about this ugly truth by the people they lead (Clance and Imes 1978).[1] The imposter phenomenon is an internal struggle but there may be very real environmental conditions that contribute to it, particularly for leaders of color and other oppressed identity groups in white-dominant cultural spaces. Research shows that 70% of us experience imposter phenomenon at some point in our careers (Wilding 2020).[2] We may all feel like imposters sometimes, but it becomes a self-limiting mindset when it significantly impacts performance.

Consider Miles's story:

> Miles rose quickly into school leadership because of his many strengths. In four years he transitioned from teacher's aide to teacher and then to dean of culture—a meteoric rise. Two years later Miles was named principal of his school when the current principal became a regional superintendent. The move made sense to staff, students, and families, who overwhelmingly trust and respect Miles. Miles is mostly proud and excited to find himself in the school leader's seat with such overwhelming support. There is a part of him, however—a voice in his ear—reminding him that he is hiding some ugly things that all of those people don't know.

That voice tells Miles that he is different from other leaders in the organization; he doesn't share the same background or fit the personality archetype. He feels like a bull in a china shop in leader cohort meetings when he opens his mouth. Rough around the edges. He looks to his own school leadership team and knows that his academic APs are more skilled and knowledgeable about curriculum and instruction, especially on reading (which he has never taught). "As a matter of fact," says the voice, "every leader you know spikes in some skillset. You don't spike in any."

As the months go by and he makes small mistakes that confirm what the voice is telling him about his shortcomings, Miles leadership shifts. He is quiet when staff aren't meeting expectations. He avoids confrontation because he is not sure he's right. He imagines his manager and their manager critiquing him behind closed doors and he closes himself off to them. His staff is confused by his actions and gradually lose confidence in the absence of clear vision and leadership decisions. Members of the leadership team react to the void in different ways. Some grow more tentative themselves, while others openly criticize Miles and focus on excelling in their own spheres of influence. The school begins to feel like it is running on autopilot, with cliques and loud voices wielding the most influence. Miles begins to dread walking through the door every day. Other staff don't feel much different.

Read this chapter if:

- ☐ You question your ability to do your job, but you suspect that is at least partly in your head.
- ☐ You focus too much on your losses and not enough on your wins.
- ☐ You perseverate on what others are saying about you behind closed doors.
- ☐ Your working environment sends implicit messages that you do not fit in because of your identities (race, gender, age, class, education, etc.).
- ☐ You do not feel like you live up to your assumptions about what a leader is supposed to be.
- ☐ Your beliefs about yourself make it hard to challenge others, make decisions, ask for help, or generally trust your staff and your managers.

Imposter Phenomenon in Education Organizations

Strong conditions for learning depend on people feeling emotionally safe enough to take risks. A key component of healthy growth mindset is one's threshold for making mistakes while learning (Dweck 2007).[3] We educators create those conditions in many ways, but chief among them is how we model growth mindset. Our intellectual risk taking and the way we handle setbacks—how we walk the walk—influence our students much more than what we might preach or teach on the subject. Emotional contagion explains why our modeling is so powerful. Our mirror neurons activate the same mirror neurons in our students and staff.

The emotional contagion of leaders who struggle with imposter phenomenon communicates the opposite of growth mindset: a fixed mindset. Their actions and emotions communicate that it is not safe to take risks, lest others see our deficiencies. It seems safer to hide our growth areas than to work on them. While staff and students may not be aware of this implicit message, it is in the air that they breathe. It becomes an obstacle to learning, particularly for the most challenged students and staff.

For leaders of color and those representing other oppressed identity groups, imposter phenomenon is inextricably linked to how power and privilege are reinforced in a school's culture and systems. Exclusive conditions in white-dominant organizational cultures can be a root cause of a leader's imposter feelings. Unfortunately, the leader's subsequent imposter-related behaviors can reinforce messages of not belonging for students and staff who share that leader's identity. In this way, a leader's imposter phenomenon can reinforce exclusive conditions for learning.

The Work Ahead

If you know that the imposter phenomenon is getting in your way, keep reading. If you do not see yourself in the preceding checklist or case study, then maybe this chapter is not for you. Ask for feedback from your manager and a few trusted staff before making that decision. If others confirm your opinion, then skip ahead to the next chapter.

This chapter is a self-contained learning journey. If you take it on, you could spend several months focusing on changing deeply engrained habits and building

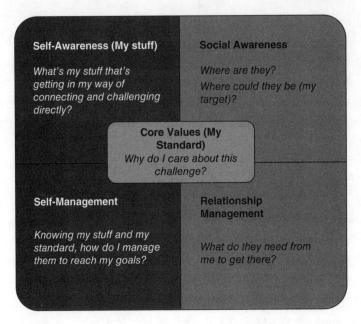

Figure 9.1: The EI 5-Square.

new adaptive muscles. Download a 5-Square learning plan template from www .noblestorygroup.com to build your plan. You will also need a journal to explore new ideas.

Let's get started.

Step 1: Start with the End in Mind

This journey starts by thinking about what success will look like when you have outgrown your imposter beliefs. Use your imagination to envision what you will be doing differently and how it will feel ideally to lead with confidence in yourself and your competency. Pay particular attention to the situations you find most challenging (the preceding checklist might help you with that) but remember that your goal is to envision your *ideal* self in these situations. To help you drill down, consider what it will it look like and feel like to:

- Make definitive decisions and stand by them.
- Challenge those who push back on expectations and decisions.
- Deliver your rationale to different-sized groups with different levels of investment.

- Challenge and empower people to own their work and stay in their lanes.
- Make mistakes, own them, and then move on.
- Admit when you don't know the answer and ask for help.
- Meet your own internal bar for success.
- Feel that you and your identities belong, and that you add strength to your organization.

You should record this reflection on the first page of your 5-Square. Journal first and then transfer to the 5-Square if journaling helps you think creatively. Give yourself uninterrupted time (at least 30 minutes) and emotional space to do this reflection. You might find it helpful to see an example vision from another 5-Square, and there is one in Appendix F. You will use this vision of success during this journey to generate awareness and strategies, and to measure your progress over time.

Step 2: Build Self-Awareness

When you have thought deeply about the leader you want to be, you are ready to hold up the mirror and explore what is getting in your way. As you think about this, push yourself to remember specific times when your imposter beliefs became obstacles to reaching your desired outcomes. It may help to revisit the checklist at the beginning of this chapter as you think of examples. Once you have two or three in mind, choose one example to use as a case study over the rest of this chapter. In coaching, we call these case studies behavioral moments. When we zoom in on these moments of emotional cause and effect, decision, and behavior, we are able to identify the chain reaction of a self-limiting mindset.

What Are Your Triggers?

First, identify the trigger moment of your case study. What happened that sparked the imposter feeling? Something—a dropped ball, someone's judgment or push back, or maybe being the only one of your identity in the room—triggered a feeling. Be as clear as you can about the specific moment in your case study, then think more broadly about how this kind of trigger shows up regularly in challenging leadership moments. Write down what comes up in the self-awareness box of your 5-Square.

What Sensations and Emotions Do You Experience?

Our triggers cause a self-limiting chain reaction that starts in our body. Neurological research shows that we process stress physiologically before we process it emotionally or intellectually. Our body is our early warning system—a fundamental aspect of self-awareness that most of us do not pay enough attention to. Think back again to your trigger moment. Where did you feel your reaction in your body? Was it pressure in the chest, burning ears, or shortness of breath? Note your physical reaction in your 5-Square.

Soon after the physical reaction comes an emotional reaction. Our emotional response to trigger moments is more complicated than we might think. In an imposter moment, you may feel afraid of judgment or frustrated with yourself. Simultaneously, you may feel resentful toward or mistrustful of others. Write down the emotions you tend to experience in these moments. Push yourself to name as many as you can.

What Stories Get in Your Way?

Our stories—the inner narratives and assumptions about ourselves, others, and context that help us make sense of the world—come next. Here we specifically focus on the stories that feed your self-limiting behaviors. In your case study, what were you telling yourself about others, yourself, and the situation that got in your way? It might help to connect each emotion with the thoughts that accompanied it. For example, if I am feeling incompetent, I may be saying to myself, "Do I really know what to do? I am not qualified, so I don't have the right to challenge."

Our Stories and Our Identities

The deeper our stories, the more connected they are to our identities. Growing up in America with our 400-year history of white male supremacy, it is inevitable that racism and sexism impact our perceptions of self. Becoming aware of how oppression plays a role in your imposter beliefs is key to overcoming them. Related to identity is context. The stronger and more exclusive the dominant culture is in a space, the more likely imposter beliefs will show up as internal obstacles for those representing other identities.

Write down all the self-limiting stories that come up in your case study moment and consider how they feed your imposter beliefs.

Then What Do You *Do*?

Your triggers, sensations and emotions, and self-limiting stories all lead you to *do* things that get in your way. These are your self-limiting behaviors. In the case study you have been unpacking, what did you do that got in your way? Consider the sequence of actions. Examine not only your words but your tone, body language, and maybe even what you did *not* say or do. Do not stop at your first or even second response. Consider all of the relevant actions in a sequence related to this moment. Write it all down in your self-awareness box of your 5-Square. We build deeper self-awareness when we really focus on all of our actions connected to one trigger moment.

What Is the Impact of Your Behaviors?

Now reflect on the full ripple effect of your actions. The impact likely goes much further than you have previously considered.

Wheatly's Green Line (see Chapter 1 and Figure 9.2) provides a helpful framework for considering impact. Start with the three circles above the line. Consider your intended leadership outcomes in your case study against your actual outcomes and the outcomes of staff and students.

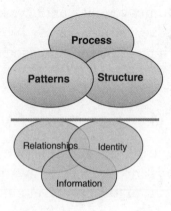

Figure 9.2: Wheatly's Six-Circle Model.

Now focus on the three circles below the line and consider the social and emotional implications of your behavior. Again, start with self and follow the ripples out. How did your actions affect your self-perception? How did your actions affect your relationships with others? How might it have affected their perceptions of themselves?

Those grappling with imposter phenomenon can usually make the cause–effect link between their behavior and what others think about them, but that is only the tip of the iceberg. The beginning of this chapter listed several ways that imposter phenomenon affects learning organizations. What is your personal version of this story? List the ripple effects of your self-limiting behaviors on the conditions for learning in your learning community.

Take a few minutes to journal. When you think you have a complete list, consider sharing with a trusted colleague or manager to see if they can think of anything you might have missed (we all have blind spots about our impact). Then record the levels of impact that matter the most in your 5-Square.

Pause and Reflect

At this point, I encourage you to take both a literal and metaphorical deep breath. Step back and offer yourself grace and gratitude for the work you have done so far. You have gone well below the surface and explored the emotional chain reaction behind your imposter mindset. It is painful to confront the self-limiting stories and behaviors and it is natural to feel down on ourself at this moment. However, when we confront personal obstacles we open the door to change and growth. With self-awareness comes an opportunity you may not have known you had: to choose a more empowering and effective way of being.

This choosing begins with building self-management strategies that can shift your stories and behaviors.

Step 3: Build Self-Management Strategies ▬▬▬

We cannot stop our triggers and our emotions; they are hardwired. However, we *can* manage triggers and emotions once we become aware of them. Self-management is about choosing how we react to triggers and emotions by choosing new stories and behaviors.

In Chapter 2, you read about the three basic self-management strategies we use in our 5-Square coaching: creating space, values-driven self-talk, and rewriting a noble story. For a deeper explanation, go back and re-read. Now we will go straight into the process of building these strategies.

Creating Space Between Trigger and Response

First, *slow down*. Creating a few seconds of space between a trigger and what we actually do is a prerequisite to accessing other strategies. This begins in our bodies as we manage sensations to create a window of time for us to slow down and think. What can you do to create space between your triggers and your actions?

- Start by considering what you already do that might serve you in trigger moments. Do you have meditative practices in your life, like yoga, prayer, or a mindfulness practice? If you do, you probably already have breathing strategies you can bring to bear. A couple of deep breaths over a matter of seconds could be all you need to help you think clearly.
- There may be other micromovements that you do already with your body that calm you down (from taking a sip of water to somehow shifting your posture). How could you more intentionally do those things in the moment? Consider the impact on your chain reaction of walking away from your computer for a glass of water, a walk around the block, or a moment with another person. If it slows you down, then it works.

Write down at least one strategy to slow down and interrupt the reaction to your trigger in the self-management box of your 5-Square

Grounding in Your Standard with Self-Coaching

Once you have slowed down and returned to your thinking brain, access your inner coach. *Building strong inner-coach voice will be* the *most important muscle you strengthen to overcome your imposter mindset*. This is because, at this moment, you have a powerful inner critic who is in control. You need to develop an even *stronger* empowering voice to overcome it. Building that voice starts with your standard.

To mine for the standard that empowers you most, go back in your case study to the self-limiting stories, behaviors, and their impact you recorded earlier in this chapter. Why do you care about rejecting those stories and leaving imposter behaviors behind? Your answers likely connect to who you want to be, what you want to accomplish, and why you do this work. In your journal, start listing all the reasons you care that come up. When you think you have a relatively complete list, review and prioritize your top five. This should be an emotional exercise that you feel in your gut.

Now, for each of your prioritized care statements, go deeper. *Why* is this statement important to you? What is that *about* for you? For each answer, try to follow with another why question. This is like peeling an onion, as there are many layers of meaning that you can uncover. Your goal here is to try to get to the core value.

Example:

I want to be seen as a strong leader. (Why?)

If I'm not seen as a strong leader, then my team won't trust me and follow me. (Why?)

People don't follow leaders who don't believe in themselves. (Why?)

If someone doesn't truly believe in themselves then why should I?

Core Value: Belief in self

You will know when you are done when you can say and feel, "This one is about (a value or value statement) for me." Do this for each of the statements that you prioritized. Then add those core values to the center square of your 5-Square.

You have just brought your power to the surface. Now think about how to harness that power in the moment with self-coaching. Take yourself back to the trigger moment in your case study. What could your inner coach have said to counter the inner critic? Which of the values you identified can orient you to your true north in the moment? Consider what that coach might tell you about these common imposter stumbling blocks:

- How you define success and failure.
- What struggling or making mistakes says about you.
- Where true validation comes from.
- What asking for help says about you.

- What the relationship is between leadership and expertise.
- What your staff and students really need from you as a leader.

After you have done some journaling, crystallize what came up for you in brief phrases that your inner coach can bring to the moment that will be easy to access. Think bumper sticker or T-shirt. Write up to five of these in your 5-Square self-management box. Some examples from leaders managing imposter mindset include:

> *I don't have to believe everything I think.*
> *They chose me for this job for my standard and my skills.*
> *Leaders don't have to be experts on everything. They have to leverage their team's expertise.*
> *Asking for help is modeling strong growth mindset.*

Finally, consider how your values relate to your identities According to the idea of intersectionality (Crenshaw 1989),[4] we all have many identities, or facets of self, that make up who we are. Some of these include gender, race, sexuality, class, ability, place of origin, and religion, but the list is really only limited by the number of ways we make sense of ourselves and each other in the world. We know that identity markers can be used to marginalize or privilege groups. Yet we also know that our identities are a source of our personal power. They weave together to create our cultures, from family culture to our many different group cultures. From these interwoven identity groups, we learn what matters to us in the world.

Re-read the list of values and inner-coach statements you just generated. Consider how your identities connect with and inform them. How can an intentional anchoring in your identities empower you to shift your imposter beliefs? Weave your identity narratives into the inner-coach statements you just wrote.

Once you feel you have two or three strong self-coaching statements, add them to the self-management box of your 5-Square.

Rewrite Noble Stories

You just wrote some new stories grounded in your power. Now we shift to some other stories that need revising: what you tell yourself about others.

You likely need to focus on two kinds of stories about others. The first stories are what *you* believe others believe *about you*. Consider the self-limiting stories you tell yourself about how others judge your intentions, performance, character, and identities. Some of your stories might be true, but many are projections of your own fears and self-limiting beliefs about struggle, expertise, and success. Go back to your self-awareness square and pull the self-limiting stories connected to other people's negative beliefs about you. If this list is incomplete, add other relevant stories. Now, *flip them*. Replace them with alternative narratives that represent the best possible stories they might believe about you.

> *What could you choose to believe about what your stakeholders believe about you that would help you connect and reach your goals?*

The second kind of stories you likely need to revise are those that assume others' worst intentions toward you. You have likely created stories about how others are out to do you harm. Go back to your self-awareness square and pull out your self-limiting stories connected to other people's intentions toward you. How could you flip these stories? What could you choose to believe about their intentions toward you that would help you connect and reach your goals?

Even if your instincts tell you that your stories about others' negative intentions are accurate, there still may be an opportunity. Could there be something about that person's experience that explains their negative intentions? Finding some point of empathy and compassion helps us engage with some level of connection that helps us reach our goals even when others are clearly in the wrong

There is one important caveat to the noble story strategy. In situations where someone is being oppressed or abused, encouraging them to find a noble story for their aggressor is wrong. A victim should not be pushed to rationalize or excuse the acts of those who cause them harm. If the process of cultivating a noble story results in someone internalizing harm done to them by others, then the strategy itself can become a form of oppression.

Write the noble stories that feel true to you in the self-management box of your 5-Square.

Self-Work: Pause and Reflect

You have now completed the left side of the 5-Square and, in doing so, you have generated a game plan for managing your stuff and harnessing your standard. If you work these strategies deliberately over time, you will overcome the imposter feelings and related behaviors that hold you back. Now we move to the right side of the 5-Square to see and engage others through a fresh lens of empowerment.

Step 4: Build Social Awareness to Diagnose Needs and Set Targets

With new self-awareness and intention to self-manage, you are prepared to see others more clearly. The first question for you to consider as you focus on others is a diagnostic one: *Where are they?* This simple question should activate your Emotional Intelligence (EI) muscles of empathy (the ability to accurately read other people's emotional state and needs), and compassion (the desire to help). Exercising these muscles together should help you diagnose needs while avoiding the blind spots that come with a defensive focus on self.

   This includes inquiring about where your team is in relation to your imposter phenomenon. How have your mindsets and behaviors impacted others? Your analysis should focus on individuals, teams, and the organization's culture as a whole. Be sure to reflect both above and below Wheatly's Green Line. You might start with your "impact" reflection in your self-awareness box. Following are some additional questions to consider:

- What self-limiting behaviors have your people adopted that connect to your imposter-driven leadership behaviors? How are these behaviors preventing them from being effective in their work and in your relationship?
- What stories do you think they believe about themselves related to this dynamic?
- What stories do you think they are telling themselves about your actions and what you believe about them?
- What default cultural norms—assumptions about the way things work—have your imposter-driven behaviors created?

- How does identity impact the dynamic? What lines of difference and power between you and your team feed this challenge for you and for them? How does this play out in specific behaviors? To what extent are they aware of these dynamics?
- What values motivate your team to do this work and be on this team? What do they care about?

Record what feels relevant to the challenges you are trying to solve in the social awareness box of your 5-Square.

Where Do They Need to Be? (Defining Your Targets)

Now that you have a working diagnosis of where your team is, you are ready to think about targets—objectives—for engaging them. The accuracy of your targets depends on the strength of the diagnosis you just recorded in your 5-Square. Your goal here to is prioritize the behaviors and mindsets you just diagnosed, and articulate intended outcomes, or changes, you hope to accomplish through your engagement. Your targets will either be behaviors, mindsets, or relational conditions that you want to shift in and with others. In your shift from imposter to empowered leader, it may help you to think about engaging others through three phases:

1. Stepping back and building awareness about the dynamics between you. This is both above- and below-the-Green-Line work. If this does *not* feel personal then you are not having the real conversation.
2. Making new agreements about how to work together. Again, this is both above- the below-the-Green-Line work. The outcomes should be observable behaviors and mindsets that create new working structures and new emotional conditions.
3. Managing and coaching your team over time to live up to new expectations and effectively manage conflict in your working relationships.

Table 9.1 shows some examples of targets. Note the direct connection between diagnosis (where they are) and the target (where they need to be).

Table 9.1: Sample targets.

Where they are (your diagnosis)		Where they need to be (your targets)
Above the Green Line		
Coming to me to solve problems and make decisions they should be able to handle themselves	➡	Independently making day-to-day decisions, executing, then coming to me afterwards to debrief
Criticizing me and other team members behind closed doors	➡	Agreeing to and living up to the norm of going directly to the person and assuming best intentions
Below the Green Line		
Unaware of the impact that identity has had on the way we are both showing up in our work together	➡	Aware of the role identity plays for us and our students
Lacking confidence in their ability because I have communicated a lack of confidence and direction	➡	Empowered, motivated, and confident to own their work
Afraid to take risks or show struggle	➡	Feeling safe to take risks and ask for help because I model both

In the social awareness box of your 5-Square, generate a target for each of the where-they-are points that you have prioritized.

Step 5: Manage Relationships to Meet Your Targets

You have now done the internal and social awareness work that prepares you to engage others as an empowered, grounded leader. It is time to use all of your new awareness and strategies to choose better ways to connect, care, and challenge to reach your targets. Each person, group, and context will require a unique blend of these three ingredients for you to make the shifts you want to make.

Use the following questions as a springboard for creative thinking about engagement. Do this thinking in the context of your personal case study, and in connection with the targets you have generated.

First return to your vision for success on the first page of your 5-Square plan to mine for strategies.

- To stir creative juices, re-read your aspirational vision from Step 1. If new ideas have emerged as you worked through this chapter, add them to the vision.
- Now read the vision again, pulling out the leadership actions that you might use to connect with, care for, and challenge your team. Add what seems important to the Relationship Management box of your 5-Square.

Now let's dig deeper into the concepts of connection, care, and challenge to deepen your engagement strategies.

What does the person or group in question need from you to feel *connected* as human beings? Make sure you are not confusing this question with what they might *want*. Connection does not always feel good, but it must feel *real*. Consider these core behaviors of connection:

- *Authenticity*—How will you show up as *you*, the human being, with no imposter-driven persona?
- *Vulnerability*—What do you need to share at an emotional level (below your Green Line) about your imposter feelings, stories, and behaviors? Consider how that sharing could make it safe for others to share with you. Make sure you self-manage to describe those real emotions without actually being *in* them in the moment. This should feel like reclaiming your power, not ceding it. It takes courage and strength to share the things that hold you back with those who contribute to the dynamic. This has likely been a missing piece of your leadership as you struggled with imposter feelings.
- *Listening*—What do you need to find out to confirm or revise your diagnosis about where they are, especially if identity plays a critical role? Consider that asking *curious* questions and listening builds connection. There is nothing more effective you can do to make another person feel truly seen and heard.

What do they need from you to feel like you *care* about them?

- What can you say or do that will show your belief in their potential to grow? How can you paint a hopeful picture of this person thriving through this change? Your new belief in your own potential to grow should shine through and inspire those you lead.

■ How can you show your investment in their growth and your relationship, *even when they make mistakes*? How can you name the noble story that you hold for them with empathy and compassion? Again, your new perspective on yourself should bring a new energy to your care for others.

How do they need you to *challenge* them to grow and meet your targets? Effective challenge is likely the key to you moving beyond your imposter-related behaviors. Remember that care and challenge should always be a both/and.

■ How will you push back on people, contexts, and cultural norms that implicitly or explicitly communicate that you don't belong because you do not fit an archetype?

■ How will you begin directly challenging others to change dysfunctional mindsets and behaviors that you let slide as you struggled with your imposter feelings? Consider how you can speak to specific behaviors, broad impact, and why you care.

■ How can you ground difficult conversations in your standard? Remember that your values are the source of your power when challenging. When you start to second guess yourself, reground yourself in your standard.

■ How and when will you name your targets (the specific shifts you want you and your team to make)? How will you come back to them if the conversation veers off course?

■ What about when the other person does not change their behavior over time? Your imposter mindset wants to make that about something you did wrong. Irrelevant! This is not about you; it is about someone else's resistance and stuff. Moving forward, how will you deliberately escalate your level of challenge and care to effectively meet the resistance? Consider crafting your most high-candor and high-care headlines in advance.

■ Beyond accountability, how will you build your team's mindsets and skills if they struggle to make the shift to your new more empowered way of leading them?

Make sure you add your new engagement strategies to your 5-Square.

Other Work: Pause and Reflect

You have just created a draft plan for shifting from leading like an imposter to leading as a confident, grounded leader. It is important to understand that this plan is not a script that you will perform in a sequence. Engaging adaptively is inherently messy and you must be ready to meet people's needs where they are, in the moment, to reach your targets. You will need to use self-management strategies to avoid the habits of mind and behavior that get in your way when you are in the mess.

Now the Real Work Begins

We have all had epiphanies about our leadership that felt like game changers, but that faded into the background of our consciousness over time. Intentional practice is what connects an epiphany to transformational change. Remember the neuroscience behind this. We change when we build new neural pathways that replace the neural superhighways of our self-limiting habits.

Your job now is to take your 5-Square plan and work it, intentionally, every day in your work. Print it out and post it somewhere in your workspace. Keep it open on your desktop. You should be re-reading it regularly, especially when preparing for the kinds of interactions that you know are hard for you. This should be a living document that evolves as you evolve. Chapter 11 will provide more guidance about how to keep your plan alive over time.

In the next and final mindset chapter, we will turn our attention to the implementer self-limiting mindset.

Endnotes

1. Clance, P.R., and Imes, S. (1978). The imposter phenomenon in high achieving women: dynamics and therapeutic intervention. *Psychotherapy Theory, Research & Practice* 15 (3).
2. Wilding, M.J. (2020). 5 ways to overcome imposter syndrome in the workplace. *Business Insider.* https://www.businessinsider.com/5-ways-to-overcome-imposter-syndrome-in-the-workplace-2020-2.
3. Dweck, C.S. (2007). *Mindset: The New Psychology of Success.* New York: Ballantine Books.
4. Crenshaw, K. (1989). Demarginalizing the intersection of race and sex: a Black feminist critique of antidiscrimination doctrine, feminist theory and antiracist politics." University of Chicago Legal Forum Vol. 1989, Iss. 1, Article 8. https://chicagounbound.uchicago.edu/cgi/viewcontent.cgi?article=1052&context=uclf.

10 The Implementer

The ability to implement common organizational systems—playbooks—is crucial to effective leadership. However, this strength can become a leadership deficit when overplayed and becomes a default way of leading. Over-implementers come to believe that the leader's primary job is to execute the best practices they are given by others. Ultimately, they rely so fully on the playbook that they lose their connection to their own values, visions, and, ultimately, their teams. Consider the case of Jodie:

> Jodie was a successful teacher because she was able to implement the common 5th grade ELA curriculum with impeccable fidelity. Her instructional coaches raved about her delivery and pacing, and her students consistently outperformed their peers. She was quickly promoted to instructional coach and then assistant principal because she was able to support others to effectively implement instructional playbooks in their classrooms. Jodie was seen as a high performer and a kind person who had some growth areas when it came to people leadership challenges. In an organization that valued instructional leadership above all, Jodie was promoted to principal after two years as assistant principal.
>
> The transition to the principalship was smooth. School systems became more efficient, and Jodie worked incredibly hard to implement the plan she and her regional superintendent had created using the organization's playbook. Her team acknowledged that Jodie was a kind boss. The school was running smoothly, but little things began to change their perceptions of their new principal. Veteran teachers who had been using instructional approaches and materials that preceded the current instructional scope and sequence were asked to change course and align to the current

system—no exceptions. Central leadership had determined a new path with school culture systems. When the new path conflicted with some of the school's effective practices and traditions, Jodie automatically shifted to align with the new approach.

Teachers and students perceived Jodie's actions as sacrificing things about their craft and their school that they held dear. When they questioned the decisions, Jodie's responses sounded like organizational rhetoric. Over time, frustrated staff spread the story that Jodie had no vision of her own and was a yes-woman for the organization. These critiques stung Jodie and sowed seeds of self-doubt about her vision.

Then, in her third year as principal, the Covid pandemic hit and the playbook went out the window. Jodie waited anxiously, frustrated at not receiving a new playbook from her leaders. However, plans shifted almost weekly with the course of the disease. Jodie felt guilty and judged because she was not delivering the next level of playbook to her team, who was also anxiously waiting. Jodie spent her summer vacation perseverating on the ticking clock, countless unknowns, and how unprepared she would be in the fall.

Read this chapter if:

- ☐ You devote most of your energy to executing the organization's playbook and very little of your energy finding your personal why.
- ☐ When your stakeholders push back against your leadership decisions, you find it hard to explain or defend your decisions in a way that matters to them.
- ☐ A common critique of your leadership is that you do not have a clear vision.
- ☐ You get stuck as a leader in the gray areas when there are no right or wrong answers.
- ☐ You can get in the rut of doing what's expected even when it does not seem to be working.
- ☐ You struggle as a leader with unexpected changes.
- ☐ You measure your success primarily by outcomes and not by your process or performance.

Implementers in Education Organizations

Our sector has gotten smarter about how to pool our resources to build and implement better and better playbooks for teacher training, curriculum, and school culture, resulting in a positive impact on student achievement. Over time, we have increasingly valued the implementer competency in our selection of leaders, and for good reason. And I want to be clear that implementing playbooks and leading from one's values are not mutually exclusive. The problem happens when they are.

When we overvalue the implementer approach and style, we risk losing two essential conditions for teaching and learning: innovation and ownership. When too much is dictated we can disempower teachers, creating passive receivers of content and instructional strategies. We risk creating the one-size-fits-all factory model of teaching and learning that does not serve so many of our learners. Given the neuroscience of emotional contagion, consider the impact of these teacher mindsets on the conditions for student learning. When teachers see themselves as passive receivers of knowledge, students will, too.

The potential negative effects of overplaying the playbook are even more pronounced for Black and brown students, low-income students, and those with disabilities. When teachers overconform to an instructional approach and content, they can leave themselves—their identities and humanity—hanging up outside the door of their classrooms. This sends the message to students that they should also leave their identities and humanity at the door. This can be devastating for students who have already received the message from our white male supremacist society that they are not welcome. This is compounded when rigid classroom norms, expectations, and instructional approaches exclude students' own cultural norms and learning styles.

The Work Ahead

If you know that overplaying the playbook is getting in your way, keep reading. If you do not see yourself in the preceding checklist or case study, then maybe this chapter is not for you. Ask for feedback from your manager and a few trusted staff before making that decision. If others confirm your opinion, then skip ahead to the next chapter.

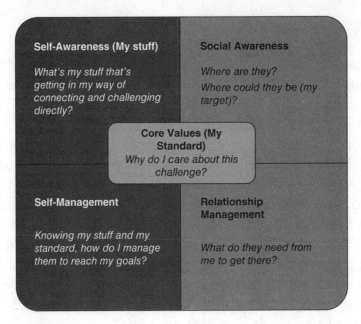

Self-Awareness (My stuff)

What's my stuff that's getting in my way of connecting and challenging directly?

Social Awareness

Where are they?
Where could they be (my target)?

Core Values (My Standard)
Why do I care about this challenge?

Self-Management

Knowing my stuff and my standard, how do I manage them to reach my goals?

Relationship Management

What do they need from me to get there?

Figure 10.1: The EI 5-Square.

This chapter is a self-contained learning journey. If you take it on, you could spend several months focusing on changing deeply engrained habits and building new adaptive muscles. Download a 5-Square learning plan template from www .noblestorygroup.com to build your plan. You will also need a journal to explore new thoughts and strategies.

Let's get started.

Step 1: Start with the End in Mind

Start by doing some aspirational thinking about what success will look like when you have moved beyond your over-implementer obstacles. Imagine what you will be doing differently and how it will ideally feel to lead from your values—your standard—and your vision. Pay particular attention to the situations you find most challenging (the preceding checklist might help you with that), but remember that your goal is to envision your *ideal* self in these situations. Remember that implementing and leading from values are not mutually exclusive. Your vision should include times when you implement *from* your values. To help you drill down, consider the following questions. What will it look like and feel like to:

- Be clear about your core values and your standard in the moment?
- Deliberately align your standards to the decisions you make?
- Challenge those who push back against your decisions with a *why* that comes from your standard?
- Deliberately choose each aspect of the playbook, aligning each decision to your standard?
- Connect with and challenge your stakeholders to find their standard in your decisions and in the playbook?
- Balance implementation with innovation in your leadership and in your team's work?

Record this reflection on the first page of your 5-Square. Journal first if that helps you think creatively. Give yourself uninterrupted time (at least 30 minutes) and emotional space to do this reflection. You might find it helpful to see an example vision from another 5-Square, and there is one in Appendix G. This aspirational thinking will become the vision of excellence that you use to generate awareness and strategies, and to measure your progress over time.

Step 2: Build Self-Awareness

When you have thought about the leader you want to be, you are ready to hold up the mirror and build awareness about what is getting in your way. As you think about this, think about specific times when your default decision to implement the playbook became an obstacle to reaching your desired outcomes. It may help to revisit the checklist at the beginning of this chapter as you think of examples. Once you have a representative example in mind, you will use it as a case study over the rest of this chapter. In coaching, we call these case studies behavioral moments. When we zoom in on these moments of emotional cause and effect, decision, and behavior, we are able to identify the chain reaction of a self-limiting mindset.

What Are Your Triggers?

First, identify the trigger moment of your case study. What happened in the exact moment that you decided you would automatically implement the protocol or practice? Something—how you received the playbook, a conversation with a manager or colleague, a voice in your head—triggered a feeling. What was the trigger moment for you? For Jodie in our case study, the trigger moment was when her larger-than-life superintendent unveiled the new playbook in a principal cohort meeting. Be as clear as you can about the specific moment of default decision in your case study, then think more broadly about how this kind of trigger shows up regularly in challenging leadership moments. Write down what comes up in the self-awareness box of your 5-Square.

What Sensations and Emotions Do You Experience?

Our triggers cause a self-limiting chain reaction that starts in our body. We process stress physiologically before we process it emotionally or intellectually. Our body is our early warning system—a fundamental aspect of self-awareness that we tend to overlook. Think back again to your trigger moment. Where did you feel your reaction in your body? Was it heat in your belly? A shortness of breath? A surge of energy in your chest? Note your physical reaction in the self-awareness box of your 5-Square.

Soon after the physical reaction comes an emotional reaction. Our emotional response to trigger moments is more complicated than we might think. In this implementer moment of decision, you may feel unsure about some parts of the protocol, or anxious about how your team will receive this new plan. Simultaneously, you may feel relief and gratitude that you don't have to figure this protocol out yourself! Write down the emotions you tend to experience in these moments in the self-awareness box. Push yourself to name as many as you can.

What Stories Get in Your Way?

Our stories come next—the inner narratives and assumptions about ourselves, others, and context that help us make sense of the world. Here, specifically focus on the stories that feed your self-limiting implementer behaviors. In your case study, what were you telling yourself about others, yourself, and the situation that led to your default decision to implement the playbook? It might help to connect each emotion with the thoughts that accompanied it. For example, if I am feeling anxious, the story might be, "How am I going to get my team to buy into this?" If I am feeling relief, my story might be, "I am so glad I don't have to think about this and can just *do* it!" Both examples are self-limiting stories because they distract you as a leader from thinking about what matters most in this moment—your standard.

Our Stories and Our Identities

The deeper our stories, the more connected they are to our identities. Growing up in America with our 400-year history of white male supremacy, it is inevitable that white cultural norms play a role in our self-limiting stories. According to Tema Okun in her 2019 article, the assumption that there is "one right way" and that groups should conform to that right way (as opposed to welcoming multiple ways to achieve an outcome) is a white cultural norm.[1] While the belief in "one way" may work for those of us who grew up with it, the norm will create dissonance for those from cultures with different ways of doing things. Consider how your valuing of "one right way" plays a role in your implementer mindset.

Write down all the self-limiting stories that came up in the self-awareness box of your 5-Square.

Then What Do You *Do*?

Your triggers, sensations and emotions, and self-limiting stories all lead you to *do* things that get in your way. These are your self-limiting behaviors. For default implementers these behaviors include some version of automatically complying with the organizational protocol and then influencing others to do the same, but in ways that may cause harm to individuals, culture, and outcomes. What they do *not* include—the crucial missing behavior—is reflecting on how the structure and decision align with your standard. In the case study you have been unpacking, what did you do that got in your way, from the moment you made the decision to move forward with the protocol through the many phases of implementation? Consider both the sequence of actions in decision-making and in follow-up interactions with your team over time. Think about both what you did and what you did not do that you wish you did. Write it all down in your self-awareness box.

What Is the Impact of Your Behaviors?

Now reflect on the full ripple effect of your actions. The impact likely goes much further than you have previously considered.

Wheatly's Green Line (see Chapter 1 and Figure 10.2) provides a helpful framework for considering impact. Start with the three circles above the line. Consider your intended leadership outcomes in your case study against your actual outcomes and the outcomes of staff and students.

Now focus on the three circles below the line and consider the social and emotional implications of your behavior. Again, start with self and follow the ripples out. How did your actions affect your self-perception? How did your actions affect your relationships with others? How might it have affected their perceptions of themselves?

Those who automatically implement can usually make the cause-effect link between their behavior and others' critiques about their vision, but that is only one personal level of a much broader impact. The beginning of this chapter listed several ways that default implementing impacts learning organizations. What is your personal version of this story? List all the ripple effects of your self-limiting behaviors on the conditions for learning in your learning community. You should be considering ways your actions disempower and exclude, particularly through the lens of identity, power, and privilege.

Take a few minutes to journal. When you think you have a pretty exhaustive list, consider sharing with a trusted colleague or manager to see if they can think of anything you might have missed (we all have blind spots about our impact). Then record the levels of impact that matter the most in your 5-Square.

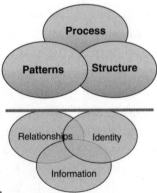

Figure 10.2: Wheatly's Six-Circle Model.

Pause and Reflect

At this point, I encourage you to take both a literal and metaphorical deep breath. Step back and offer yourself both grace and gratitude for the work you have done so far. It is painful to confront the stories we tell ourselves and the impact that our actions have on ourselves and those around us. It is natural to feel down on ourselves at this moment. However, when we confront deep and personal obstacles we open the door to change and growth. With self-awareness comes an opportunity you may not have known you had: to choose a more empowering and effective way of being.

This choosing begins with building new self-management strategies that can shift your stories and behaviors.

Step 3: Build Self-Management Strategies

We cannot stop our triggers and our emotions; they are hardwired. However, we can *manage* triggers and emotions once we become aware of them. Self-management is about choosing how we react to triggers and emotions by choosing new stories and behaviors.

In Chapter 2, you read about the three basic self-management strategies we use in our 5-Square coaching: creating space, values-driven self-talk, and rewriting a noble story. For a deeper explanation, go back and re-read. Now we will go straight into the process of building these strategies.

Create Space Between Trigger and Response

First, *slow down*. Creating a few seconds of space between our triggers and what we actually do is a prerequisite to accessing other self-management strategies. This begins in our bodies, managing sensations to create a window of time to interrupt our emotional hijack and come back to our thinking brains. What can you do to create space between your triggers and your actions?

- Start by considering what you already do that might serve you in trigger moments. Do you already have meditative practices in your life, like yoga, prayer, or a mindfulness practice? If you do, you probably already have breathing strategies you can bring to bear. A couple of deep breaths over a matter of seconds could be all you need to regain your ability to think clearly.

- There may be other micromovements that you do already with your body that calm you down (from taking a sip of water to shifting your posture). Micromovements are most effective when they connect directly to the part of your body where you feel your trigger. If you feel it in your shoulders, is there a shoulder flex that might work? If you ball up your fists, what finger movements might release tension?
- Interrupting the moment with a new activity also works if you have the time. Consider the impact on your chain reaction of walking away from your computer for a glass of water, a walk around the block, or a moment with another person or a pet. If it slows you down, then it works.

Write down at least one strategy to slow down and interrupt the reaction to your trigger in the self-management box of your 5-Square

Ground in Your Standard with Self-Coaching

 Once you have slowed down and returned to your thinking brain, access your inner coach. *Building a strong inner coach voice that is grounded in your standard—your values—will be* the *most important thing you do to overcome your implementer self-limiting mindset.* This is because, right now, you are out of practice with accessing your standard in the moments of decision-making as a leader.

Remember the rudder metaphor from Chapter 3 (see Figure 10.3)? Without its rudder. a boat goes in circles, no matter how high tech the rest of its components. No matter how smart and skilled we are, when we do not lead from our standard we too go in circles. School leaders make many adaptive decisions every day, and each one has multiple right answers. As a leader you can make decisions that are not wrong, but that do not move you or your team forward on a path. The strength of

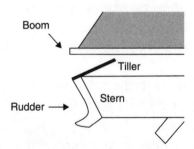

Figure 10.3: The rudder.

the connection between your standard and your decisions determines how straight a path you are on. Stakeholders see that path as your vision in action.

When we see our job as implementing the playbook, we tend to stop making the effort to connect our decisions to our standard. Not using that muscle leads to atrophy. The playbook does not always have an answer for a problem, or our teams push back against the playbook, so you can feel lost. This is why your primary task is to strengthen the muscle of connecting to standard in the decision-making moment.

The first step is to build awareness of the values at the core of your standard. To mine for these values, start with the self-limiting stories and behaviors from your 5-Square self-awareness reflection. Why do you care about *not* believing those stories and acting out those behaviors anymore? Your answers likely connect to who you want to be as a leader, what you want to accomplish, and what you really believe about teaching and learning. In your journal, start listing all the reasons you care that come up. When you think you have a relatively complete list, review and prioritize your top five. This should be an emotional exercise that connects you to your gut.

Now, for each of your prioritized care statements, go deeper. *Why* is this statement important to you? What is that *about* for you? For each answer, try to follow with another why question. Peel the onion; there are many layers of meaning that you can uncover. Your goal here is to try to get to core values.

Example:

I want to be seen as a strong leader. (Why?)

I want to feel like, and be seen as, running *my* school. (Why?)

Because I believe strong school leaders own every aspect of their learning communities. (Why?)

Because when you own everything, you are really measuring everything against who you are and your own beliefs . . . your authentic self.

Core Value: Authenticity

Experiment with this "why" conversation and see what it surfaces. You will know when you are done when you can say and feel, "This one is about (a value or value statement) for me." Don't overthink this—it's more of an emotional than logical exercise. Do this for each of the journal statements that you prioritized and then add those core values to the center square of your 5-Square.

You have just practiced surfacing your power. Now think about how to harness that power in the moment with self-coaching. Take yourself back to the trigger moment in your case study. What could your inner coach have said to activate your leadership rudder? Consider what your inner coach might tell you about:

■ What you believe about ownership and authenticity.
■ What you believe about teaching and learning and the core conditions for both.
■ What your staff and students really need to move toward their goals relative to this decision.
■ How this decision connects to what is at your core as a person.

Write down what comes up in your journal.

Now, consider how your values relate to your identities. According to the idea of intersectionality (Crenshaw 1989),[2] we all have many identities, or facets of self, that make up who we are. Some of these include gender, race, sexuality, class, ability, place of origin, and religion, but the list is really only limited by the number of ways we make sense of ourselves and each other in the world. We know that identity markers can be used to marginalize or privilege groups. Yet we also know that our identities are a source of our personal power. They weave together to create our cultures, from family culture to our many different group cultures. From these interwoven identity groups, we learn what matters to us in the world.

Re-read the list of values and inner-coach statements you just generated. Consider how your identities connect with and inform them. How can an intentional anchoring in your identities empower you to shift your implementer stories and behaviors? Weave your identity narratives into the inner-coach statements you just wrote.

Finally, crystallize what means the most to you in brief phrases that your inner coach can bring to the moment, and that will be easy to access. Think bumper sticker or T-shirt. Write up to five of these in your 5-Square self-management box. Some examples from leaders managing implementer mindset include:

What's your standard and what's your stuff in this?
Why do you care?
They chose you for this job because of your standard. Now lead from it!

If this were your child, what would you want?

How are you creating the conditions for strong teaching and learning for all students here?

Rewrite Noble Stories

Now we shift to stories that need revising related to what you tell yourself about others.

As an over-implementer, you likely tell yourself self-limiting stories about two groups: 1) those you assume criticize you for over-implementing, and 2) those you believe expect you to implement the whole playbook. There is probably a fear-based story you have for each group. What do they believe about you as a leader? What are you afraid they would think and do if you *did* ground your decisions in your values? Give these questions some thought, then go back and add them to your other self-limiting stories in the self-awareness box of your 5-square.

Now, *flip your stories*. Replace these fear-based "worst case scenarios" with alternative narratives that emphasize the most affirming stories each group could possibly think about you leading from your standard. The key question is this:

What could you choose to believe your stakeholders think about you leading more from your standard that would help you overcome your default implementer tendencies?

The answers to this question are your noble stories. They are another form of self-coaching. Add the stories that will support you the most when you are triggered to your self-management square.

Self-Work: Pause and Reflect

You have now completed the left side of the 5-Square and, in doing so, you have generated a game plan for managing your default implementer "stuff" and instead grounding your leadership in your standard. If you work these strategies deliberately over time, you will begin to shift habits of mind you may have thought to be fixed.

Now we move to the right side of the 5-Square to tackle the default implementer habits at play between you and others.

Step 4: Build Social Awareness to Diagnose Needs and Set Targets

 With your new self-awareness and intention to self-manage, you are prepared to see others more clearly. As you shift your focus from self to others, the first question for you to consider is a diagnostic one: *Where are they?* This simple question activates cognitive empathy: your ability to accurately read other people's emotional state and needs. Taking perspective will help you diagnose others' inner obstacles and help you determine your targets for engaging them.

You should ask this question in relation to your implementer growth area. Your analysis should focus on individuals, teams, and your organization's culture as a whole. Be sure to reflect both above and below Wheatly's Green Line. You might start with the "impact" reflection you added to your self-awareness box. Following are some additional questions to consider:

- What default cultural norms—assumptions about the way things work—have your implementer-driven behaviors created?
- How might overplaying implementation over time have created bad habits for your team around compliance? Or potentially have weakened adaptability muscles?
- What stories do some of your team have about your vision and relationship with the organization that may not be serving you?
- What stories might your team have about what *you* believe about *them* based on what competencies you have and have not valued and celebrated over time?
- How might your team be feeling about their level of involvement in decision-making and creative freedom in the school and in their classrooms?
- How does identity impact the dynamic here? What lines of privilege and power between you and your team feed this challenge for you and for them? Remember that "one right way" is considered a white supremacist norm. How might people who value "many right ways" be impacted by this norm, especially when they represent nondominant identities.
- What does your team care about? How could you leverage their standard to tap into their motivation?

Record what feels relevant to the challenges you are trying to solve in the Social Awareness box of your 5-Square.

Where Do They Need to Be? (Defining Your Targets)

Now that you have a working diagnosis of where your team is, you are ready to think about targets—objectives—for engaging them. The accuracy of your targets depends on the strength of the diagnosis you just recorded in your 5-Square. Your goal here is to prioritize the behaviors and mindsets you just diagnosed, and articulate intended outcomes, or changes, you hope to accomplish through your engagement. Your targets should include behaviors, mindsets, or relational conditions that you want to work on with them. Shifting your team's perceptions should be a theme. If you could rewrite the stories they tell themselves about you as a leader and themselves as educators in your school, what would the new stories be?

Table 10.1 shows some examples of targets. Note the direct connection between diagnosis (where they are) and the target (where they need to be).

Add the targets you will prioritize to the social awareness box of your 5-Square.

Step 5: Manage Relationships to Meet Your Targets

You have now done the internal work and perspective-taking to prepare yourself to engage others as a standards-driven leader. This is where the rubber meets the road. You are ready to use all of your new awareness and strategies to choose better ways to connect, care, and challenge to reach your targets. Each person, group, and context will require a unique blend of these three ingredients for you to make the shifts you want to make.

Use the following questions as a springboard for creative thinking about engagement. Do this thinking in the context of your personal case study, and in connection with the targets you have generated.

Table 10.1: Sample targets.

Where they are (your diagnosis)		Where they need to be (your targets)
Above the Green Line		
Questioning schoolwide decisions and not fully committing, then implementing haphazardly	➡	Fully committing to schoolwide decisions and implementing them with fidelity
Waiting to be told what to do in moments of adaptive challenge in which they should be making their own decisions	➡	Solving problems on their own and turning to each other for support when they need it
Below the Green Line		
Perceive me as not having vision, or not leading from my vision, and being a "yes" person	➡	Believing that I make leadership decisions from my own standard, my *why*
Feeling disempowered in their craft and contributions to our school	➡	Believing that there are meaningful ways in which they are empowered to innovate and contribute to decisions (especially on the *how*)
Feeling that they don't have a voice, and that their identities are not accepted in our school	➡	Feeling that their identity-based strengths are valued as important contributors to our collective success, and that we as a team are aware of the equity dangers of "one right way"

First return to your vision for success on the first page of your 5-Square plan:

- To get your creative juices flowing, re-read your aspirational vision from Step 1. If new ideas about how you would ideally be leading have come up while working through this chapter, add them to the vision.
- Now read the vision again, pulling out the leadership actions that you might use to connect with, care for, and challenge your team. Add what resonates most to the relationship management box of your 5-Square.

Now let's dig deeper into the concepts of connection, care, and challenge to deepen your engagement strategies.

What does the person or group in question need from you to feel *connected* as human beings? Make sure you are not confusing this question with what they might *want*. Connection does not always feel good, but it must feel *real*. Consider these core behaviors of connection:

- *Authenticity*—How will you show up as *you*, the human being, without a manufactured persona?
- *Vulnerability*—What do you need to share at an emotional level (below your Green Line) about your overreliance on implementing the game plan and your intentions to lead more deeply from your vision? Consider how that sharing could make it safe for others to share with you. Make sure you self-manage to describe those real emotions without actually being *in* them in the moment. This should feel like claiming your power, not ceding it. It takes courage and strength to share the things that hold you back. You should also see this as an opportunity to shift perceptions by adding a new chapter to others' story about you.
- *Listening to person*—What do you need to find out to confirm or revise your diagnosis about where they are, especially if equity is at play? What harms has your "one right way" behavior caused? Consider that asking *curious* questions and listening builds connection. There is nothing more effective you can do to make another person feel truly seen and heard.
- *Listening to issues*—How can you self-manage to truly listen to and consider other points of view on decisions?
- *Values connection*—The opposite of rote implementing is values-driven decision-making. How can you surface others' standard and connect yours with theirs when considering decisions, particularly when you may not see eye to eye on an issue?

Now consider what they need from you to feel like you *care* about them? Remember that care in the 5-Square is not just about empathy, but also your belief in people's ability to grow and your investment in helping them grow.

- What can you say or do to affirm and value others' standards and strengths?
- How can you reflect your noble story back to them?
- How can you create meaningful ways for people to innovate and contribute to the direction of your school?

- How can you create meaningful spaces for people to provide input at the right time and on the issues they care about?
- Whether you agree or disagree, how can you acknowledge that there is not one right way?
- How can you advocate for and protect what your team cares about the most?

Finally, how do you need to *challenge* your team to meet your targets? Effective challenge is likely the key to you moving beyond being perceived as a default implementer. Remember that care and challenge should always be a both/and.

- How will you share your decisions, whether they align to the playbook or not, firmly grounded in your standard?
- How will you directly challenge others when they wrongfully accuse you of default implementing? You cannot let this narrative stand if it is not true about a decision! Consider how you can speak to their specific behaviors, their impact on you and the team, and why you care about this accusation.
- How can you be seen fighting for what you deeply believe is right for your school, students, staff, and families, even when others disagree with you? You best challenge the implementer narrative when people experience your standard and passion.
- How will your challenge escalate with people who are unable to shift their perception of you as an implementer even as you grow into leading from your values and vision?

Make sure you add all of your new Relationship Management strategies to your 5-Square.

Other Work: Pause and Reflect

You have just created a plan to shift from default implementing to leading from your standard. It is important to understand that this plan is not a script you will perform in a sequence. Engaging in adaptive challenges with others is inherently messy and you must choose the right balance of connection, care, and challenge in the moment to reach your targets. It will take deliberate self-management to avoid the habits of mind and behavior that get in your way.

Now the Real Work Begins

We have all had epiphanies about our leadership that felt like game changers, but that faded into the background of our consciousness over time. Intentional practice is what connects new awareness to transformational change. Remember the neuroscience behind this. We change when we build new neural pathways that replace the neural superhighways of our self-limiting habits.

Your job now is to take your 5-Square plan and work it, intentionally, every day into your work. Print it out and post it somewhere in your workspace. Keep it open on your desktop. You should be re-reading it regularly, especially when preparing for the kinds of interactions that you know are hard for you. This should be a living document that evolves as you evolve. The next (and final) chapter will provide more guidance about how to keep your plan alive over time.

Endnotes

1. Okun, T. (2019). White Supremacy Culture. DRworksBook. www.dismantlingracism.org.
2. Crenshaw, K. (1989). Demarginalizing the intersection of race and sex: a Black feminist critique of antidiscrimination doctrine, feminist theory and antiracist politics. *University of Chicago Legal Forum* Vol. 1989, Iss. 1, Article 8. https://chicagounbound.uchicago.edu/cgi/viewcontent.cgi?article=1052&context=uclf.

III Staying Focused Over Time

Chapter 11: Working Your 5-Square for Lasting Behavior Change

11 Working Your 5-Square for Lasting Behavior Change

You have probably read at least one other chapter in this book and used that chapter to create your own 5-Square—your own internal and interpersonal plan for shifting a mindset and behaviors that have been an obstacle to reaching your full potential as a leader. Hopefully you arrive at this chapter with new awareness about yourself and your communities that will allow you to leverage your standard and manage your stuff so that you see others more clearly, set clearer and stronger adaptive leadership targets, and choose ways to engage others more effectively to achieve those targets. You have identified habits of mind and behavior that don't serve you, and you have a plan.

From a neuroscience perspective, you have identified neural superhighways created over the course of your life that do not serve you, and you are beginning to carve out a new neural pathway to replace it. It's a footpath right now, but the good news is that you can turn that pathway into a new highway while the old highway withers into an old country road. The not-so-good news is that the process takes a long time and requires a lot of very intentional practice.

Several years ago I decided that I had enough personal baggage to merit going to therapy. It was a wonderful and challenging experience, therapy. I had some major epiphanies about where some of my "less functional" behaviors come from. One of them—being overcritical of and micromanaging my kids—was one I wanted to change. Unfortunately, despite what felt like life-changing new awareness about my parenting behavior, I still hear myself nagging my kids when they don't clear their breakfast dishes or borrow my clothes without asking. Therein lies the hard truth about self-awareness and self-management: building new self-awareness (even rock-your-world self-awareness) will not in itself change our behavior.

So, while you have new awareness and a plan, your new leadership competency journey has just begun. Now you have to work it. Over the rest of this chapter you will develop a plan for working your 5-Square over time. You should treat this like any other important project plan for which you leverage your personal organization system to achieve your goals.

Build Your System

Your goal is to focus on this growth intention over time. That means holding your new awareness and working your internal and interpersonal strategies in your everyday work. What can you do every day, week, or month that will support you to maintain this kind of focus? The following are some strategies that have worked with leaders I have coached.

Set Measurable and Time-Bound Goals

How will you know if you are growing? What would you expect to see and feel? What would you expect others to be saying and doing? And how can you measure all of this? Craft a handful of goals and metrics you could apply over time. Most may be informal, but you may also have some more formal metrics (leadership 360s, organizational culture surveys) that you might use. Once you have listed your goals, schedule times that you will make space to reflect on progress. Yes, put these dates on your calendar and hold time to reflect. What doesn't get scheduled and measured doesn't get done.

Use Your Technology

We have a brave new world of apps and devices that help us track our steps, calories, screen time, and just about anything else we want to track. How could you leverage your tech to help you stay focused on practicing your new strategies? The starting line would be calendar reminders, but the sky (and your tech savvy) is the limit.

Work Your 5-Square

You have put a lot of work into creating a robust plan of action. Now it is time to *use* it. My hope for you is that this 5-Square plan lives in your everyday work.

You have it visually present as a reminder. It is a tool you can consult to prepare for a challenge. It is there to reflect on and even improve after a challenge. The more you use it, the more your new habit becomes engrained in your brain. How can you make your 5-Square a living, breathing tool?

Create Mindful Space

I promise you that you won't be able to make the changes you desire if you never slow down. This work takes emotional space. How will you create the space to slow down, recharge your emotional battery, and just get grounded? A brief (10 minutes or less) daily mindfulness practice is one example. Walking, running, swimming, and any other number of solo physical activities also count. You might go back to your work from Chapter 3 to find your perfect activity. Whatever you choose, make sure it meets the goal of you disconnecting from the rat race and just being with yourself with no agenda.

Build Your Support Network

No matter how robust our personal systems and how deep our personal commitment is to change, we more effectively focus on big goals when we have others supporting us. A group of trusted people across roles and life contexts can provide encouragement, community, mindful focus, feedback, and accountability when we invite them into our change process. Consider what it would look and feel like to share what you are working on and the content of your 5-Square with your support network. Think about how your partner, friends, or even your kids could bring awareness to your moments of challenge and success and remind you of your strategies in your personal life. Think about how your manager and/or coach could incorporate your 5-Square into your regular check-ins, particularly when the two of you are grappling together with adaptive problem solving. Consider ways that your colleagues could become peer coaches, or what a professional learning community would look like working on a common self-limiting belief together.

Now take this community concept to the next level. Imagine what it would look and sound like to invite your teachers, staff, and students into this transformative, personal learning journey. How does it feel to think about that? Do you think that letting them in on your plan would diminish you? How would you react in their place? Would hearing from your leader that she wants to be more effective and at the same time for her and you to be happier seem negative? Or would it be a plus for your learning community? The answer brings you back to a core premise of this book.

Social–Emotional Leadership: Creating the Conditions for Adult Social–Emotional Learning

I started *The Noble School Leader* with the claim that the book is about social–emotional learning, and that by engaging in social–emotional learning a leader becomes a social–emotional leader. It is the *how* of social–emotional leadership. School leaders create the conditions for adult social–emotional learning, first and foremost by doing their own social–emotional learning. Social–emotional learning conditions really are emotional conditions, and leaders create these conditions in their community through their day-to-day behavior. How teachers, staff, and students experience our example and our emotional contagion determines the permission, the safety, and the inspiration they feel to do their own social–emotional learning.

A social–emotional learning community where all students feel empowered to learn is predicated on their teachers feeling empowered to learn. A social–emotional learning community where adults feel empowered to learn is one in which their leaders are seen learning and growing over time. The social–emotional learning you have begun in this book is the key to your social–emotional leadership. Doing the work intentionally and *publicly* with your learning community is how you create the conditions for the children and adults you lead to reach their potential.

Appendices
Introduction

In the seven chapters of Part Two, "Working the 5-Square," you built your own 5-Square learning plans to shift mindsets and behaviors that are getting in your way. Here I include example 5-Square learning plans for each of these seven leadership obstacles. Each plan is a composite of actual learning plans generated by leaders I have coached who worked on that specific obstacle themselves. These examples are not intended to be the "right answer" to all the reflective questions asked in each chapter. The awareness and strategies generated in your 5-Square are not technical skills or knowledge that others can replicate. Rather, these examples are included to illustrate the level of depth and breadth of thinking you are aiming for. They also provide an example of how information can be organized in the template for those who appreciate structural guidance.

Appendix A: Transactional Leader Sample 5-Square Development Plan

Aspirational Leadership Headline

I want to recognize the adaptive needs of my people in context and effectively engage with them to move us forward toward our goals.

Vision for Success

What I Will Be Doing/Saying

- Asking curious questions, above and below the Green Line, to figure out where people are.
- Actively listening with diagnostic empathy at an emotional and values level.
- Looking at every decision through the technical and adaptive lenses.
- Thinking about the impact of decisions and words across my web of stakeholders.
- Stopping and effectively changing course in the moment when I sense the real conversation has shifted below the Green Line.
- Be present and aware of my own emotions as a radar.
- Share my emotions as data, without being in them, to connect at a human level.

How I Will Feel When I'm Leading This Way

- Present
- Grounded in my values and emotions in the moment
- Energized
- Calm
- Purposeful

What Others Will Be Doing/Saying

- Sharing their emotions and values with me.
- Opening up because I am listening.
- Giving me a second chance because my actions show a shift.

What Others Will Be Feeling

- Like they can bring more of themselves to work.
- Trusting me at a human level.
- Connected with me; we have a real relationship.

Self-Awareness (Our Stuff)	Social Awareness
Triggers: People react in a messy emotional way and push back against expectations. **Emotions:** Surprised. Frustrated (them and me). Impatient/urgent. Disappointed (them). Unsuccessful/incompetent (me). Afraid. Stuck. **Self-limiting stories:** Where is this coming from?! So not necessary. Why can't they just do what is expected of them? We are adults! They should be able to do their jobs without this emotional drama! They are not being professional. *And* I don't know what to do to move this person forward. I am bad at these situations. I feel stuck.	**Where is this person/team** right now? (consider emotions, beliefs/mindsets, values, identity, and behaviors) <ul><li>Not meeting deadlines.</li><li>Not communicating about obstacles.</li><li>Feeling like I am not professionally and personally invested in them.</li><li>Not invested in the work that is late.</li><li>Not feeling safe to be honest for fear of consequences.</li><li>Unhappy at work.</li></ul>

<u>Identify:</u>

- I was educated and trained in the white cultural norms or urgency and objectivity.
- As a child, conflict was not surfaced. We responded with icy silence.

<u>Behaviors:</u>

- Push forward in the work without addressing people's needs. Ignore conflicts.
- Allow subtext to grow.
- Allow dysfunctional team behaviors to keep moving fast.
- Pay little attention to the team's narrative, then be surprised by conflict.

<u>Impact:</u>

- Damage relationships.
- Create resentments, conflicts.
- Allow others to create a negative narrative about me, the school.
- Ultimately, damage the psychological safety of the learning space.

Where can they be/Your target (consider emotions, beliefs/mindsets, values, identity, and behaviors)

- Feeling seen, heard, and valued by me.
- Trusting that I will not judge them for their struggle.
- Understanding the value of the late work to the team and kids.
- Happy and thriving at work.

Values (Our Standard)

(Consider your core values holistically as well as in this context. Consider the connection to your identity.)

- Psychological safety—We need it to learn and grow. These are emotional conditions, so I need to pay attention to emotions.
- Growth mindset—I believe and act like a leader who believes anyone can grow.
- Equity leader—The BIPOC leaders I manage feel that I set them up for success. They feel prepared to lead.

Self-Management

How will you manage your triggers? (consider strategies like breathing, self-talk, anchoring in values, planning ahead)

Deep breath—into the irritation and impatience

Self-coaching

Slow down and listen below the Green Line.

Your job is to create safety and trust.

It's not about you. what do *they* need?

What *noble story* do you need to believe about this person/group to effectively connect and reach your targets?

Everyone wants to be successful and do right by our kids. They may need something different than you need to get there.

Relationship Management

What does this person need from you to meet the target?

Connect:

- Stop talking, listen with curiosity, and ask curious questions about where they are.
- Get curious about their lives.
- Share where I am, naming my real emotions.
- Own my stuff that might be getting in thew way.

Care personally:

- Affirm their values, strengths, and potential.
- Normalize struggle—it's how we grow.
- Show care about their lives, their humanity.

Challenge directly:

- Name their behavior, its impact, and why I care
- Challenge them to own their outcomes and performance
- Challenge them to recommit to our relationship just as I am doing

Appendix B: Unintended Enabler 5-Square Development Plan

Aspirational Leadership Headline

I want to lead an urgent, joyful team that trusts each other to lean into healthy conflict in order to get further faster.

Vision for Success

What I Will Be Doing/Saying

- Saying what is on my mind without a filter, knowing that if I am misunderstood, we will work through it.
  - This is what I want to say right now, and we'll work through the meaning of it together.
- Figuring out what people need in the moment.
- Most of the time we are together we are in that high-energy sprint together.
- Naming my standard in the moment when it is not being met.
- Having a clear plan to escalate my challenge when my standard is repeatedly not met over time, either intentionally or unintentionally.

How I Will Feel When I'm Leading This Way:

- Trusting
- Fearless
- More energized
- Healthy discomfort
- Excited about the next opportunity to move the work forward
- Excited about the next meeting

What Others Will Be Doing/Saying

- Free flow of ideas and communication.
- Healthy debate . . . productive conflict to get at the truth of what's really happening. All or most of the time.
- People are showing up authentically,
- Giving 100% consistently.
- Not sitting back and waiting for their turn . . . jumping in.

How Others Will Feel When I Am Leading This Way

- Brave, courageous, unchained, free
- Trusting
- Refreshed . . . relieved
- Intense, edgy discovery . . . productive nervousness
- Enlightened
- Energized
- Engaged
- Looking forward to our time together
- Joyful

Self-Awareness (Our Stuff)	Social Awareness
Triggers:	**Where is this person/team** right now? (Consider emotions, beliefs/mindsets, values, identity, and behaviors)
No response (silence), blank stares. Good people suffering. Perception that I might or did hurt someone.	■ Not meeting deadlines.
Emotions:	■ Spreading negativity with colleagues.
Remorse/regret. Fear. Confusion. Indecision. Shame. Resentment. Incompetence.	■ Not invested in tasks,
Self-limiting stories:	■ Not aware of the impact of their behavior.
Their silence means I messed up or hurt them. Maybe I'm wrong and being unreasonable in my expectations. If I say this, I will damage our relationship. They may even quit. But they need to do their job! And I am so bad at difficult conversations. I am so bad at this.	■ Not invested in our relationship, or feeling connected with me.
	■ Not feeling held accountable, especially across identity lines.
Identity:	**Where can they be/Your Target** (Consider emotions, beliefs/mindsets, values, identity, and behaviors)
■ Raised in a conflict averse family. Publicly we were taught to make everyone feel good.	■ Meeting deadlines.
■ Privilege guilt—I am the recipient of inequitable, racist privilege.	■ Invested in our working relationship and feeling connected and accountable.
Behaviors:	■ Understanding and valuing the impact of their behavior on themselves, their team, and kids.
Silence. Sugarcoating the message. Let small things become big things. Hold different people to different standards.	■ Feeling challenged and like they are growing.
Impact:	
■ Team left unsure of where they stand with me, which creates self-doubt.	
■ I lose credibility as an inconsistent leader.	
■ Adult and student culture chaotic due to lack of read expectations.	

Values (Our Standard)

(Consider your core values holistically and in the current context. Consider the connection to your identities.)

- ■ Personal alignment—Living in sync with my values and identity to reach my full potential.
- ■ Equity—I am not creating a more just world by holding BIPOC people to a lower standard. *That* makes me part of the problem.
- ■ Growth—Challenge is a key ingredient to learning and growing.

Self-Management	Relationship Management

Self-Management

How will you manage your triggers? (consider strategies like breathing, self-talk, anchoring in values, planning ahead)

Breathe and relax my shoulders. Count to three.

Self-coaching:

- ■ People can't grow without challenge. That's your job.
- ■ Equity leadership requires high standards, not lowering the bar.

What *noble story* do you need to believe about this person/group to effectively connect and reach your targets?

People want to grow and do a good job. They want and expect challenge to help them get there.

Relationship Management

What does this person need from you to meet the target?

Connect:

- ■ Name the real issues and be real about how I feel about them.
- ■ Then listen and ask curious questions to see where they are.
- ■ Own my part, if any, in the problem.

Care personally:

- ■ Affirm values, strengths.
- ■ Affirm my belief in their potential.

Challenge directly:

- ■ Name their unproductive behavior, its impact, and why I care.
- ■ Name crystal clear expectations and how I will hold them accountable
- ■ Challenge them to own their stuff.
- ■ Challenge them to recommit to our working relationship.
- ■ Restate impact and expectations over time if behavior continues. Have a plan for escalating.

Appendix C: Negative Controller Sample 5-Square Development Plan

Aspirational Vision

I want to build strong relationships with all kinds of people who allow me to truly connect with them, even when I am being direct and holding them accountable.

What I Am Doing

- I am able to flip the switch back and forth between authentic personal conversation then jump into the content.
- Truly listening. Listening completely.
- Asking more questions. Probing. I'm interested in finding the root cause.
- Responding by sharing my own emotions, hopes, and challenges.
- Smiling (affect).

What I Am Feeling

- Valuing the personal conversation.
- At ease and successful in the personal conversation.
- Different level of connection.
- Sports teammate metaphor . . . I trust on a deeper level.
- Sense of accomplishment.

What Others Are Doing

- Smiling.
- Behaviors that show that they're clearly engaged.
- Asking for next steps, proactively asking for when the follow-up will be.
- Saying thank you.
- Self-reporting success . . . authentically sharing things they actually feel good about.

What Others Are Feeling

- Supported . . . My leader understands and value my contributions, work, effort, persistence.
- The job is still tough, but I feel really supported and more optimistic about the outcome.
- Valued. My leader thinks I am great.

Self-Awareness (Our Stuff)	Social Awareness
Triggers: Educators not meeting expectations and/or complaining/getting frustrated, putting themselves before kids. _Emotions:_ Frustrated. Disgusted and disappointed. Insecure. Afraid. Hopeless. Incompetent. _Self-limiting stories:_ I shouldn't have to teach adults how to be adults. That isn't my job. You're a grown-up! You shouldn't need empathy. If I want something to really work at this school, I have to do it myself. And am I doing enough? Is this my fault? _Identity:_ A small number of deeply committed teachers are the reason I am here today. I owe my success to their love and going above and beyond for me.	**Where is this person/team** right now? (consider emotions, beliefs/mindsets, values, identity, and behaviors) ■ Not feeling cared for or trusted, especially across our lines of difference (race). ■ Not feeling safe to grow, take risks. ■ Not trusting each other, me. ■ Coming to me to make every little decision. ■ Working really hard and believing in kids and mission.

Behaviors:

- Do other people's work for them.
- Engage adults in an impatient transactional (vs. developmental) way.
- Write off people who I perceive to be making excuses

Impact:

- Adults don't feel like I care about or believe in them or trust them.
- Not creating conditions where my people can grow.
- Adults are suffering and kids don't get the teachers they need.

Where can they be/Your Target (consider emotions, beliefs/mindsets, values, identity, and behaviors)

- Feeling cared for, believing they can do it.
- Feeling successful and optimistic at work.
- Resilient—getting back up after struggling.
- Owning decisions, being honest about challenges.
- Having fun.

Values (Our Standard)

(Consider your core values holistically as well as in the negative controller context, and the connection of these values to your identities.)

- **Equity**—Our kids deserve the best and I will do *anything* for *every* kid. I am here because some teachers did that for me. It takes strong teachers and adults to do that, and it's my job to make my adults strong for my kids.
- **Development**—it's my job to help educators reach their potential.

Self-Management

How will you manage your triggers? (consider strategies like breathing, self-talk, anchoring in values, planning ahead)

Create space

- Take a deep breath to slow down.
- Take time before to ground (choose time and place).

Self-talk

- Our kids won't get the best if I don't develop my team.
- People need to know that I believe in them to grow, and I can't fake it.
- How would I engage them if they were a student?
- Every interaction I have is an opportunity for someone to learn. Stop taking that away.

Relationship Management

What does this person need from you to meet the target?

Connect:

- Listen curiously and ask questions.
- Take in feedback without getting upset.
- Share my own struggles and emotions connected to current challenges as well as our relationship.

Care personally:

- Affirm challenges and emotions.
- Focus more on wins than struggles.
- Express care, value, belief (like I do with kids).
- Normalize struggle (it's how we grow and learn).

What *noble story* do you need to believe about this person/group to effectively connect and reach your targets?	Challenge directly:
■ Remember why I hired them, and what they have done recently that's great.	■ Build structures around feedback to make it less personal and more developmental.
■ Adults are just like kids, they want to win	■ Directly name behaviors that don't reach our bar and name impact on kids and staff.
■ Their actions are a resistance strategy.	■ Ground in our common values. (This is about ___)
■ This is not a reflection of who they are.	

Appendix D: Pacesetter Sample 5-Square Development Plan

Aspirational Leadership Headline

I want to create and sustain healthy sacrifice-renewal cycles and support my team to do the same.

Vision for Success

What I Will Be Doing/Saying

- Prioritizing myself as much as or more than they prioritize the work.
- Building healthy baseline routines of self-care and elevate them to sacred priorities.
- Turning the work off when it is time for self.
- Creating periods of renewal to restart healthy habits after making deliberate choices to sacrifice during periods of challenge.
- Planning deliberate renewal periods around the predictable cycles of a school year.
- Not doing other people's work. Being clear about roles and responsibilities and effectively directing work to the right people.
- Managing up to right-size the work for myself and my team. Saying no at the right times.
- Playing the long game. In prolonged times of sacrifice—like leading through turnaround or a pandemic—then I am building even stronger boundaries around sacred time for self-care.

- Accepting that the work is never done, so the goal is strong prioritization. Making proactive and game-time decisions about what deserves my time and what will have to wait, get delegated, or not get done at all.
- Not letting short-term urgency cloud my long-term lens and my equity lens, and helping my team to do the same. Creating a collective value of taking time and creating space for the important work that requires it.

How I Will Feel When I'm Leading This Way

- Grounded
- Healthy tension between sacrifice and renewal
- Empowered, steering my ship
- At peace (giving myself grace)
- Proud (self-affirmed)
- Energized
- Successful (meeting my new definition for achievement)

What Others Will Be Doing/Saying

- Engaging productively and respectfully in the sacrifice and renewal tension with me.
- Respecting my boundaries.
- Inspired to work on their own mindsets and boundaries .
- Owning their work in their clear roles and responsbilities, and not doing other people's work.
- Not letting short-term urgency cloud their long-term and equity lenses.

What Others Will Be Feeling

- Valuing healthy sacrifice-renewal cycles
- Valued as a collaborator in creating more healthy organizational culture and structures
- Accepting and respecting of my and others' boundaries
- Empowered to prioritize renewal in their lives
- Healthy
- Grounded
- Successful

Self-Awareness (Our Stuff)	Social Awareness
Triggers: Finding out my students are underperforming or struggling somehow. More bad news about or changes at work. An emergency I can resolve.	**Where is this person/team** right now? (consider emotions, beliefs/mindsets, values, identity, and behaviors)

Self-Awareness (Our Stuff)

Triggers:

Finding out my students are underperforming or struggling somehow. More bad news about or changes at work. An emergency I can resolve.

Emotions:

- Fears: what are you afraid will happen if you *do* start prioritizing self-care and renewal?

Ashamed, judged, incompetent, ineffective, compromising my integrity

- What positive emotions do you get from pacesetters behaviors?

Pride, achievement, belonging, self-affirmation, values-driven contentment

Self-limiting stories:

- If I prioritize self, then I'm not an activist, I will not be seen as worthy by others in my organization, and I will not achieve the outcomes I set out to achieve. I will ultimately put myself before kids who are the victim of structural inequality.

- I feel successful when I do things I'm good at (teach 8th grade lit vs. lead, do email instead of difficult conversations). I feel worthy when people see me sacrificing because the culture rewards that. I feel like I am living my mission as an activist/social justice warrior when I am sacrificing.

Behaviors:

- Work too much. Sacrificing when I should be renewing.
- Carrying the emotional loads of others
- Doing other people's work

Social Awareness

Where is this person/team right now? (consider emotions, beliefs/mindsets, values, identity, and behaviors)

Four lenses:

1. What obstacles have I created for/in others? What obstacles have they created for me?
2. What obstacles are endemic in our culture?
3. What obstacles are endemic in our organizational structures?
4. What obstacles are endemic in our sector? Governing bodies? City? Country?

What mindsets and behaviors are evidence of these obstacles?

What blind spots do individuals/groups have that are keeping us stuck?

How might identity and equity be at play?

- White cultural norm of urgency = culture and power structure aligned to prioritizing short-term need over equity.
- Identity, power, and privilege → leaders at the top most likely to hold cultural norm of urgency most strongly and have the most blind spots about impact.
- People with the answers (holding/valuing alternative norms) more likely to be BIPOC, and not have the power in the organization to bring their solutions to the table.

Identity:	Where can they be/your target (consider emotions, beliefs/mindsets, values, identity, and behaviors)
■ White guilt—If I am not sacrificing for my students and community, then I am sinking back into my privilege and perpetuating racism. ■ BIPOC guilt—If I am not sacrificing for my students and community, then I am not doing enough for my people. ■ White cultural norm of urgency—short-term over long-term and over equity.	1. Hold and defend my personal boundaries 2. Advocate/manage up to right-size load for self and team 3. Effectively empower others to do their own work and carry their own loads 4. Raise awareness one-to-one about pacesetter behavior and mindset and build new mindset/skill to build self practices and effective renewal cycles.
Impact: ■ Doing other people's work enables them and keeps me from getting to the work of your position. ■ Perpetuating the pacesetter culture (emotional contagion). My behavior becomes expectation for others (midnight emails, last to leave the building). ■ Overwhelm plus burnout weakens conditions for learning. What do our most vulnerable learners need? ■ Reduced capacity from burnout impacts outcomes. ■ Attrition has significant long-term negative impact on outcomes.	5. Raise others awareness about the pacesetter culture and behavior as a group, then build culture and revise structures to support self-care practices and strong sacrifice/renewal cycles (change management).

Values (Our Standard)

(Consider your core values as a person, as well as why you care in this context. Also consider connections to your identities.)

Competing commitments

Mission: Impact, social justice, activism. + achievement (feeling successful) + reputation (feeling worthy) + urgency

vs.

Personal happiness + reaching full potential + sustainability (for self and others)

When does your standard become your stuff? When the behaviors your values dictate do not achieve the goals you are trying to achieve.

Self-Management

How will you manage your triggers? (consider strategies like breathing, self-talk, anchoring in values, planning ahead)

- Proactively build robust plan for baseline self-care.
- Breath into the moment of choice.
- Self-talk to live into strong boundaries for prioritizing self-care. (*My renewal is necessary for me to do my best for kids. And I want to live a fulfilling life.*)
- Self-talk to turn it off during self-time. (*I worked for 10 hours. If I do this personal thing, it's okay. And there will always be more work. Do it when you're fresh.*)
- Self-talk to effectively delegate work to the right team members. (*If you do their work, you can't do yours, and nobody else can do your work.*)

What *noble story* do you need to believe about this person/group to effectively connect and reach your targets?

- My team wants to be empowered to own their own work. They want to grow and realize their potential.
- My team wants me to take care of myself and help them take care of themselves
- My team and my students are strong enough and resilient enough to carry their own emotional load. They don't need me to do that for them. Doing so is actually enabling and paternalistic.

Relationship Management

What does this person need from you to meet the target?

Connect:

- Listen to where others are with their sustainability challenges.
- Share my experience with sacrifice syndrome and my aspirations for self-care and effective sacrifice/renewal cycles both vulnerably and with candor.
- Invite others to share their experiences with sacrifice syndrome and also their aspirations.
- Connect on common values.

Care personally:

- Proactively create clear goals, roles, and responsibilities for staff to clarify who owns what work.
- Affirm the fears and values that support sacrifice syndrome but challenge them.
- Paint a picture for a both/and.

Challenge directly:

- Call out the competing commitments at the heart of the problem to push to surface fears and address them.
- Push people to consider short-term vs. long-term outcomes and the equity cost of urgency when analyzing current practice and culture.
- Challenge stories that underplay or omit the negative impact of pacesetter behaviors, culture, and systems on outcomes.

Appendix E: Doer Sample 5-Square Development Plan

Aspirational Leadership Headline

I want to do only my work and effectively direct the doers in service of their growth and our students.

Vision for Success

What I Will Be Doing/Saying

- Crystal clear about my role and the roles and responsibilities of my colleagues and direct reports.
- Staying in my lane—self-managing to not take on others' work.
- Delegating proactively and effectively.
- Prioritizing time to do proactive planning.
- Communicating time-sensitive information in advance to stakeholders.
- Managing up to manage my role and responsibility and that of the people I lead.
- Right-sizing expectations.
- Challenging and empowering people to own their work and stay in their lanes.

How I Will Feel When I'm Leading This Way

- Clear
- Calm and focused
- Outward focused
- Energized

- Aligned to my value of growing people
- Respected
- Competent

What Others Will Be Doing/Saying

- Owning their roles and outcomes.
- Focused on getting better.
- Seeing my delegation as empowering them and investing in their growth.
- Coming to me for advice and coaching rather than to take on their work.

What Others Will Be Feeling

- Confident and proud of their ability to do their job.
- Feeling like they are growing.
- Believed in and invested in by me.

Self-Awareness (Our Stuff)	Social Awareness
Triggers: A task unfinished, done poorly, or not assigned. A struggling team member. Emotions: Irritation, disappointment, superiority Anticipation, excitement, competent Overwhelmed, incompetent, anxious Self-limiting stories: This person can't do this task effectively. If you want something done well, you have to do it yourself. It will be easier for me to just do this. I am good at this, and it feels good to be successful. My team will judge me if they don't see me in the trenches. But I can't keep working this hard long term. This job is unsustainable.	Where is this person/team right now? (consider emotions, beliefs/mindsets, values, identity, and behaviors) - Frustrated at me for disempowering them. - Enabled and unaware—they have become dependent on me to solve their problems and make decisions. They expect me to do for them. - Lacking confidence due to my doing their work. - Unaware of the impact on their outcomes and growth of the dynamic.

How might my identities be at play?

White supremacist culture norms I am acting out: perfectionism, only one right way, paternalism, power hoarding, individualism, I'm the only one. I have always turned inward and worked harder under stress. It was how I grew up.

Behaviors:

Default to taking on unassigned tasks. Taking over other people's work when they struggle. Doing work that was mine in the past but is in someone else's role and responsibility now. Dropping balls in core role. Working all the time.

Impact:

Self: Overwhelmed, in sacrifice syndrome, dropping balls, not doing the proactive "directing" work of the leader to set clear path for others. Not have a long-term vision or cohesive strategy for the school.

Staff: Disempowered, feeling not trusted, not successful. Unclear and feeling frustrated and anxious about lack of clarity. Not getting developed.

Students: Experience confusion, anxiety of unclear roles of staff second hand.

Where can they be/your target (consider emotions, beliefs/mindsets, values, identity and behaviors)

- Aware of the dynamic and its impact.
- Empowered and motivated to own the parts of their job that I have been doing.
- Rebuilding their confidence that they can do it.
- Feeling believed in and that I am investing in their growth.
- Understanding and respecting the limits of my role in terms of doing.

Values (Our Standard)

(Consider your core values as a person, as well as why you care in this context. Also consider connections to your identities.)

Achievement: getting to the right outcomes and meeting high expectations

Growth: mine and others

Equity and closing the opportunity gap: for self and others

Self-Management

How will you manage your triggers? (consider strategies like breathing, self-talk, anchoring in values, planning ahead)

Breathe into the guilt and urge to help.

Plan ahead—calendar ahead to prioritize time.

Self-talk

- If I do this what will I *not* do?
- Fight the guilt!
- Is this my job or someone else's job? Should I be directing or doing?
- The work will never be done. What's most important right now?
- If I take their work, I take their power and their learning from them.
- If I take their work, I am upholding white supremacist norms and damaging learning conditions.
- Does this have to be great or just good enough?
- Part of my job is proactive thinking and planning, which happens by myself, at a desk, behind closed doors.

What *noble story* do you need to believe about this person/group to effectively connect and reach your targets?

- My team is capable of learning to do their work really well. It's my job to get them there.
- Everyone wants to grow and be empowered to do their work.
- My team will respect me for directing just as much or more than doing.

Relationship Management

What does this person need from you to meet the target?

Connect:

- Step-back moment to name it and own the dynamic.
- Share my own vulnerable story as a doer (standard, stuff, impact).
- Listen and question to confirm "where they are."

Care personally:

- Belief in their ability.
- Positivity and optimism: painting a hopeful and motivating picture of what could be.
- Clarify roles and responsibilities.
- Belief in their ability to do, and investment in helping them get there.

Challenge directly:

- Set a new expectation and hold self and others accountable.
- Name it when others don't meet the standard and coach to build capacity.
- Say no when others ask you to do their work.
- Delegate the right tasks to the right people.

Appendix F: Imposter Sample 5-Square Development Plan

Aspirational Leadership Headline

I want to lead from a place of confidence, belief in myself, and growth mindset for myself and my team.

Vision for Success

What I Will Be Doing/Saying

- Standing up in front of people and communicating the decision I made and why. And sustaining that narrative over time.
- Sticking to my decisions and vision even when some people don't like it.
- Stepping back, self-managing, and redirecting people who are not meeting the standard in the moment.
- Owning my own mistakes or lack of knowledge in the moment and communicating to staff that I can still lead effectively through that.
- Normalizing making mistakes as part of learning and growing.
- Asking people to make an effort to think beyond themselves and think of the team. What do I need to do to get you on board? To be a team player?
- Challenging with decision points. If you can't put your personal preference to the side and go with the team, this might not be the place for you.

How I Will Feel When I'm Leading This Way

- Clear
- Confident, believing in myself
- Self-grace—allowing myself to be imperfect and make mistakes
- Optimistic
- Connected to people, the whole
- About the decision—at peace, comfortable having made it

What Others Will Be Doing/Saying

- Trust me enough to listen and engage without feeling dissonance boiling over.
- Feeling affirmed, but also seeing their part in the problem.
- See making mistakes as part of learning and growing.

What Others Will Be Feeling

- Excited, hopeful . . .
- Trusting me, believing that we can do this together
- Motivated to move forward in a new way
- Respecting me
- Safe to make well-intentioned mistakes

Self-Awareness (Our Stuff)	Social Awareness
<u>Triggers:</u> Others doing better than me. Others questioning my decisions. Dropping balls. Feeling unprepared. Being the only one of my identities in the room. Condescension. When I am unclear about my role in a situation or don't know the answer. <u>Emotions:</u> Afraid, ashamed, judged by self and others, incompetent, insulted, resentful, embarrassed, angry with myself, not trusted.	**Where is this person/team** right now? (consider emotions, beliefs/mindsets, values, identity and behaviors) - Looking to me for guidance (even if they don't know it). - Wanting to be empowered to do their job (not me do it for them). - Blind spots that they need my help to work through. - Frustrated. Defensive. Feeling ineffective. Confused about what they need to do better. - Frustrated and anxious about lack of direction or clarity. - Caught in bad habits due to lack of guidance. - Identity-based stories about how I see them or how they see me (confirmation bias).

Self-limiting stories:

Do I really know what to do? I am not qualified, so I don't have the right to challenge. Everyone can see right through me. I don't fit in here. The leader has to have all the answers and be polished and professional. What are my bosses/people saying about me behind closed doors? I am not good at anything important. Struggle = failure. Success = perfection. Having to work so hard = incompetence (this should be easy for me). I should be an expert in everything.

Identity connection:

Imposter may be a by-product of identity-based marginalization over time.

Behaviors: fight or flight

Stay silent. Avoid confrontation. Take it out on others. Knee jerk, defensive, impulsive words/actions. Don't follow through. Don't hold people accountable. Don't share my ideas and vision. Don't ask for help or collaborate. Don't trust others. I see only losses (not wins). I try to compensate by overworking. Turn inward and isolate.

Impact:

I lower expectations for staff. Our vision and direction becomes unclear. We do not row together. Not aligned. Adults feel unsafe due to lack of clarity and steady hand at the wheel. I alienate myself from my team. I am miserable and feel alone.

Where can they be/your target (consider emotions, beliefs/mindsets, values, identity, and behaviors)

- Clear about roles, vision, decisions, expectations.
- Aware of the dynamic between us and working together to correct it (norming).
- Aware of their growth areas and motivated to work on them.
- Aware of how our identities contributed to this, and norming on moving forward.
- Feeling good about *us*, feeling prepared and empowered to do their job, feeling more confident about me as a leader and our school's direction.

Values (Our Standard)

(Consider your core values holistically and related to this challenge, and how they connect to your identities.)

- Ownership—it's my job.
- Growth—for me, for my team.
- Vulnerability—to grow you need to be vulnerable. The conditions need to be safe for others to be vulnerable.
- Achievement—always getting better.
- Impact—I want my actions to have the most possible impact for kids.

Self-Management	Relationship Management
How will you manage your triggers? (consider strategies like breathing, self-talk, anchoring in values, planning ahead)	**What does this person need from you to meet the target?**
Breathe. Power movement.	**Connect: step back conversation**
Self-talk:	<ul><li>Share my fears/stories with teammates and norm on trust.</li><li>Share my imposter story and what I'm doing about it.</li><li>Listen to confirm where they are. Ask questions to probe for their awareness of their stuff in this, and what they can do about it.</li><li>Ask for help.</li></ul>
<ul><li>Be a champion for kids.</li><li>It's your job.</li><li>It's not about you.</li><li>If I don't say it now, we all pay for it later.</li><li>What's the worst thing that can happen?</li><li>I was chosen for this job because I have real skills and a strong standard.</li><li>Leaders don't have to know everything and be perfect. They have to be resilient and get there eventually.</li><li>I do not have to believe everything I think. I do not have to believe my inner critic.</li><li>Feedback is not personal. It's about growth.</li></ul>	**Care personally:** <ul><li>Own my impact.</li><li>Affirm investment and belief in them.</li><li>Invite them to collaborate with me to fix dynamics (contracting/norming).</li><li>Affirm what I need to do and change for them to be successful.</li><li>Create clarity (the path) where I have previously created ambiguity.</li><li>Centering BIPOC in spaces . . . increase belonging.</li></ul>

- (re-define) Success = effort, resiliency, growth, as well as outcomes.
- (re-define) Leader = head learner, director (not doer and expert of everything).
- Asking for help = leadership competency (adaptive).
- I am not the only one; 70% of people experience this at some point in their careers.

What *noble story* do you need to believe about this person/group to effectively connect and reach your targets?

- They want to get better.
- This isn't their vision either.
- I can call up the best of them, too.

Pushing people may not feel good in the moment, but it could shift things for them in a way that they will thank me for later.

- People believe in me, and they want me to succeed. They will not write me off if I don't know everything, or if I make a mistake.
- When people give me feedback it's not personal. They want or need something, or they are trying to support me to get better.

Challenge directly:

- Advocate for what I need in our working relationship to be successful.
- Clearly name their growth areas: behavior → impact → values.
- Set clear expectations and vision for accountability and development.
- Get them to commit to moving forward with new agreements and expectations (decision point).

Appendix G:
The Implementer
Sample 5-Square
Development Plan

Aspirational Leadership Headline

I want to lead from my vision, integrating the playbook where it aligns with my vision and moving beyond the playbook where it doesn't align.

Vision for Success

What I Will Be Doing/Saying

- Getting clearer and clearer about my core values—my standard—in the moment and aligning that standard to my decisions.
- Pressure testing structures, organizational systems, and "this is just what we do" against my values and my vision.
- I deliberately *choose* each aspect of the playbook, taking the time to internally align each structure to my standard.
- When some aspect of the playbook does not seem to align with my standard, I engage across my web to advocate for an alternative that does.
- When explaining my decisions, whether they are to implement or not implement the playbook, I do so from my standard and my why.

- When I have made a values-based decision on a tactic, I connect with and challenge my team to make sure that they also align their values to our path forward. If necessary, we engage in conflict, but then we all commit.
- If my stakeholders push back out of negative feelings toward the organization or about the playbook, I am confident in challenging from my standard.
- I am able to lead beyond, or without, the playbook through adaptive challenges. I can be adaptable.
- I do not let my or my team's adaptability competency atrophy by overpracticing the implementation competency. We are aware of that danger. I create opportunities for my team to create and try new tactics and approaches, experiment, and struggle.

How I Will Feel When I'm Leading This Way

- Confident, empowered
- Grounded
- Balanced
- In touch with my gut
- Healthy tension
- Like a leader

What Others Will Be Doing/Saying

- Reflecting on their own standard and how decisions in the moment connect to that.
- If they push back, they eventually understand, respect, and get on board with my decisions.
- While they are strong implementers, they also innovate and feel empowered in their craft.

What Others Will Be Feeling

- Confident in me. Safe.
- Clear about where I stand.
- On board with decisions.
- Positive about and ownership of the playbook.
- Empowered to contribute and innovate.

Self-Awareness (Our Stuff)	Social Awareness

Self-Awareness (Our Stuff)

Triggers:

A change in expectations (new leader, partner, project, time, context). Unexpected challenge (an emergency + deadline, health challenge, pandemic, financial crisis). Struggle, setback, failure. Pushback on the playbook from staff or families.

Emotions:

Self-judgment, shame, fear of failure

Anger, blame, resentment

Judgment, frustration, indecision

Self-limiting stories:

Internalize: What is wrong with me? Why can't I get my team to follow the plan? Is there something wrong with the plan? I'm not good enough.

Externalize: I blame others, the situation to protect ego. What is wrong with them?! Why do they have to question our path? We need to row together. This resistance is just going to get in our way and slow us down. They need to conform/comply! Time for challenge. To get them to comply.

Identity:

Just one right way. That is how I was raised. Rule following.

Behaviors:

- Lose composure, confidence.
- Lash out, self-isolate.
- Hide behind excuses or even lie about outcomes.
- Keep doing what isn't working (the rut).
- Give up.
- Pressure stakeholders to comply without listening to understand their points of view.

Social Awareness

Where is this person/team right now? Diagnose their needs.

- Some have the story that I don't have my own vision and am a "yes" person to the organization.
- Feeling disempowered to practice the creative side of their craft.
- Feeling a lack of connection because they are not involved in decision-making conversations.
- Feeling disenchanted with me, the school, the organization because they don't feel we are making decisions for the right reasons (lack of *why*).
- Some are used to implementing, so when the time comes to get adaptive many are stuck.

Identity implications:

- People whose cultural norms are more collaborative, group-process focused will feel our living white cultural norm of "one right way" as repressive, especially if driven by a c-level white leadership. They may feel excluded, without a voice.
- Also, if "one right way" is what is praised and valued, then their strengths—creativity, collaboration, innovation—are not celebrated.

■ Comply without internalizing. Put all energy into implementing and very little into aligning with personal vision and values.

Impact:

■ Perceived as not having my own vision. Create a passive, disempowered team. Discourage innovation. Message that learning = passive "receiving" of knowledge. Teaching = one-size-fits-all "factory" model.

■ Favoring one style/set of norms over another. Excluding. Likely missing the equity lens. Missing important context-specific factors.

Where can they be? (your target)

1. Perceiving that I am making leadership decisions from my standard, my *why*.

2. Conflict then commit.

3. Perceiving that there are meaningful ways in which they are empowered to be creative and make their own or collaborative decisions. The *what* may be out of their hands sometimes but the *how* is very much theirs.

4. Feel that their strengths are highly valued.

5. Perceive that I, and we as a team, are aware of the equity dangers of "one right way."

Values (Our Standard)

(Consider core values and values in implementer, as well as identity, connection.)

To support me in crisis when playbook becomes obsolete in a crisis:

■ Growth mindset (Carol Dweck): change and struggle = opportunity to learn and grow.

■ Failure = quitting. Success = persevering and growing (*not* failure = negative outcome; Success = positive outcome).

■ Adaptability: nimble beats strong every day.

■ Achievement motive can be a competing commitment that gets in the way.

■ Equity: what people need in the moment might not be what's in the playbook.

To support me when balancing implementation with own vision

■ Self-actualization: I care about reaching my full potential as a leader and human being.

■ Authenticity: leading in a way that is aligned to my beliefs.

■ Achievement: I care about being effective and reach goals.

■ Reputation: I care about being seen as a strong leader.

■ Ownership" I care about this being *my* school and *my* decisions . . . not being a middle manager.

Self-Management

How will you manage your triggers? (consider strategies like breathing, self-talk, anchoring in values, planning ahead)

Breathe and stretch, arms to the ceiling (power pose)

Self-Coaching

- My beliefs—my standard—are strong, valid and will make the school stronger if I act from them.
- Success = persevering and growing.
- Nimble beats strong every day.
- I am here to be a leader, not a middle manager.

What *noble story* do you need to believe about this person/group to effectively connect?

- They believe in my ability to grow as a leader.
- They believe I have a vision, and they want me to share it with them.
- They will follow me and believe in me if I share and lead from my beliefs.

Relationship Management

What do they need from you to meet your targets?

Connect:

- Vulnerability—naming emotional reality. Owning my implementer struggles.
- Ask for help—run toward others when I'm stuck.
- Listen to meet people where they are in their emotions and their values.
- Listen to other ideas/ways.
- Acknowledge there is not just one right way.
- Appeal to common values, hopes, and fears.

Care personally:

- Express gratitude.
- Show care through trusting others when vulnerable.
- Affirm others' values and identity-based strengths.
- Create truly meaningful ways for people to live into their values of innovation and contribution.
- Protect the team and advocate for what they care about the most.

Challenge directly:

- Self-advocate—manage up to get what the team needs (past fear of judgment of a possible no).
- Speak from my deeper why about decisions.
- Challenge resistance from my standard.
- Fight for what I believe is right for my kids/staff.
- Challenge my team when they wrongfully accuse me of just complying with organizational mandates. Make it explicit when I truly own organizational decisions.

Index